D1555512

TESTIMONIES FOR THE CHURCH

VOLUME NINE

TESTIMONIES

FOR

THE CHURCH

VOLUME NINE
Comprising Testimony Number 37

by
ELLEN G. WHITE

PACIFIC PRESS PUBLISHING ASSOCIATION
Boise, Idaho
Oshawa, Ontario, Canada

Copyright, 1948, by the
Ellen G. White Publications

Printed in United States of America

96 97 98 99 00

CONTENTS

SECTION TWO

Literature in Service

SECTION THREE

The Work in the Cities

SECTION FOUR

The Health Work

SECTION FIVE

The Spirit of Unity

SECTION SIX

Among the Colored People

SECTION SEVEN

The Religious Liberty Work

SECTION EIGHT

Timely Counsels

THE TIMES OF VOLUME NINE

As we look at the times of volume 9 we view a five-year span extending to the late summer of 1909. In Mrs. White's experience this period is opened and closed with trips from her home in St. Helena, California, to the East to attend important meetings. For the denomination it is a time of full recovery from the crisis of 1902-03 and of extending the work, of launching new enterprises, and of establishing new institutions.

Following important meetings in Michigan in the spring of 1904, Mrs. White visited the South and then made her way to Washington, D. C., where steps were being taken to provide buildings for the work which was being established at the nation's capital. There was a new headquarters building to be erected, the Review and Herald must be provided with a home, a sanitarium was to be built, and a college established. The fact that Mrs. White made her home in Washington for some months, where she could give counsel regarding the work, as these four enterprises were gotten under way, was a great encouragement to the workers. It also exerted a far-reaching influence throughout the denomination in establishing the confidence of the church members that God had led in the transfer of the administration and publishing interests to the nation's capital.

This was a period of rapid advancement in the development of our medical work on the Pacific Coast. Sanitariums were opened in National City, Glendale, and Loma Linda, California. From the first, Loma Linda seemed destined to become a training center for medical workers at some future time to do the work for the denomination begun at Battle Creek. During the critical years of the establishment of the medical college, Mrs. White made frequent visits to Southern California, where she could give personal counsel and encouragement, and could assist in the laying of plans for the advancing work. It was utterances, based upon the revelations given her of God, that led us step by step eventually to the establishment of a fully recognized medical college. So insurmountable were the obstacles that, had it not been for the faith and confidence inspired by the frequent counsels which came through the spirit of prophecy, the enterprise would never have survived.

These important interests that took Mrs. White much from her home and her writing, resulted in a great delay in the issuance of books she hoped could soon be in the field doing their work. *The Ministry of Healing* was the only Ellen G. White book newly issued during this five-year period.

The work of the denomination had by this time grown too large for us to mention in detail the various advance steps. The message was now belting the globe, missionaries were being sent out in increasing numbers, more institutions devoted to educational, publishing, and medical interests were being established. The message was truly reaching the ends of the earth.

It brought great rejoicing to the heart of Ellen White to meet with the representatives of the world-wide work as they gathered in Washington, D.C., in the spring of 1909 for the General Conference session. This was her last trip East—this the last General Conference session she attended. She was now eighty-one years of age and had given a long life of service to the cause of God. She had seen the work grow from the struggling beginning days when there were only a handful who kept the Sabbath and who looked for the soon coming of the Lord. Now they numbered 85,000, and there were 1,200 ordained and licensed minister. As Ellen White stood before the General Conference, she was led to speak on certain subjects of great importance which must be reviewed. Among these was health reform. For forty-five years she had led out in teaching the great principles of healthful living which had been presented to her in vision. She had seen the fruitage of this teaching. However, there were some who still held back, there were some who were inclined to extremes, and so she reviewed our position and teachings point by point. This statement made before the General Conference forms an important chapter of volume 9.

Another topic upon which she chose to speak was that of the medical college of Loma Linda. She set forth the objectives of that institution and appealed for the co-operation of all workers and laity in making this work a success. This important statement is also a part of volume 9.

Mrs. White had seen the work of the administration of the church develop from a committee of three which was appointed in 1863 to take charge of the General Conference, to its present status of organization with General Conference departments and with Division and Union Conference organizations dividing the responsibilities among hundreds who carried the burden of the work in various parts of the world field. In her closing words she pleaded for unity and consecration. In her written statements she dealt with the authority of the General Conference and the importance of the actions taken by the General Conference in full session. She wrote of the distribution of responsibility and the need of humility and of faith. These counsels form an important part of the closing section of volume 9.

At the turn of the century Mrs. White had begun to appeal for a renewed interest in the evangelizing of the millions in the great metropolitan centers of the world. These needs had been emphasized again and again in the counsels which had been sent to the leading workers. In response to these messages, interests in city work was revived. Large centers were entered. Many evangelistic efforts were held, old churches were strengthened, and new churches were established. To preserve the appeals for this work and the counsels as to its conduct in permanent form, an entire section of volume 9 is devoted to this important subject.

We were in days, too, when the various enterprises which were entered into called for the talents and energies of our lay members. It began to be clear that this work could never be finished unless the laity vigorously united with the ministry in carrying the message to the world. The work of laymen took on new importance. In the last two volumes of the *Testimonies* increasing emphasis had been placed upon the work of the laymen, and this is brought to a climax in volume 9. Following a picture of the last crisis and events to take place in the closing scenes of earth's history, several chapters are devoted to the call for every Seventh-day Adventist to take an active part in evangelism, in home missionary work, and in the circulation of literature.

There were two other lines of detailed counsel which are represented in this volume for the first time in the *Testimonies,* though considerable instruction had been given through the years relating to them. The first has to do with the work among the colored people. The second has to do with to religious liberty work. It was largely in response to the appeals made by Ellen White in the articles in the *Review* in the middle nineties that workers and laymen pushed into the great Southland and began their ministry, some in educational lines, some in medical lines, some in preaching the message, and others in quietly living the message as homes were established in regions which had not yet received the light. Still others had joined in this work in response to the appeals in volume 7. The workers faced many problems. Plans must be laid for advancement. New issues must be met, especially those relating to the work where there was race antagonism. Through the critical years counsel had been given which served as safe guidance for the work, and to make this counsel a permanent record to serve the church, it was included in volume 9.

The religious liberty work was a line of endeavor in which we had been engaged for many years. Some were inclined to take extreme positions urging that true Sabbathkeeping meant that one must make it prominent to those about him that we labored on Sunday. In some regions this led to persecution. The Lord in His goodness sent messages to this people to give us a balanced conception of questions of this kind. These, too, appear in this volume in the section entitled, "The Religious Liberty Work," opening with the chapter, "A Time of Trial Before Us," and closing with the chapter, "Words of Caution." So volume 9, drawing together counsels new and old, reiterating certain lines of instruction, giving details of counsel in other lines, encouraging to service, pointing out the dangers of extremes, leading to confidence in organization and pointing to the reward of earnest effort, became the cap-sheaf of the *Testimonies for the Church.*

The work of Ellen White did not close with the issuance of *Testimonies for the Church,* volume 9. Addressing herself more closely to her work of book preparation during the succeeding five years, she brought out *Acts of the Apostles* in 1911 and *Counsels to Parents, Teachers, and Students* in 1913. She also did her final work on manuscripts for the new edition of *Gospel Workers* and *Life Sketches,* published in 1915, and *Prophets and Kings,* which came from the press in 1916.

Especially did she take delight in the special efforts which were made to warn the cities, and from time to time there came from her pen messages of counsel and instruction regarding this important phase of our work. The steady progress of the cause around the world was marked by this now aging messenger of the Lord residing among the quiet hills of Northern California. Although she knew her labors were nearly finished, she had no fears for the future of the work of God, for as she stated: "Whether or not my life is spared, my writings will constantly speak, and their work will go forward as long as time shall last."—*Writing and Sending Out of the "Testimonies for the Church,"* pages 13, 14.

As plans were laid for the General Conference session of 1913, Mrs. White would have been pleased to have attended, but in her advancing age this seemed inadvisable. Not being able to present an oral message, she wrote two communications to be read to the delegates and church members assembled. In the second message, which was read by the president of the General Conference to the conference in session on the morning of May 27, she reviewed the experience of past years, and rejoiced in the marked evidences that God had led His people. Then, looking ahead, she called for renewed efforts in soul-saving work and appealed again for the unwarned cities. Looking into the future she saw the triumph of the church and expressed words of courage:

"I have words of encouragement for you, my brethren. We are to move forward in faith and hope, expecting large things from God. The enemy will seek in every way to hinder the efforts that are being made to advance the truth, but in the strength of the Lord you may gain success. Let no discouraging words be spoken, but only such words as will tend to strengthen and sustain your fellow workers. . . .

"My interest in the general work is still as deep as ever, and I greatly desire that the cause of present truth shall steadily advance in all parts of the world. . . .

"I pray earnestly that the work we do at this time shall impress itself deeply on heart and mind and soul. Perplexities will increase; but let us, as believers in God, encourage one another. Let us not lower the standard, but keep it lifted high, looking to Him who is the author and finisher of our faith. When in the night season I am unable to sleep, I lift my heart in prayer to God, and He strengthens me, and gives me the assurance that He is with His ministering servants in the home field and in distant lands. I am encouraged and blessed as I realize that the God of Israel is still guiding His people, and that He will continue to be with them, even to the end. . . .

"The Lord desires to see the work of proclaiming the third angel's message carried forward with increasing efficiency. As He has worked in all ages to give victories to His people, so in this age He longs to carry to a triumphant fulfillment His purposes for His church. He bids His believing saints to advance unitedly, going from strength to greater strength, from faith to increased assurance and confidence in the truth and righteousness of His cause.

"We are to stand firm as a rock to the principles of the word of God, remembering that God is with us to give us strength to meet each new experience. Let us ever maintain in our lives the principles of righteousness, that we may go forward from strength to strength in the name of the Lord. We are to hold as very sacred the faith that has been substantiated by the instruction and approval of the Spirit of God from our earliest experience until the present time. We are to cherish as very precious the work that the Lord has been carrying forward through His commandment-keeping people, and which, through the power of His grace, will grow stronger and more efficient as time advances. The enemy is seeking to becloud the discernment of God's people, and to weaken their efficiency, but if they will labor as the Spirit of God shall direct, He will open doors of opportunity before them for the work of building up the old waste places. Their experience will be one of constant growth, until the Lord shall descend from heaven with power and great glory to set His seal of final triumph upon His faithful ones.

"The work that lies before us is one that will put to the

stretch every power of the human being. It will call for the exercise of strong faith and constant vigilance. At times the difficulties that we shall meet will be most disheartening. The very greatness of the task will appall us. And yet, with God's help, His servants will finally triumph."—Reported in *The General Conference Bulletin,* May 28, 1913, pages 164, 165.

In the times of the nine volumes of *Testimonies for the Church* written over a period of fifty-five years the church continually grew and developed and prospered. The counsel given afforded safe guidance, the reproof and correction led many straying feet back to the paths of righteousness, the words of cheer and encouragement revived many a faint heart, and the picture of the reward of the faithful spurred thousands to the determination to reach the goal set before us.

Looking ahead, we must ever remember the words recorded in *Life Sketches,* page 196:

"We have nothing to fear for the future, except as we shall forget the way the Lord has led us, and His teaching in our past history."

THE TRUSTEES OF THE
ELLEN G. WHITE PUBLICATIONS.

FOR THE COMING OF THE KING

> "Yet a little while and He that
> shall come will come and will
> not tarry." Hebrews 10:37.

THE LAST CRISIS

We are living in the time of the end. The fast fulfilling signs of the times declare that the coming of Christ is near at hand. The days in which we live are solemn and important. The Spirit of God is gradually but surely being withdrawn from the earth. Plagues and judgments are already filling upon the despisers of the grace of God. The calamities by land and sea, the unsettled state of society, the alarms of war, are portentous. They forecast approaching events of the greatest magnitude.

The agencies of evil are combining their forces and consolidating. They are strengthening for the last great crisis. Great changes are soon to take place in our world, and the final movements will be rapid ones.

The condition of things in the world shows that troublous times are right upon us. The daily papers are full of indications of a terrible conflict in the near future. Bold robberies are of frequent occurrence. Strikes are common. Thefts and murders are committed on every hand. Men possessed of demons are taking the lives of men, women, and little children. Men have become infatuated with vice, and every species of evil prevails.

The enemy has succeeded in perverting justice and in filling men's hearts with the desire for selfish gain.

"Justice standeth afar off; for truth is fallen in the street, and equity cannot enter." Isaiah 59:14. In the great cities there are multitudes living in poverty and wretchedness, well-nigh destitute of food, shelter, and clothing; while in the same cities are those who have more than heart could wish, who live luxuriously, spending their money on richly furnished houses, on personal adornment, or worse still, upon the gratification of sensual appetites, upon liquor, tobacco, and other things that destroy the powers of the brain, unbalance the mind, and debase the soul. The cries of starving humanity are coming up before God, while by every species of oppression and extortion men are piling up colossal fortunes.

On one occasion, when in New York City, I was in the night season called upon to behold buildings rising story after story toward heaven. These buildings were warranted to be fireproof, and they were erected to glorify their owners and builders. Higher and still higher these buildings rose, and in them the most costly material was used. Those to whom these buildings belonged were not asking themselves: "How can we best glorify God?" The Lord was not in their thoughts.

I thought: "Oh, that those who are thus investing their means could see their course as God sees it! They are piling up magnificent buildings, but how foolish in the sight of the Ruler of the universe is their planning and devising. They are not studying with all the powers of heart and mind how they may glorify God. They have lost sight of this, the first duty of man."

As these lofty buildings went up, the owners rejoiced with ambitious pride that they had money to use in gratifying self and provoking the envy of their neighbors. Much of the money that they thus invested had been obtained through exaction, through grinding down the poor. They forgot that in heaven an account of every business transaction is kept; every unjust deal, every fraudulent act, is there recorded. The time is coming when in their fraud and insolence men will reach a point that the Lord will not permit them to pass, and they will learn that there is a limit to the forbearance of Jehovah.

The scene that next passed before me was an alarm of fire. Men looked at the lofty and supposedly fire-proof buildings and said: "They are perfectly safe." But these buildings were consumed as if made of pitch. The fire engines could do nothing to stay the destruction. The firemen were unable to operate the engines.

I am instructed that when the Lord's time comes, should no change have taken place in the hearts of proud, ambitious human beings, men will find that the hand that had been strong to save will be strong to destroy. No earthly power can stay the hand of God. No material can be used in the erection of buildings that will preserve them from destruction when God's appointed time comes to send retribution on men for their disregard of His law and for their selfish ambition.

There are not many, even among educators and statesmen, who comprehend the causes that underlie the present state of society. Those who hold the reins of government are not able to solve the problem of moral corruption, poverty, pauperism, and increasing crime. They are struggling in vain to place business operations on a more secure basis. If men would give more heed to the teaching of God's word, they would find a solution of the problems that perplex them.

The Scriptures describe the condition of the world just before Christ's second coming. Of the men who by robbery and extortion are amassing great riches, it is written: "Ye have heaped treasure together for the last days. Behold, the hire of the laborers who have reaped down your fields, which is of you kept back by fraud, crieth: and the cries of them which have reaped are entered into the ears of the Lord of Sabaoth. Ye have lived in pleasure on the earth, and been wanton; ye have nourished your hearts, as in a day of slaughter. Ye have condemned and killed the just; and he doth not resist you." James 5:3-6.

But who reads the warnings given by the fast fulfilling signs of the times? What impression is made upon worldlings? What change is seen in their attitude? No more than was seen in the attitude of the inhabitants of the Noachian world. Absorbed in worldly business and pleasure, the antediluvians "knew not until the Flood came, and took them all away." Matthew 24:39. They had heaven-sent warnings, but they refused to listen. And today the world, utterly regardless of the warning voice of God, is hurrying on to eternal ruin.

The world is stirred with the spirit of war. The prophecy of the eleventh chapter of Daniel has nearly reached its complete fulfillment. Soon the scenes of trouble spoken of in the prophecies will take place.

"Behold, the Lord maketh the earth empty, and maketh it waste, and turneth it upside down, and scattereth abroad the inhabitants thereof. . . . Because they have transgressed the laws, changed the ordinance, broken the everlasting covenant. Therefore hath the curse devoured the earth, and they that dwell therein are desolate. . . . The mirth of tabrets ceaseth, the noise of them that rejoice endeth, the joy of the harp ceaseth." Isaiah 24:1-8.

"Alas for the day! for the day of the Lord is at hand, and as a destruction from the Almighty shall it come. . . . The seed is rotten under their clods, the garners are laid desolate, the barns are broken down; for the corn is withered. How do the beasts groan! the herds of cattle are perplexed, because they have no pasture; yea, the flocks of sheep are made desolate." "The vine is dried up, and the fig tree languisheth; the pomegranate tree, the palm tree also, and the apple tree, even all the trees of the field, are withered: because joy is withered away from the sons of men." Joel 1:15-18, 12.

"I am pained at my very heart; . . . I cannot hold my peace, because thou hast heard, O my soul, the sound of the trumpet, the alarm of war. Destruction upon destruction is cried; for the whole land is spoiled." Jeremiah 4:19, 20.

"I beheld the earth, and, lo, it was without form, and void; and the heavens, and they had no light. I beheld the mountains, and, lo, they trembled, and all the hills moved lightly. I beheld, and, lo, there was no man, and all the birds of the heavens were fled. I beheld, and, lo, the fruitful place was a wilderness, and all the cities thereof were broken down." Verses 23-26.

"Alas! for that day is great, so that none is like it: it is even the time of Jacob's trouble; but he shall be saved out of it." Jeremiah 30:7.

Not all in this world have taken sides with the enemy against God. Not all have become disloyal. There are a faithful few who are true to God; for John writes: "Here are they that keep the commandments of God, and the faith of Jesus." Revelation 14:12. Soon the battle will be waged fiercely between those who serve God and those who serve Him not. Soon everything that can be shaken will be shaken, that those things that cannot be shaken may remain.

Satan is a diligent Bible student. He knows that his time is short, and he seeks at every point to counterwork the work of the Lord upon this earth. It is impossible to give any idea of the experience of the people of God who shall be alive upon the earth when celestial glory and a repetition of the persecutions of the past are blended. They will walk in the light proceeding from the throne of God. By means of the angels there will be constant communication between heaven and earth. And Satan, surrounded by evil angels, and claiming to be God, will work miracles of all kinds, to deceive, if possible, the very elect. God's people will not find their safety in working miracles, for Satan will counterfeit the miracles that will be wrought. God's tried and tested people will find their power in the sign spoken of in Exodus 31:12-18. They are to take their stand on the living word: "It is written." This is the only foundation upon which they can stand securely. Those who have broken their covenant with God will in that day be without God and without hope.

The worshipers of God will be especially distinguished by their regard for the fourth commandment, since this is the sign of God's creative power and the witness to His claim upon man's reverence and homage. The wicked will be distinguished by their efforts to tear down the Creator's memorial and to exalt the institution of Rome. In the issue of the conflict all Christendom will be divided into two great classes, those who keep the commandments of God and the faith of Jesus, and those who worship the beast and his image, and receive his mark. Although church and state will unite their power to compel all, "both small and great, rich and poor, free and bond," to receive the mark of the beast, yet the people of God will not receive it. Revelation 13:16. The prophet of Patmos beholds "them that had gotten the victory over the beast, and over his image, and over his mark, and over the number of his name, stand on the sea of glass, having the harps of God," and singing the song of Moses and the Lamb. Revelation 15:2.

Fearful tests and trials await the people of God. The spirit of war is stirring the nations from one end of the earth to the other. But in the midst of the time of trouble that is coming,—a time of trouble such as has not been since there was a nation,—God's chosen people will stand unmoved. Satan and his host cannot destroy them, for angels that excel in strength will protect them.

God's word to His people is: "Come out from among them, and be ye separate, . . . and touch not the unclean thing; and I will receive you, and will be a Father unto you, and ye shall be My sons and daughters." "Ye are a chosen generation, a royal priesthood, an holy nation, a peculiar people; that ye should show forth the praises of Him who hath called you out of darkness into His marvelous light." 2 Corinthians 6:17, 18; 1 Peter 2:9. God's people are to be distinguished as a people who serve Him fully, wholeheartedly, taking no honor to themselves, and remembering that by a most solemn covenant they have bound themselves to serve the Lord and Him only.

"The Lord spake unto Moses, saying, Speak thou also unto the children of Israel, saying, Verily My Sabbaths ye shall keep: for it is a sign between Me and you throughout your generations; that ye may know that I am the Lord that doth sanctify you. Ye shall keep the Sabbath therefore; for it is holy unto you: everyone that defileth it shall surely be put to death: for whosoever doeth any work therein, that soul shall be cut off from among his people. Six days may work be done; but in the seventh is the Sabbath of rest, holy to the Lord: whosoever doeth any work in the Sabbath day, he shall surely be put to death. Wherefore the children of Israel shall keep the Sabbath, to observe the Sabbath throughout their generations, for a perpetual covenant. It is a sign between Me and the children of Israel forever: for in six days the Lord made heaven and earth, and on the seventh day He rested, and was refreshed." Exodus 31:12-17.

Do not these words point us out as God's denominated people? and do they not declare to us that so long as time shall last, we are to cherish the sacred, denominational distinction placed upon us? The children of Israel were to observe the Sabbath throughout their generations "for a perpetual covenant." The Sabbath has lost none of its meaning. It is still the sign between God and His people, and it will be so forever.

CALLED TO BE WITNESSES

In a special sense Seventh-day Adventists have been set in the world as watchmen and light bearers. To them has been entrusted the last warning for a perishing world. On them is shining wonderful light from the word of God. They have been given a work of the most solemn import—the proclamation of the first, second, and third angels' messages. There is no other work of so great importance. They are to allow nothing else to absorb their attention.

The most solemn truths ever entrusted to mortals have been given us to proclaim to the world. The proclamation of these truths is to be our work. The world is to be warned, and God's people are to be true to the trust committed to them. They are not to engage in speculation, neither are they to enter into business enterprises with unbelievers; for this would hinder them in their God-given work.

Christ says of His people: "Ye are the light of the world." Matthew 5:14. It is not a small matter that the counsels and plans of God have been so clearly opened to us. It is a wonderful privilege to be able to understand the will of God as revealed in the sure word of prophecy. This places on us a heavy responsibility. God expects us to impart to others the knowledge that He has given us. It is His purpose that divine and human instrumentalities shall unite in the proclamation of the warning message.

So far as his opportunities extend, everyone who has received the light of truth is under the same responsibility as was the prophet of Israel to whom came the word: "Son of man, I have set thee a watchman unto the house of Israel; therefore thou shalt hear the word at My mouth, and warn them from Me. When I say unto the wicked, O wicked man, thou shalt surely die; if thou dost not speak to warn the wicked from his way, that wicked man shall die in his iniquity; but his blood will I require at thine hand. Nevertheless, if thou warn the wicked of his way to turn from it; if he do not turn from his way, he shall die in his iniquity; but thou hast delivered thy soul." Ezekiel 33:7-9.

Are we to wait until the fulfillment of the prophecies of the end before we say anything concerning them? Of what value will our words be then? Shall we wait until God's judgments fall upon the transgressor before we tell him how to avoid them? Where is our faith in the word of God? Must we see things foretold come to pass before we will believe what He has said? In clear, distinct rays light has come to us, showing us that the great day of the Lord is near at hand, "even at the doors." Let us read and understand before it is too late.

We are to be consecrated channels, through which the heavenly life is to flow to others. The Holy Spirit is to animate and pervade the whole church, purifying and cementing hearts. Those who have been buried with Christ in baptism are to rise to newness of life, giving a living representation of the life of Christ. Upon us is laid a sacred charge. The commission has been given us: "Go ye therefore, and make disciples of all nations, baptizing them in the name of the Father, and of the Son, and of the Holy Ghost: teaching them to observe all things whatsoever I have commanded you: and, lo, I am with you always even unto the end of the world." Matthew 28:19, 20, margin. You are dedicated to the work of making known the gospel of salvation. Heaven's perfection is to be your power.

A HOLY LIFE

It is not only by preaching the truth, not only by distributing literature, that we are to witness for God. Let us remember that a Christlike life is the most powerful argument that can be advanced in favor of Christianity, and that a cheap Christian character works more harm in the world than the character of a worldling. Not all the books written can serve the purpose of a holy life. Men will believe, not what the minister preaches, but what the church lives. Too often the influence of the sermon preached from the pulpit is counteracted by the sermon preached in the lives of those who claim to be advocates of truth.

It is the purpose of God to glorify Himself in His people before the world. He expects those who bear the name of Christ to represent Him in thought, word, and deed. Their thoughts are to be pure and their words noble and uplifting, drawing those around them nearer the Saviour. The religion of Christ is to be interwoven with all that they do and say. Their every business transaction is to be fragrant with the presence of God.

Sin is a hateful thing. It marred the moral beauty of a large number of the angels. It entered our world and well-nigh obliterated the moral image of God in man. But in His great love, God provided a way whereby man might regain the position from which he fell in yielding to the tempter. Christ came to stand at the head of humanity, to work out in our behalf a perfect character. Those who receive Him are born again.

Christ saw humanity, through the working of the mighty growth of sin, possessed by the prince of the power of the air and putting forth gigantic strength in exploits of evil. He saw also that a mightier power was to meet and conquer Satan. "Now is the judgment of this world," He said, "now shall the prince of this world be cast out." John 12:31. He saw that if human beings believed on Him, they would be given power against the host of fallen angels, whose name is legion. Christ strengthened His soul with the thought that, by the wonderful sacrifice which He was about to make, the prince of this world was to be cast out and men and women placed where, through the grace of God, they could regain what they had lost.

The life that Christ lived in this world, men and women can live through His power and under His instruction. In their conflict with Satan they may have all the help that He had. They may be more than conquerors through Him who loved them and gave Himself for them.

The lives of professing Christians who do not live the Christ life are a mockery to religion. Everyone whose name is registered on the church roll is under obligation to represent Christ by revealing the inward adorning of a meek and quiet spirit. They are to be His witnesses, making known the advantages of walking and working as Christ has given them example. The truth for this time is to appear in its power in the lives of those who believe it, and is to be imparted to the world. Believers are to represent in their lives its power to sanctify and ennoble.

CHRIST'S REPRESENTATIVES

The inhabitants of the heavenly universe expect the followers of Christ to shine as lights in the world. They are to show forth the power of the grace that Christ died to give men. God expects those who profess to be Christians to reveal in their lives the highest development of Christianity. They are recognized representatives of Christ, and they are to show that Christianity is a reality. They are to be men of faith, men of courage, whole-souled men, who, without questioning, trust in God and His promises.

All who would enter the city of God must during their earthly life set forth Christ in their dealings. It is this that constitutes them the messengers of Christ, His witnesses. They are to bear a plain, decided testimony against all evil practices, pointing sinners to the Lamb of God, who taketh away the sin of the world. He gives to all who receive Him, power to become the sons of God. Regeneration is the only path by which we can enter the city of God. It is narrow, and the gate by which we enter is strait; but along it we are to lead men and women and children, teaching them that, in order to be saved, they must have a new heart and a new spirit. The old, hereditary traits of character must be overcome. The natural desires of the soul must be changed. All deception, all falsifying, all evilspeaking, must be put away. The new life, which makes men and women Christlike, is to be lived.

STEADFAST ADHERENCE TO THE TRUTH

There must be no pretense in the lives of those who have so sacred and solemn a message as we have been called to bear. The world is watching Seventh-day Adventists because it knows something of their profession of faith and of their high standard, and when it sees those who do not live up to their profession, it points at them with scorn.

Those who love Jesus will bring all in their lives into harmony with His will. They have chosen to be on the Lord's side, and their lives are to stand out in vivid contrast with the lives of worldlings. The tempter will come to them with his blandishments and bribes, saying: "All this will I give thee if thou wilt worship me." But they know that he has nothing worth receiving, and they refuse to yield to his temptations. Through the grace of God they are enabled to keep their purity of principle unsullied. Holy angels are close beside them, and Christ is revealed in their steadfast adherence to the truth. They are Christ's minutemen, bearing, as true witnesses, a decided testimony in favor of the truth. They show that there is a spiritual power that can enable men and women not to swerve an inch from truth and justice for all the gifts that men can bestow. Such ones, wherever they may be, will be honored of heaven because they have conformed their lives to the will of God, caring not what sacrifices they are called upon to make.

A WORLD-WIDE MESSAGE

The light that God has given His people is not to be shut up within the churches that already know the truth. It is to be shed abroad into the dark places of the earth. Those who walk in the light as Christ is in the light will co-operate with the Saviour by revealing to others what He has revealed to them. It is God's purpose that the truth for this time shall be made known to every kindred and nation and tongue and people. In the world today men and women are absorbed in the search for worldly gain and worldly pleasure. There are thousands upon thousands who give no time or thought to the salvation of the soul. The time has come when the message of Christ's soon coming is to sound throughout the world.

Unmistakable evidences point to the nearness of the end. The warning is to be given in certain tones. The way must be prepared for the coming of the Prince of Peace in the clouds of heaven. There is much to be done in the cities that have not yet heard the truth for this time. We are not to establish institutions to rival in size and splendor the institutions of the world; but in the name of the Lord, with the untiring perseverance and unflagging zeal that Christ brought into His labors, we are to carry forward the work of the Lord.

As a people we greatly need to humble our hearts before God, pleading His forgiveness for our neglect to fulfill the gospel commission. We have made large centers in a few places, leaving unworked many important cities. Let us now take up the work appointed us and proclaim the message that is to arouse men and women to a sense of their danger. If every Seventh-day Adventist had done the work laid upon him, the number of believers would now be much larger than it is. In all the cities of America there would be those who had been led to heed the message to obey the Law of God.

In some places the message regarding the observance of the Sabbath has been set forth with clearness and power, while other places have been left without warning. Will not those who know the truth awake to the responsibilities resting upon them? My brethren, you cannot afford to bury yourselves in worldly enterprises or interests. You cannot afford to neglect the commission given you by the Saviour.

Everything in the universe calls upon those who know the truth to consecrate themselves unreservedly to the proclamation of the truth as it has been made known to them in the third angel's message. That which we see and hear calls us to our duty. The working of satanic agencies calls every Christian to stand in his lot.

THE KIND OF WORKERS NEEDED

The work given us is a great and important one, and in it are needed wise, unselfish men, men who understand what it means to give themselves to unselfish effort to save souls. But there is no need for the service of men who are lukewarm, for such men Christ cannot use. Men and women are needed whose hearts are touched with human suffering and whose lives give evidence that they are receiving and imparting light and life and grace.

The people of God are to come close to Christ in self-denial and sacrifice, their one aim being to give the message of mercy to all the world. Some will work in one way and some in another, as the Lord shall call and lead them. But they are all to strive together, seeking to make the work a perfect whole. With pen and voice they are to labor for Him. The printed word of truth is to be translated into different languages and carried to the ends of the earth.

My heart is often burdened because so many who might work are doing nothing. They are the sport of Satan's temptations. Every church member who has a knowledge of the truth is expected to work while the day lasts; for the night cometh, wherein no man can work. Erelong we shall understand what that night means. The Spirit of God is being grieved away from the earth. The nations are angry with one another. Widespread preparations are being made for war. The night is at hand. Let the church arouse and go forth to do her appointed work. Every believer, educated or uneducated, can bear the message.

Eternity stretches before us. The curtain is about to

be lifted. What are we thinking of, that we cling to our selfish love of ease, while all around us souls are perishing? Have our hearts become utterly callous? Can we not see and understand that we have a work to do in behalf of others? My brethren and sisters, are you among those who, having eyes, see not, and having ears, hear not? Is it in vain that God has given you a knowledge of His will? Is it in vain that He has sent you warning after warning of the nearness of the end? Do you believe the declarations of His word concerning what is coming upon the world? Do you believe that God's judgments are hanging over the inhabitants of the earth? How, then, can you sit at ease, careless and indifferent?

Every day that passes brings us nearer the end. Does it bring us also near to God? Are we watching unto prayer? Those with whom we associate day by day need our help, our guidance. They may be in such a condition of mind that a word in season will be sent home by the Holy Spirit as a nail in a sure place. Tomorrow some of these souls may be where we can never reach them again. What is our influence over these fellow travelers? What effort do we make to win them to Christ?

Time is short, and our forces must be organized to do a larger work. Laborers are needed who comprehend the greatness of the work and who will engage in it, not for the wages they receive, but from a realization of the nearness of the end. The time demands greater efficiency and deeper consecration. Oh, I am so full of this subject that I cry to God: "Raise up and send forth messengers filled with a sense of their responsibility, messengers in whose hearts self-idolatry, which lies at the foundation of all sin, has been crucified."

AN IMPRESSIVE SCENE

In the visions of the night a very impressive scene passed before me. I saw an immense ball of fire fall among some beautiful mansions, causing their instant destruction. I heard someone say: "We knew that the judgments of God were coming upon the earth, but we did not know that they would come so soon." Others, with agonized voices, said: "You knew! Why then did you not tell us? We did not know." On every side I heard similar words of reproach spoken.

In great distress I awoke. I went to sleep again, and I seemed to be in a large gathering. One of authority was addressing the company, before whom was spread out a map of the world. He said that the map pictured God's vineyard, which must be cultivated. As light from heaven shone upon anyone, that one was to reflect the light to others. Lights were to be kindled in many places, and from these lights still other lights were to be kindled.

The words were repeated: "Ye are the salt of the earth: but if the salt have lost his savor, wherewith shall it be salted? it is thenceforth good for nothing, but to be cast out, and to be trodden underfoot of men. Ye are the light of the world. A city that is set on an hill cannot be hid. Neither do men light a candle, and put it under a bushel, but on a candlestick; and it giveth light unto all that are in the house. Let your light so shine before men, that they may see your good works, and glorify your Father which is in heaven." Matthew 5:13-16.

I saw jets of light shining from cities and villages, and from the high places and the low places of the earth. God's word was obeyed, and as a result there were memorials for Him in every city and village. His truth was proclaimed throughout the world.

Then this map was removed and another put in its place. On it light was shining from a few places only. The rest of the world was in darkness, with only a glimmer of light here and there. Our Instructor said: "This darkness is the result of men's following their own course. They have cherished hereditary and cultivated tendencies to evil. They have made questioning and faultfinding and accusing the chief business of their lives. Their hearts are not right with God. They have hidden their light under a bushel."

If every soldier of Christ had done his duty, if every watchman on the walls of Zion had given the trumpet a certain sound, the world might ere this have heard the message of warning. But the work is years behind. While men have slept, Satan has stolen a march upon us.

Putting our trust in God, we are to move steadily forward, doing His work with unselfishness, in humble dependence upon Him, committing ourselves and our present and future to His wise providence, holding the beginning of our confidence firm unto the end, remembering that it is not because of our worthiness that we receive the blessings of heaven, but because of the worthiness of Christ, and our acceptance, through faith in Him, of God's abounding grace.

HOME MISSIONARY WORK

God expects personal service from everyone to whom He has entrusted a knowledge of the truth for this time. Not all can go as missionaries to foreign lands, but all can be home missionaries in their families and neighborhoods. There are many ways in which church members may give the message to those around them. One of the most successful is by living helpful, unselfish, Christian lives. Those who are fighting the battle of life at great odds may be refreshed and strengthened by little attentions which cost nothing. Kindly words simply spoken, little attentions simply bestowed, will sweep away the clouds of temptation and doubt that gather over the soul. The true heart expression of Christlike sympathy, given in simplicity, has power to open the door of hearts that need the simple, delicate touch of the spirit of Christ.

Christ accepts, oh, so gladly! every human agency that is surrendered to Him. He brings the human into union with the divine, that He may communicate to the world the mysteries of incarnate love. Talk it, pray it, sing it, fill the world with the message of His truth, and keep pressing on into the regions beyond.

Heavenly intelligences are waiting to cooperate with human instrumentalities, that they may reveal to the world what human beings may become and what, through their influence, they may accomplish for the saving of souls that are ready to perish. He who is truly converted will be so filled with the love of God that he will long to impart to others the joy that he himself possesses. The Lord desires His church to show forth to the world the beauty of holiness. She is to demonstrate the power of Christian religion. Heaven is to be reflected in the character of the Christian. The song of gratitude and praise is to be heard by those in darkness. For the good tidings of the gospel, for its promises and assurances, we are to express our gratitude by seeking to do others good. The doing of this work will bring rays of heavenly righteousness to wearied, perplexed, suffering souls. It is as a fountain opened for the wayworn, thirsty traveler. At every work of mercy, every work of love, angels of God are present.

OUR EXAMPLE

Christ's work is to be our example. Constantly He went about doing good. In the temple and the synagogues, in the streets of the cities, in the marketplace and the workshop, by the seaside and among the hills, He preached the gospel and healed the sick. His life was one of unselfish service, and it is to be our lessonbook. His tender, pitying love rebukes our selfishness and heartlessness.

Wherever Christ went, He scattered blessings in His path. How many who claim to believe on Him have learned His lessons of kindness, of tender pity, of unselfish love? Hear His voice speaking to the weak, the weary, the helpless: "Come unto Me, all ye that labor and are heavy-laden, and I will give you rest." Matthew 11:28. There was no wearying of His patience, no repressing of His love.

Christ calls upon us to labor patiently and perseveringly for the thousands perishing in their sins, scattered in all lands, like wrecks on a desert shore. Those who share in Christ's glory must share also in His ministry, helping the weak, the wretched, and the despondent.

Let those who take up this work make the life of Christ their constant study. Let them be intensely in earnest, using every capability in the Lord's service. Precious results will follow sincere, unselfish effort. From the Great Teacher the workers will receive the highest of all education. But those who do not impart the light they have received will one day realize that they have sustained a fearful loss.

Human beings have no right to think that there is a limit to the efforts that they are to make in the work of soulsaving. Did Christ ever become weary in His work? Did He ever draw back from sacrifice and hardship? Church members are to put forth the continuous, persevering efforts that He put forth. They are to be ever ready to spring into action in obedience to the Master's commands. Wherever we see work waiting to be done we are to take it up and do it, constantly looking unto Jesus. If our church members would heed this instruction, hundreds of souls would be won to Jesus. If every church member were a living missionary, the gospel would speedily be proclaimed in all countries, to all peoples, nations, and tongues.

THE RESULT OF WHOLEHEARTED EFFORT

Let sanctified ability be brought into the work of proclaiming the truth for this time. If the forces of the enemy gain the victory now, it will be because the churches neglect their God-given work. For years the work has been kept before us, but many have been asleep. If Seventh-day Adventists will now arouse and do the work assigned them, the truth will be presented to our neglected cities in clear, distinct lines and in the power of the Spirit.

When wholehearted work is done, the efficacy of the

grace of Christ will be seen. The watchmen on the walls of Zion are to be wide awake, and they are to arouse others. God's people are to be so earnest and faithful in their work for Him that all selfishness will be separated from their lives. His workers will then see eye to eye, and the arm of the Lord, the power of which was seen in the life of Christ, will be revealed. Confidence will be restored, and there will be unity in the churches throughout our ranks.

DIFFERENT LINES OF SERVICE

The Lord is calling upon His people to take up different lines of work. Those in the highways and byways of life are to hear the gospel message. Church members are to do evangelistic work in the homes of their neighbors who have not yet received full evidence of the truth for this time.

God calls for Christian families to go into communities that are in darkness and error, and work wisely and perseveringly for the Master. To answer this call requires self-sacrifice. While many are waiting to have every obstacle removed, souls are dying without hope and without God in the world. Many, very many, for the sake of worldly advantage, for the sake of acquiring scientific knowledge, will venture into pestilential regions and endure hardship and privation. Where are those who are willing to do this for the sake of telling others of the Saviour? Where are the men and women who will move into regions that are in need of the gospel, that they may point those in darkness to the Redeemer?

CIRCULATING OUR PUBLICATIONS

Many of God's people are to go forth with our publications into places where the third angel's message has never been proclaimed. Our books are to be published in many different languages. With these books, humble, faithful men are to go out as colporteur-evangelists, bearing the truth to those who would otherwise never be enlightened. Those who take up this line of work are to go prepared to do medical missionary work. The sick and suffering are to be helped. Many for whom this work of mercy is done will hear and accept the words of life.

The work of the canvasser-evangelist, whose heart is imbued with the Holy Spirit, is fraught with wonderful possibilities for good. The presentation of the truth, in love and simplicity, from house to house, is in harmony with the instruction that Christ gave His disciples when He sent them out on their first missionary tour. By songs of praise, by humble, heartfelt prayers, many will be reached. The divine worker will be present to send conviction to hearts. "I am with you alway," is His promise. With the assurance of the abiding presence of such a helper we may labor with faith and hope and courage.

From city to city, from country to country, they are to carry the publications containing the promise of the Saviour's soon coming. These publications are to be translated into every language, for to all the world the gospel is to be preached. To every worker Christ promises the divine efficiency that will make his labors a success.

Those who have long known the truth need to seek the Lord most earnestly, that their hearts may be filled with a determination to work for their neighbors. My brethren and sisters, visit those who live near you, and by sympathy and kindness seek to reach their hearts. Be sure to work in a way that will remove prejudice instead of creating it. And remember that those who know the truth for this time and yet confine their efforts to their own churches, refusing to work for their unconverted neighbors, will be called to account for unfulfilled duties.

Lend your neighbors some of our smaller books. If their interest is awakened, take some of the larger books. Show them *Christ's Object Lessons.* Tell them its history, and ask them if they do not want a copy. If they already have it, ask them if they do not want to read other books of a similar nature. If possible, secure an opportunity to teach them the truth. Beside all waters you are to sow the seeds of truth, though not knowing which shall prosper, this or that.

HOUSE-TO-HOUSE WORK

In many states there are settlements of industrious, well-to-do farmers, who have never had the truth for this time. Such places should be worked. Let our lay members take up this line of service. By lending or selling books, by distributing papers, and by holding Bible readings, our lay members could do much in their own neighhorhoods. Filled with love for souls they could proclaim the message with such power that many would be converted.

Two Bible workers were seated in a family. With the open Bible before them, they presented the Lord Jesus Christ as the sin-pardoning Saviour. Earnest prayer was offered to God, and hearts were softened and subdued by the influence of the Spirit of God. Their prayers were uttered with freshness and power. As the word of God was explained, I saw that a soft, radiant light illumined the Scriptures, and I said, softly: "Go out into the highways and hedges, and compel them to come in, that My house may be filled." Luke 14:23.

The precious light was communicated from neighbor to neighbor. Family altars which had been broken down were again erected, and many were converted.

My brethren and sisters, give yourselves to the Lord for service. Allow no opportunity to pass unimproved. Visit the sick and suffering, and show a kindly interest in them. If possible, do something to make them more comfortable. Through this means you can reach their hearts and speak a word for Christ.

Eternity alone will reveal how far-reaching such a line of labor can be. Other lines of usefulness will open before those who are willing to do the duty nearest them. It is not learned, eloquent speakers that are needed now, but humble, Christlike men and women, who have learned from Jesus of Nazareth to be meek and lowly, and who, trusting in His strength, will go forth into the highways and hedges to give the invitation: "Come; for all things are now ready." Verse 17.

Those who are wise in agricultural lines, in tilling the soil, those who can construct simple, plain buildings, may help. They can do good work and at the same time show in their characters the high standard to which it is the privilege of this people to attain. Let farmers, financiers, builders, and those who are skilled in various other crafts, go to neglected fields, to improve the land, to establish industries, to prepare humble homes for themselves, and to give their neighbors a knowledge of the truth for this time.

WORK FOR WOMEN

There is a wide field of service for women as well as for men. The efficient cook, the seamstress, the nurse —the help of all is needed. Let the members of poor households be taught how to cook, how to make and mend their own clothing, how to nurse the sick, how to care properly for the home. Even the children should be taught to do some little errand of love and mercy for those less fortunate than themselves.

THE HOME A MISSION FIELD

Let not parents forget the great mission field that lies before them in the home. In the children committed to her every mother his a sacred charge from God. "Take this son, this daughter," God says, "and train it for Me. Give it a character polished after the similitude of a palace, that it may shine in the courts of the Lord forever." The light and glory that shine from the throne of God rest upon the faithful mother as she tries to educate her children to resist the influence of evil.

A PLACE FOR EVERYONE

There is earnest work for every pair of hands to do. Let every stroke tell for the uplifting of humanity. There are so many that need to be helped. The heart of him who lives, not to please himself, but to be a blessing to those who have so few blessings, will thrill with satisfaction. Let every idler awake and face the realities of life. Take the word of God and search its pages. If you are doers of the word, life will indeed be to you a living reality, and you will find that the reward is abundant.

The Lord has a place for everyone in His great plan. Talents that are not needed are not bestowed. Supposing that the talent is small. God has a place for it, and that one talent, if faithfully used, will do the very work God designs that it should do. The talents of the humble cottager are needed in the house-to-house labor and can accomplish more in this work than brilliant gifts.

A thousand doors of usefulness are open before us. We lament the scanty resources at present available, while various and urgent demands are pressing us for means and men. Were we thoroughly in earnest, even now we could multiply the resources a hundredfold. Selfishness and self-indulgence bar the way.

Church members, let the light shine forth. Let your voices be heard in humble prayer, in witness against intemperance, the folly, and the amusements of this world, and in the proclamation of the truth for this time. Your voice, your influence, your time—all these are gifts from God and are to be used in winning souls to Christ.

Visit your neighbors and show an interest in the salvation of their souls. Arouse every spiritual energy to action. Tell those whom you visit that the end of all things is at hand. The Lord Jesus Christ will open the door of their hearts and will make upon their minds lasting impressions.

Strive to arouse men and women from their spiritual insensibility. Tell them how you found Jesus and how blessed you have been since you gained an experience in His service. Tell them what blessing comes to you as you sit at the feet of Jesus and learn precious lessons from His word. Tell them of the gladness and joy that there is in the Christian life. Your warm, fervent words will convince them that you have found the pearl of great price. Let your cheerful, encouraging words show that you have certainly found the higher way. This is genuine missionary work, and as it is done, many will awake as from a dream.

Even while engaged in their daily employment, God's people can lead others to Christ. And while doing this they will have the precious assurance that the Saviour is close beside them. They need not think that they are left to depend on their own feeble efforts. Christ will give them words to speak that will refresh and encourage and strengthen poor, struggling souls who are in darkness. Their own faith will be strengthened as they realize that the Redeemer's promise is being fulfilled. Not only are they a blessing to others, but the work they do for Christ brings blessing to themselves.

There are many who can and should do the work of which I have spoken. My brother, my sister, what are you doing for Christ? Are you seeking to be a blessing to others? Are your lips uttering words of kindness, sympathy, and love? Are you putting forth earnest efforts to win others to the Saviour?

THE RESULT OF FAILING TO WORK

Comparatively little missionary work is done, and what is the result? The truths that Christ gave are not taught. Many of God's people are not growing in grace. Many are in an unpleasant, complaining frame of mind. Those who are not helping others to see the importance of the truth for this time must feel dissatisfied with themselves. Satan takes advantage of this feature in their experience and leads them to criticize and find fault. If they were busily engaged in seeking to know and do the will of God they would feel such a burden for perishing souls, such an unrest of mind, that they could not be restrained from fulfilling the commission: "Go ye into all the world, and preach the gospel to every creature." Mark 16:15.

AN APPEAL FOR UNTIRING EFFORT

The Lord calls upon His people to arouse out of sleep The end of all things is at hand. When those who know the truth will be laborers together with God, the fruits of righteousness will appear. By the revelation of the love of God in missionary effort many will be awakened to see the sinfulness of their own course of action. They will see that in the past their selfishness has disqualified them from being laborers together with God. The exhibition of the love of God as seen in unselfish ministry to others will be the means of leading many souls to believe the word of God just as it reads.

God desires to refresh His people by the gift of the Holy Spirit, baptizing them anew in His love. There is no need for a dearth of the Spirit in the church. After Christ's ascension the Holy Spirit came upon the waiting, praying, believing disciples with a fullness and power that reached every heart. In the future the earth is to be lightened with the glory of God. A holy influence is to go forth to the world from those who are sanctified through the truth. The earth is to be encircled with an atmosphere of grace. The Holy Spirit is to work on human hearts, taking the things of God and showing them to men.

MISSIONARY FAMILIES

Very much more might be done for Christ if all who have the light of truth would practice the truth. There are whole families who might be missionaries, engaging in personal labor, toiling for the Master with busy hands and active brains, devising new methods for the success of His work. There are earnest, prudent, warmhearted men and women who could do much for Christ if they would give themselves to God, drawing near to Him and seeking Him with the whole heart.

My brethren and sisters, take an active part in the work of soulsaving. This work will give life and vigor to the mental and spiritual powers. Light from Christ will shine into the mind. The Saviour will abide in your hearts, and in His light you will see light.

Consecrate yourselves wholly to the work of God. He is your strength, and He will be at your right hand, helping you to carry on His merciful designs. By personal labor reach those around you. Become acquainted with them. Preaching will not do the work that needs to be done. Angels of God attend you to the dwellings of those you visit. This work cannot be done by proxy. Money lent or given will not accomplish it. Sermons will not do it. By visiting the people, talking, praying, sympathizing with them, you will win hearts. This is the highest missionary work that you can do. To do it, you will need resolute, persevering faith, unwearying patience, and a deep love for souls.

Find access to the people in whose neighborhood you live. As you tell them of the truth, use words of Christlike sympathy. Remember that the Lord Jesus is the Master Worker. He waters the seed sown. He puts into your minds words that will reach hearts. Expect that God will sustain the consecrated, unselfish worker. Obedience, childlike faith, trust in God—these will bring peace and joy. Work disinterestedly, lovingly, patiently, for all with whom you are brought into contact. Show no impatience. Utter not one unkind word. Let the love of Christ be in your hearts, the law of kindness on your lips.

It is a mystery that there are not hundreds at work where now there is but one. The heavenly universe is astonished at the apathy, the coldness, the listlessness of those who profess to be sons and daughters of God. In the truth there is a living power. Go forth in faith, and proclaim the truth as if you believed it. Let those for whom you labor see that to you it is indeed a living reality.

DEVELOPMENT THROUGH SERVICE

Those who give their lives to Christlike ministry know the meaning of true happiness. Their interests and their prayers reach far beyond self. They themselves are growing as they try to help others. They become familiar with the largest plans, the most stirring enterprises, and how can they but grow when they place themselves in the divine channel of light and blessing? Such ones receive wisdom from heaven. They become more and more identified with Christ in all His plans. There is no opportunity for spiritual stagnation. Selfish ambition and self-seeking are rebuked by constant contact with the absorbing interests, the elevated aspirations, which belong to high and holy activities.

THE NEED OF EARNEST EFFORT

In the power of the Spirit the delegated servants of Christ are to bear witness for their Leader. The yearning desire of the Saviour for the salvation of sinners is to mark all their efforts. The gracious invitation, first given by Christ, is to be taken up by human voices and sounded throughout the world: "Whosoever will, let him take the water of life freely." Revelation 22:17. The church is to say: "Come." Every power in the church is to be actively engaged on the side of Christ. The followers of Christ are to combine in a strong effort to call the attention of the world to the fast-fulfilling prophecies of the word of God. Infidelity and spiritualism are gaining a strong hold in the world. Shall those to whom great light has been given be cold and faithless now?

We are on the very verge of the time of trouble, and perplexities that are scarcely dreamed of are before us. A power from beneath is leading men to war against Heaven. Human beings have confederated with satanic agencies to make void the law of God. The inhabitants of the world are fast becoming as the inhabitants of the world in Noah's day, who were swept away by the Flood, and as the inhabitants of Sodom, who were consumed by fire from heaven. The powers of Satan are at work to keep minds diverted from eternal realities. The enemy has arranged matters to suit his own purposes. Worldly business, sports, the fashions of the day—these things occupy the minds of men and women. Amusements and unprofitable reading spoil the judgment. In the broad road that leads to eternal ruin there walks a long procession. The world, filled with violence, reveling, and drunkenness, is converting the church. The law of God, the divine standard of righteousness, is declared to be of no effect.

At this time—a time of overwhelming iniquity—a new life, coming from the Source of all life, is to take possession of those who have the love of God in their hearts, and they are to go forth to proclaim with power the message of a crucified and risen Saviour. They are to put forth earnest, untiring efforts to save souls. Their example is to be such that it will have a telling influence for good on those around them. They are to count all things but loss for the excellency of the knowledge of Christ Jesus our Lord.

Intense earnestness should now take possession of us. Our slumbering energies should be aroused to untiring effort. Consecrated workers should go forth into the field clearing the King's highway, and gaining victories in new places. My brother, my sister, is it nothing to you to know that every day souls are going down into the grave unwarned and unsaved, ignorant of their need of eternal life and of the atonement made for them by the Saviour? Is it nothing to you that soon the world is to meet Jehovah over His broken law? Heavenly angels marvel that those who for so many years have had the light, have not carried the torch of truth into the dark places of the earth.

The infinite value of the sacrifice required for our redemption reveals the fact that sin is a tremendous evil. God might have wiped out this foul blot upon creation by sweeping the sinner from the face of the earth. But He "so loved the world, that He gave His only-begotten Son, that whosoever believeth in Him should not perish, but have everlasting life." John 3:16. Then why are we not more in earnest? Why are so large a number idle?

Why are not all who profess to love God, seeking to enlighten their neighbors and their associates, that they may no longer neglect so great salvation?

A LACK OF SYMPATHY

Among professing Christians of today there is a fearful lack of the sympathy that should be felt for souls unsaved. Unless our hearts beat in unison with the heart of Christ, how can we understand the sacredness and importance of the work to which we are called by the words: "Watch for . . . souls, as they that must give account"? We talk of Christian missions. The sound of our voices is heard, but do we feel Christ's tender heart longing for souls?

The Saviour was an untiring worker. He did not measure His work by hours. His time, His heart, His strength, were given to labor for the benefit of humanity. Entire days were devoted to labor, and entire nights were spent in prayer, that He might be braced to meet the wily foe in all his deceptive working, and fortified to do His work of uplifting and restoring humanity.

The man who loves God does not measure his work by the eight-hour system. He works at all hours and is never off duty. As he has opportunity he does good. Everywhere, at all times and in all places, he finds opportunity to work for God. He carries fragrance with him wherever he goes. A wholesome atmosphere surrounds his soul. The beauty of his well-ordered life and godly conversation inspires in others faith and hope and courage.

It is heart missionaries that are needed. Spasmodic efforts will do little good. We must arrest the attention. We must be deeply in earnest.

By aggressive warfare, in the midst of opposition,

peril, loss, and human suffering, the work of soulsaving is to be carried forward. At a certain battle, when one of the regiments of the attacking force was being beaten back by the hordes of the enemy, the ensign in front stood his ground as the troops retreated. The captain shouted to him to bring back the colors, but the reply of the ensign was: "Bring the men up to the colors!" This is the work that devolves upon every faithful standard-bearer—to bring the men up to the colors. The Lord calls for wholeheartedness. We all know that the sin of many professing Christians is that they lack the courage and energy to bring themselves and those connected with them up to the standard.

From all countries the Macedonian cry is sounding: "Come over, . . . and help us." God has opened fields before us, and if human agencies would but co-operate with divine agencies, many, many souls would be won to the truth. But the Lord's professing people have been sleeping over their allotted work, and in many places it remains comparatively untouched. God has sent message after message to arouse our people to do something, and to do it now. But to the call, "Whom shall I send?" there have been few to respond, "Here am I; send me." Isaiah 6:8.

When the reproach of indolence and slothfulness shall have been wiped away from the church, the Spirit of the Lord will be graciously manifested. Divine power will be revealed. The church will see the providential working of the Lord of hosts. The light of truth will shine forth in clear, strong rays, and, as in the time of the apostles, many souls will turn from error to truth. The earth will be lighted with the glory of the Lord.

Heavenly angels have long been waiting for human agents—the members of the church—to co-operate with them in the great work to be done. They are waiting for you. So vast is the field, so comprehensive the design, that every sanctified heart will be pressed into service as an instrument of divine power.

At the same time there will be a power working from beneath. While God's agents of mercy work through consecrated human beings, Satan sets his agencies in operation, laying under tribute all who will submit to his control. There will be lords many and gods many. The cry will be heard, "Lo, here is Christ," and, "Lo, there is Christ." The deep plotting of Satan will reveal itself everywhere for the purpose of diverting the attention of men and women from present duty. There will be signs and wonders. But the eye of faith will discern in all these manifestations harbingers of the grand and awful future, and the triumphs that await the people of God.

Work, oh, work, keeping eternity in view! Bear in mind that every power must be sanctified. A great work is to be done. Let the prayer go forth from unfeigned lips: "God be merciful unto us, and bless us; and cause His face to shine upon us. . . . That Thy way may be known upon earth, Thy saving health among all nations." Psalm 67:1, 2.

Those who realize, even in a limited degree, what redemption means to them and to their fellow men, will walk by faith and will comprehend in some measure the vast needs of humanity. Their hearts will be moved to compassion as they see the widespread destitution in our world—the destitution of the multitudes who are suffering for food and clothing, and the moral destitution of thousands who are under the shadow of a terrible doom, in comparison with which physical suffering fades into nothingness.

Let church members bear in mind that the fact that their names are registered on the church books will not save them. They must show themselves approved of God, workmen that need not be ashamed. Day by day they are to build their characters in accordance with Christ's directions. They are to abide in Him, constantly exercising faith in Him. Thus they will grow up to the full stature of men and women in Christ—wholesome, cheerful, grateful Christians, led by God into clearer and still clearer light. If this is not their experience, they will be among those whose voices will one day be raised in the bitter lamentation: "The harvest is past, the summer is ended, and my soul is not saved! Why did I not flee to the Stronghold for refuge? Why have I trifled with my soul's salvation, and done despite to the Spirit of grace?"

"The great day of the Lord is near, it is near, and hasteth greatly." Zephaniah 1:14. Let us be shod with the gospel shoes, ready to march at a moment's notice. Every hour, every minute, is precious. We have no time to spend in self-gratification. All around us there are souls perishing in sin. Every day there is something to do for our Lord and Master. Every day we are to point souls to the Lamb of God, who taketh away the sin of the world.

"Be ye also ready; for in such an hour as we think not the Son of man cometh." Matthew 24:44. Go to your rest at night with every sin confessed. Thus we did when in 1844 we expected to meet our Lord. And now this great event is nearer than when we first believed. Be ye always ready, in the evening, in the morning, and at noon, that when the cry is heard, "Behold, the Bridegroom cometh; go ye out to meet Him," you may, even though awakened out of sleep, go forth to meet Him with your lamps trimmed and burning.

"FREELY YE HAVE RECEIVED, FREELY GIVE"

Self-sacrifice is the keynote of the teachings of Christ. Often it is presented and enjoined in language that seems authoritative, because God sees that there is no other way to save man than to cut away from his life the selfishness which, if retained, would degrade the whole being.

Christ became poor that we might be partakers of the "far more exceeding and eternal weight of glory." 2 Corinthians 4:17. We are to practice the same self-sacrifice that led Him to give Himself up to the death of the cross, to make it possible for human beings to have eternal life. In all our expenditure of means we are to strive to fulfill the purpose of Him who is the alpha and omega of all Christian effort.

We are to place in the Lord's treasury all the means that we can spare. For this means, needy, unworked fields are calling. From many lands is sounding the cry, "Come over, . . . and help us." Our church members should feel a deep interest in home and foreign missions. Great blessings will come to them as they make self-sacrificing efforts to plant the standard of truth in new territory. The money invested in this work will bring rich returns. New converts, rejoicing in the light received from the word, will in their turn give of their means to carry the light of truth to others.

GOD'S BENEVOLENCE

God gives to us regularly, freely, abundantly. Every earthly blessing is from His hand. What if the Lord should cease to bestow His gifts upon us? What a cry of wretchedness, suffering, and want would go up from the earth! We need daily the unfailing flow of Jehovah's goodness.

This world was established and is sustained by the compassionate love of the Creator. God is the giver of all we have. He calls upon us to return to Him a portion of the abundance He has bestowed on us. Think of the care He gives the earth, sending the rain and sunshine in their season, to cause vegetation to flourish. He bestows His favors on the just and on the unjust. Shall not the recipients of His blessings show their gratitude by giving of their means to help suffering humanity?

There are many souls to be brought to the saving knowledge of the truth. The prodigal is far from his Father's house, perishing with hunger. He is to be the object of our compassion. Do you ask: "How does God regard those who are perishing in their sins?" I point you to Calvary. God "gave His only-begotten Son, that whosoever believeth in Him should not perish, but have everlasting life." John 3:16. Think of the Saviour's matchless love. While we were yet sinners, Christ died to save us from eternal death. In return for the great love wherewith Christ has loved you, you are to bring to Him your thank offering. You are to make a gratitude offering of yourself. Your time, your talents, your means—all are to flow to the world in a tide of love for the saving of the lost. Jesus has made it possible for you to accept His love and in happy co-operation with Him to work under its fragrant influence. He requires you to use your possessions in unselfish service, that His plan for the salvation of souls shall be carried forward with power. He expects you to give your undivided energies to His work.

Would you make your property secure? Place it in the hand that bears the nailprint of the crucifixion. Retain it in your possession, and it will be to your eternal loss. Give it to God, and from that moment it bears His inscription. It is sealed with His immutability. Would you enjoy your substance? Then use it for the blessing of the suffering.

THE WORLD'S NEED OF HELP

The magnitude of our work calls for willing liberality on the part of the people of God. In Africa, in China, in India, there are thousands, yes, millions, who have not heard the message of the truth for this time. They must be warned. The islands of the sea are waiting for a knowledge of God. In these islands schools are to be established to prepare students to go to higher schools within reach, there to be educated and trained, and sent back to their island homes to give to others the light they have received.

In our own country there is much to be done. There are many cities to be entered and warned. Evangelists should be finding their way into all the places where the minds of men are agitated over the question of Sunday legislation and the teaching of religion in the public schools. It is the neglect of Seventh-day Adventists to improve these providential opportunities that is hindering the advancement of the cause.

The Lord has made us His stewards. He has placed His means in our hands for faithful distribution. He asks us to render to Him His own. He has reserved the tithe as His sacred portion to be used in sending the gospel to all parts of the world. My brethren and sisters, confess and forsake your selfishness, and bring to the Lord your gifts and offerings. Bring Him also the tithe that you have withheld. Come confessing your neglect.

Prove the Lord, as He has invited you to do. "I will rebuke the devourer for your sakes, and he shall not destroy the fruits of your ground; neither shall your vine cast her fruit before the time in the field, saith the Lord of hosts." Malachi 3:11.

OUR SELFISHNESS A HINDRANCE TO GOD'S WORK

Instruction has been given me that there is a withholding of the tithe that should be faithfully brought into the Lord's treasury for the support of ministers and missionaries who are opening the Scriptures to the people and working from house to house. The work of evangelizing the world has been greatly hindered by personal selfishness. Some, even among professing Christians, are unable to see that the work of the gospel is to be supported by the means that Christ has given them. Money is needed in order that the work done all over the world may be carried forward. Thousands upon thousands are perishing in sin, and a lack of means is hindering the proclamation of the truth that is to be carried to all nations and kindreds and tongues and people. There are men ready to go forth as the Lord's messengers, but because of a lack of means in the treasury they cannot be sent to the places where the people are begging for someone to come and teach them the truth.

There are many in our world who are longing to hear the word of life. But how can they hear without a preacher? And how can those sent to teach them live without support? God would have the lives of His workers carefully sustained. They are His property, and He is dishonored when they are compelled to labor in a way that injures their health. He is dishonored, also, when for lack of means workers cannot be sent to destitute fields.

In place of complaining of the officers of the General Conference because they cannot respond to the multiplied calls for men and means, let our church members bear a living testimony to the power of the truth by denying self and giving liberally for the advancement of the work. Let our sisters save by refusing to put expensive trimmings on their garments. Let every unnecessary expense be cut down. Let every family bring their tithes and offerings to the Lord.

GOD'S ALMONERS

Those who are truly converted will regard themselves as God's almoners and will dispense, for the advancement of the work, the means He has placed in their hands. If Christ's words were obeyed, there would be sufficient means in His treasury for the needs of His cause. He has entrusted to men and women an abundance of means for the carrying forward of His plan of mercy and benevolence. He bids His stewards of means invest their money in the work of feeding the hungry, clothing the naked, and preaching the gospel to the poor. Perfection of character cannot possibly be attained without self-sacrifice.

Never was there a more important time in the history of our work than the present. The message of the third chapter of Malachi comes to us, holding up before us the need of honesty in our relations to the Lord and His work. My brethren, the money that you use to buy and sell and get gain will be a curse to you if you withhold from the Lord that which is His. The means entrusted to you for the advancement of the Lord's work should be used in sending the gospel to all parts of the world.

We are Christ's witnesses, and we are not to allow

worldly interests and plans to absorb our time and attention. There are higher interests at stake. "Seek ye first
the kingdom of God, and His righteousness." Matthew
6:33. Christ gave Himself willingly and cheerfully to the
carrying out of the will of God. He became obedient unto
death, even the death of the cross. In view of all that He
has done, should we feel it a hardship to deny self? Shall
we draw back from being partakers of Christ's
sufferings? His death ought to stir every fiber of our beings, making us willing to consecrate to His work all that
we have and are. As we think of all that He has done for
us, our hearts should be filled with gratitude and love,
and we should renounce all selfishness. What duty could
the heart refuse to perform under the constraining influence of the love of Christ?

Shall we not, by self-denial, do all that we can to advance God's enterprise of mercy? Can we behold the divine condescension, the suffering endured by the Son of
God, without being filled with a desire to be allowed to
sacrifice something for Him? Is it not a high honor to be
allowed to co-operate with Him? He left His heavenly
home to seek for us. Shall we not become His undershepherds, to seek for the lost and straying? Shall we
not reveal in our lives His divine tenderness and compassion?

The Lord desires His people to be thoughtful and care-
taking. He desires them to practice economy in everything. If the workers in the mission fields could have the
means that is used in expensive furnishings and in personal adornment, the triumphs of the cross of Christ
would be greatly extended.

Not all can make large offerings, not all can do great
works, magnificent deeds; but all can practice self-denial,
all can reveal the unselfishness of the Saviour. Some can

bring large gifts to the Lord's treasury; others can bring only mites; but every gift brought in sincerity is accepted by the Lord.

We plead for the money that is spent on needless things. My brethren and sisters, waste not your money in purchasing unnecessary things. You may think these little sums do not amount to much, but many littles will make a great whole. Cut off every extravagant expenditure. Indulge in nothing that is simply for display. Your money means the salvation of souls. Let there be systematic giving on the part of all. Some may be unable to give a large sum, but all can lay aside each week something for the Master. Let the children act their part. Let parents teach their children to save their pennies to give to the Lord. The gospel ministry is to be supported by self-denial and sacrifice. Through the self-denying efforts of God's people others will be brought into the faith, and these in turn will help to increase the offerings made for the carrying forward of the Lord's work.

Unmistakable evidences point to the nearness of the end. The way must be prepared for the coming of the Prince of Peace. Let not our church members complain because they are so often called upon to give. What is it that makes the frequent calls a necessity? Is it not the rapid increase of missionary enterprises? Shall we, by refusing to give, retard the growth of these enterprises? Shall we forget that we are laborers together with God? From every church, prayers should ascend to God for an increase of devotion and liberality. My brethren and sisters, do not plead for retrenchment in evangelical work. So long as there are souls to save, our interest in the work of soulsaving is to know no abating. The church cannot abridge her task without denying her Master. Not all can go as missionaries to foreign lands, but all can give of their means for the carrying forward of foreign missions.

There are new fields to be entered, and we must have your help. Shall we ignore the commission given us, and thus forfeit the fulfillment of the promise accompanying the commission? Shall the people of God become careless and indifferent, and refuse to give of their means for the advancement of His work? Can they do this without severing their connection with Him? They may think thus to economize, but it is a fearful economy that places them where they are separated from God.

My brethren and sisters, it is too late to devote your time and strength to self-serving. Let not the last day find you destitute of the heavenly treasure. Seek to push the triumphs of the cross, seek to enlighten souls, labor for the salvation of your fellow beings, and your work will abide the trying test of fire.

Every true, self-sacrificing worker for God is willing to spend and be spent for the sake of others. Christ says: "He that loveth his life shall lose it; and he that hateth his life in this world shall keep it unto life eternal." John 12:25. By earnest, thoughtful efforts to help where help is needed, the true Christian shows his love for God and for his fellow beings. He may lose his life in service; but when Christ comes to gather His jewels to Himself, he will find it again.

My brethren and sisters, do not spend a large amount of time and money on self, for the sake of appearance. Those who do this are obliged to leave undone many things that would have comforted others, sending a warm glow to their weary spirits. We all need to learn how to improve faithfully the opportunities that so often come to us to bring light and hope into the lives of others. How can we improve these opportunities if our thoughts are centered on self? He who is self-centered loses countless opportunities for doing that which would have brought blessing to himself and others. It is the duty of the servant of Christ, under every circumstance, to ask himself, What can I do to help others? Having done his best, he is to leave the consequences with God.

God has provided for everyone pleasure that may be enjoyed by rich and poor alike—the pleasure found in cultivating pureness of thought and unselfishness of action, the pleasure that comes from speaking sympathizing words and doing kindly deeds. From those who perform such service, the light of Christ shines to brighten lives darkened by many sorrows.

The temptation may come to you to invest your money in land. Perhaps your children will advise you to do this. But can you not show a better way? Has not your money been entrusted to you to be traded upon wisely, and put out to usury, that when the Lord comes, He may find the talents doubled? Can you not see that He wants you to use your means in helping to build meeting houses and to establish sanitariums?

We need now to esteem souls above money. If you know of a higher work in this world than the work of soulsaving, a work which will bring better results for the investment of means, will you not tell us of it, that we may measure its value?

I fear that many of our people do not realize the importance of God's work. One to whom I wrote for money answered thus: "I received your letter asking me to lend you some money. But there was a piece of land that the children thought it advisable for me to purchase, and I have invested my spare means in this land." How much better would it have been for this brother to invest his money in establishing sanitariums, in which witness is borne to the truth for this time, or in schools, which will provide for our youth the best influences, and in which they can be trained to become missionaries for God.

My brethren and sisters, invest your means in the establishment of Christian missions, from which the light of truth will shine forth, drawing souls to God. One soul, truly converted, becoming a missionary for God, will win other souls to the Saviour.

God Himself originated plans for the advancement of His work, and He has provided His people with a surplus of means, that when He calls for help, they may respond, saying: "Lord, Thy pound hath gained other pounds."

If those to whom God's money has been entrusted will be faithful in bringing the means lent them to the Lord's treasury, His work will make rapid advancement. Many souls will be won to the cause of truth, and the day of Christ's coming will be hastened. Men and women are to be brought under the influence of true, earnest, wholehearted workers, who labor for souls as they that must give an account. All who are baptized into a measure of the apostolic spirit will be constrained to become God's missionaries. If they will be true, firm in the faith, if they will not sell their Lord for gain, but will ever acknowledge the divine supremacy and superintendence, God will prepare the way before them and will greatly bless them. He will help them to represent His goodness, love, and mercy. And the glory of the Lord will be their rearward. There will be joy in the heavenly courts, and joy, pure, heavenly joy, will fill the hearts of the workers. To save perishing souls they will be willing to spend and be spent, and their hearts will be filled with love and thanksgiving. The consciousness of God's presence will purify and ennoble their experience, enriching and strengthening them. The grace of heaven will be revealed in their work, in the conquests achieved in winning souls to Christ.

So God's work in our world is to be carried forward. Faithful stewards are to place the Lord's money in His treasury, that workers may be sent to all parts of the world. The church here below is to serve God with self-denial and sacrifice. Thus the work is to be carried forward and the most glorious triumphs won.

Love for lost souls brought Christ to Calvary's cross. Love for souls will lead us to self-denial and sacrifice, for the saving of that which is lost. And as Christ's followers give back to the Lord His own, they are accumulating treasure which will be theirs when they hear the words: "Well done, thou good and faithful servant: . . . enter thou into the joy of thy Lord," "who for the joy that was set before Him endured the cross, despising the shame, and is set down at the right hand of the throne of God." Matthew 25:21; Hebrews 12:2. The joy of seeing souls eternally saved will be the reward of all who follow in the steps of the Redeemer.

"He that spared not His own Son, but delivered Him up for us all, how shall He not with Him also freely give us all things?" Romans 8:32.

It was a costly sacrifice that the Lord of heaven made. Divine benevolence was stirred to its unfathomable depths; it was impossible for God to give more. He "so loved the world, that He gave His only-begotten Son, that whosoever believeth in Him should not perish, but have everlasting life." John 3:16. Why is our gratitude so limited? It is only as a ripple on the surface, compared with the great tide of love that flows to us from the Father.

The signs that foretell the second coming of Christ are fast fulfilling. Shall the people be left in ignorance of the great event before them and have to meet that awful day unprepared? Heaven has made a complete offering for the salvation of the world. Shall those who profess to love God and keep His commandments be indifferent to the souls of men? No, no! they cannot be.

With untiring zeal those who have received the light of present truth should go forth to give this light to those who sit in darkness. With consecrated efforts, by self-denial and self-sacrifice, they are to labor in the strength of the God of Israel. This message is to be carried to foreign lands; it is to be given to the cities and towns of our own country. The weary and the heavy-laden are longing for the message of truth that will give them rest and peace in Christ. Who will carry the message to those who have never heard it? Who will seek the joy and glory of God by drawing sinners to the feet of Him who gave His life a sacrifice for every soul? Who will lift up the Saviour before men as "the Lamb of God, which taketh away the sin of the world"? John 1:29.

LITERATURE IN SERVICE *

"The Lord gave the word:
great was the company of those
that published it." Psalm
68:11.

OUR PUBLICATIONS

The great and wonderful work of the last gospel message is to be carried on now as it has never been before. The world is to receive the light of truth through an evangelizing ministry of the word in our books and periodicals. Our publications are to show that the end of all things is at hand. I am bidden to say to our publishing houses: "Lift up the standard; lift it up higher. Proclaim the third angel's message, that it may be heard by all the world. Let it be seen that 'here are they that keep the commandments of God, and the faith of Jesus.' Revelation 14:12. Let our literature give the message as a witness to all the world."

Our workers should now be encouraged to give their first attention to books that deal with the evidences of our faith—books that teach the doctrines of the Bible and that will prepare a people to stand in the trying times before us. Having brought a people to the enlightenment of the truth by prayerful labor in Bible instruction, and through a wise use of our publications, we are to teach them to become laborers in word and doctrine. We are to encourage them to scatter the books that deal with Bible subjects—books the teachings of which will prepare a people to stand, having their loins girded with truth and their lamps burning.

We have been asleep, as it were, regarding the work

* A portion of this matter was published first in 1908.

that may be accomplished by the circulation of well-prepared literature. Let us now, by the wise use of periodicals and books, preach the word with determined energy, that the world may understand the message that Christ gave to John on the Isle of Patmos. Let every human intelligence who professes the name of Christ testify: "The end of all things is at hand; prepare to meet thy God."

Our publications should go everywhere. Let them be issued in many languages. The third angel's message is to be given through this medium and through the living teacher. You who believe the truth for this time, wake up. It is your duty now to bring in all the means possible to help those who understand the truth to proclaim it. Part of the money that comes in from the sale of our publications should be used to increase our facilities for the production of more literature that will open blind eyes and break up the fallow ground of the heart.

There is danger of entering into commercialism and becoming so engrossed in worldly business that the truths of the word of God in their purity and power will not be brought into the life. The love of trade and gain is becoming more and more prevalent. My brethren, let your souls be truly converted. If ever there was a time when we needed to understand our responsibilities, it is now, when truth is fallen in the streets and, equity cannot enter. Satan has come down with great power to work with all deceivableness of unrighteousness in them that perish; and everything that can be shaken will be shaken, and those things that cannot be shaken will remain. The Lord is coming very soon, and we are entering into scenes of calamity. Satanic agencies, though unseen, are working to destroy human life. But if our life is hid with Christ in God, we shall see of His grace and salvation. Christ is coming to establish His kingdom on the earth. Let our tongues be sanctified and used to glorify Him. Let us work now as we have never worked before. We are exhorted to "be instant in season, out of season." 2 Timothy 4:2. We are to make openings for the presentation of the truth. We are to improve every opportunity of drawing souls to Christ.

As a people we are to be reconverted, our lives sanctified to declare the truth as it is in Jesus. In the work of scattering our publications, we can speak of a Saviour's love from a warm and throbbing heart. God alone has the power to forgive sins; if we do not speak this message to the unconverted, our neglect may prove their ruin. Blessed, soul-saving Bible truths are published in our papers. There are many who can help in the work of selling our periodicals. The Lord calls upon all of us to seek to save perishing souls. Satan is at work to deceive the very elect, and now is our time to work with vigilance. Our books and papers are to be brought before the notice of the people; the gospel of present truth is to be given to our cities without delay. Shall we not arouse to our duties?

If we are making the life and teachings of Christ our study, every passing event will furnish a text for an impressive discourse. It was thus the Saviour preached the gospel in the highways and byways; and as He spoke, the little group that listened to Him swelled to a great company. Present-day evangelists are to be workers together with Christ. These, just as verily as the first disciples, have the assurance: "All power is given unto Me in heaven and in earth. Go ye therefore, and teach all nations, baptizing them in the name of the Father, and of the Son, and of the Holy Ghost: teaching them to observe all things whatsoever I have commanded you:

and, lo, I am with you alway, even unto the end of the world." Matthew 28:18-20.

The work to be carried on by the people of God is declared in the words of Inspiration: "Behold, I send My messenger before Thy face, which shall prepare Thy way before Thee. The voice of one crying in the wilderness, Prepare ye the way of the Lord, make His paths straight." Mark 1:2, 3. "Behold My servant, whom I uphold; Mine elect, in whom My soul delighteth, I have put My Spirit upon Him. He shall bring forth judgment to the Gentiles. . . . He shall not fail nor be discouraged, till He have set judgment in the earth and the isles shall wait for His law." Isaiah 42:1-4.

God invites all men to the fullest investigation of the claims of His law. His word is sacred and infinite. The cause of truth is to go forth as a lamp that burneth. Earnest study of the word of God will reveal the truth. Sin and wrong will not be sustained, but the law of God will be vindicated. "Thus saith God the Lord, He that created the heavens, and stretched them out; He that spread forth the earth, and that which cometh out of it; He that giveth breath unto the people upon it, and spirit to them that walk therein: I the Lord have called thee in righteousness, and will hold thine hand, and will keep thee, and give thee for a covenant of the people, for a light of the Gentiles; to open the blind eyes, to bring out the prisoners from the prison, and them that sit in darkness out of the prison house." Verse 5-7. Christians are to seek their light from the word of God and then in faith go forth to give that light to those who sit in darkness.

Sanitarium, California, May 24, 1908.

CIRCULATE THE PUBLICATIONS

In the night of March 2, 1907, many things were revealed to me regarding the value of our publications on present truth and the small effort that is being made by our brethren and sisters in the churches for their wide circulation.

I have been repeatedly shown that our presses should now be constantly employed in publishing light and truth. This is a time of spiritual darkness in the churches of the world. Ignorance of divine things has hidden God and the truth from view. The forces of evil are gathering in strength. Satan flatters his co-workers that he will do a work that will captivate the world. While partial inactivity has come upon the church, Satan and his hosts are intensely active. The professed Christian churches are not converting the world; for they are themselves corrupted with selfishness and pride, and need to feel the converting power of God in their midst before they can lead others to a purer or higher standard.

AN ENCOURAGING EXPERIENCE

The afternoon of March 2 I spent in counsel with Brother and Sister S. N. Haskell, discussing the work in Oakland and their plans to go East to spend some time in South Lancaster. After our visit I was weary and retired early. I was suffering with rheumatism in my left side and could get no rest because of the pain. I turned from side to side, trying to find ease from the suffering. There was a pain in my heart that portended no good for me. At last I fell asleep.

About half past nine I attempted to turn myself, and as I did so, I became aware that my body was entirely free from pain. As I turned from side to side, and moved my hands, I experienced an extraordinary freedom and lightness that I cannot describe. The room was filled with light, a most beautiful, soft, azure light, and I seemed to be in the arms of heavenly beings.

This peculiar light I have experienced in the past in times of special blessing, but this time it was more distinct, more impressive, and I felt such peace, peace so full and abundant no words can express it. I raised myself into a sitting posture, and I saw that I was surrounded by a bright cloud, white as snow, the edges of which were tinged with a deep pink. The softest, sweetest music was filling the air, and I recognized the music as the singing of the angels. Then a Voice spoke to me, saying: "Fear not; I am your Saviour. Holy angels are all about you."

"Then this is heaven," I said, "and now I can be at rest. I shall have no more messages to bear, no more misrepresentations to endure. Everything will be easy now, and I shall enjoy peace and rest. Oh, what inexpressible peace fills my soul! Is this indeed heaven? Am I one of God's little children? and shall I always have this peace?"

The Voice replied: "Your work is not yet done."

Again I fell asleep, and when I awoke I heard music, and I wanted to sing. Then someone passed my door, and I wondered if that person saw the light. After a time the light passed away, but the peace remained.

After a while I fell asleep again. This time I seemed to be in a council meeting where our book work was being discussed. There were a number of our brethren present, leaders in our work, and Elder Haskell and his wife were there consulting together and with the brethren about the circulation of our books, tracts, and periodicals.

Elder Haskell was presenting strong reasons why the books which contain the knowledge that has been communicated to Sister White—the books containing the special message to come to the world at this present time—should be more freely circulated. "Why," he inquired, "do not our people appreciate and circulate more widely the books bearing the divine credentials? Why is not a specialty made of the books containing the warnings regarding Satan's work? Why do we not give greater effort to circulating the books that point out Satan's plans to counterwork the work of God, that uncover his plans and point out his deceptions? The moral evils of his deceptions are to be removed by opening the eyes of the people so that they shall discern the situation and the dangers of our times; so that they shall make diligent effort to lay hold by faith upon Christ and His righteousness."

A messenger from heaven stood in our midst, and he spoke words of warning and instruction. He made us clearly understand that the gospel of the kingdom is the message for which the world is perishing and that this message, as contained in our publications already in print and those yet to be issued, should be circulated among the people who are nigh and afar off.

DANGERS IN SPECULATIVE STUDY

The light of truth which God designs shall come to the people of the world at this time is not that which the world's men of learning are seeking to impart, for these men in their research often arrive at erroneous conclusions and in their study of many authors become enthused with theories that are of satanic origin. Satan, clothed in the garb of an angel of light, presents for the study of the human mind subjects which seem very interesting and which are full of scientific mystery. In the investigation of these subjects, men are led to accept erroneous conclusions and to unite with seducing spirits in the work of propounding new theories which lead away from the truth.

There is danger that the false sentiments expressed in the books that they have been reading will sometimes be interwoven by our ministers, teachers, and editors with their arguments, discourses, and publications, under the belief that they are the same in principle as the teachings of the Spirit of truth. The book *Living Temple* is an illustration of this work, the writer of which declared in its support that its teachings were the same as those found in the writings of Mrs. White. Again and again we shall be called to meet the influence of men who are studying sciences of satanic origin, through which Satan is working to make a nonentity of God and of Christ.

The Father and the Son each have a personality. Christ declared: "I and My Father are one." Yet it was the Son of God who came to the world in human form. Laying aside His royal robe and kingly crown, He clothed His divinity with humanity, that humanity through His infinite sacrifice might become partakers of the divine nature and escape the corruption that is in the world through lust.

Christ was tempted in all points as man is tempted, but at no time did He bring against the tempter a railing accusation. To every temptation He presented the word of the Lord. "It is written" was His never-failing weapon. We, as the representatives of Christ, are to meet every thrust of the enemy with the word of the living

God. Never should we allow ourselves to follow the trail of the serpent by using his scientific arguments. Satan can never gain advantage of the child of God who relies on the word of God as his defense.

Our Counselor impressed deeply on our minds that God's commandment-keeping people must be sanctified through the truth and that truth must ever be given the foremost place. We must not forget that Satan still lives to exercise his deceptive power through false science.

Christ was the Majesty of heaven, the Prince of life; yet He humbled Himself as a man and became obedient to every law of God. He passed over the ground that every man must tread who takes His name, and came forth from His trial pure and untainted by sin. He was our example in all things.

The first advent of Christ and His life of ministry are not studied as they should be. His life was one of self-denial, in which truth in all its noble qualities was expressed. He lived to bless humanity by every good word and work.

DIGNITY OF THE BOOK WORK

The work of bookmaking is a grand and good work; but it has not always stood in the high and holy position that God designed it should occupy, because self has been interwoven with the work of some who have engaged in it. The book work should be the means of quickly giving the sacred light of present truth to the world. The publications that come forth from our presses today are to be of such a character as to strengthen every pin and pillar of the faith that was established by the word of God and by the revelations of His Spirit.

The truth that God has given for His people in these last days should keep them firm when there come into the church those who present false theories. The truth that has stood firm against the attacks of the enemy for more than half a century must still be the confidence and comfort of God's people.

Our evidence to nonprofessors that we have the truth of the word of God will be given in a life of strict self-denial. We must not make a mockery of our faith, but ever keep before us the example of Him who, though He was the Prince of heaven, stooped to a life of self-denial and sacrifice to vindicate the righteousness of His Father's word. Let us each resolve to do our best, that the light of our good works may shine forth to the world.

UNITY IN PROGRESS

Perfect agreement should exist in the plans laid for the publication of our books and periodicals, that the light which they contain may be quickly carried everywhere to the nominal churches and to the world. Much more should have been accomplished in the sale of our books than we see accomplished today.

Our ministers should call upon the church members to let the truth triumph. "Arise, shine; for thy light is come, and the glory of the Lord is risen upon thee. For, behold, the darkness shall cover the earth, and gross darkness the people: but the Lord shall arise upon thee, and His glory shall be seen upon thee. And the Gentiles shall come to thy light, and kings to the brightness of thy rising." Isaiah 60:1-3. Unity and love will accomplish wonderful things for the believers. Will not our churches arouse and give the last warning message to the world?

OUR RELIEF BOOKS

Christ's Object Lessons is a book that speaks for itself, and it has accomplished a good work. As it has been sold, and the object of its sale related, money has been received that has relieved the indebtedness of our schools. But more than this, many by reading the book have been blessed by its lessons of truth, and many others will be blessed by reading it.

The book *Ministry of Healing* may do the same work for our sanitariums and health institutions that *Christ's Object Lessons* has done for our schools. This book contains the wisdom of the Great Physician. To me it has been a precious privilege to donate my work on these books to the cause of God. In the future there should be well-planned and persevering efforts made to increase their sale.

LIFT THE DEBTS

God designs that we shall learn lessons from the failures of the past. It is not pleasing to Him to have debts rest upon His institutions. We have reached the time when we must give character to the work by refusing to erect large and costly buildings. We are not to copy the mistakes of the past and become more and more involved in debt. We are rather to endeavor to clear off the indebtedness that still remains on our institutions. Our churches can help in this matter if they will. Those members to whom the Lord has given means can invest their money in the cause without interest or at a low rate of interest, and by their freewill offerings they can help to support the work. The Lord asks you to return cheerfully to Him a portion of the goods He has lent you, and thus become His almoners.

ANOTHER VIEW OF THE BOOK WORK

Afterward we were in camp meetings and in large meetings in our churches, where the ministers presented clearly the perils of the times in which we live and the great importance of making haste in the circulation of our literature. In response to these appeals the brethren and sisters came forward and purchased many books. Some took a few, and some purchased large quantities. Most of the purchasers paid for the books they took. A few arranged to pay afterward.

Because books were being sold at low prices, some being especially reduced for the occasion, many were purchased, and some by persons not of our faith. They said: "It must be that these books contain a message for us. These people are willing to make sacrifices in order that we may have them, and we will secure them for ourselves and our friends."

But dissatisfaction was expressed by some of our own people. One said: "A stop must be put to this work, or our business will be spoiled." As one brother was carrying away an armful of books, a canvasser laid his hand upon his arm and said: "My brother, what are you doing with so many books?" Then I heard the voice of our Counselor saying: "Forbid them not. This is a work that should be done. The end is near. Already much time has been lost, when these books should have been in circulation. Sell them far and near. Scatter them like the leaves of autumn. This work is to continue without the forbiddings of anyone. Souls are perishing out of Christ. Let them be warned of His soon appearing in the clouds of heaven."

Some of the workers continued to appear much cast down. One was weeping and said: "These are doing the publishing work an injustice by purchasing these books at so low a price; besides, this work is depriving us of some of the revenue by which our work is sustained." The Voice replied: "You are meeting with no loss. These workers who take the books at reduced prices could not obtain so ready sale for them except it be at this so-called sacrifice. Many are now purchasing for their friends and for themselves who otherwise would not think of buying."

A CAUTION

Then instruction was given to Elder Haskell that in his anxiety to supply the people with the precious truth contained in his books, in his desire that all should feel that the books are worth more than they cost, and that all should be encouraged to give them a wide circulation, he was selling his books too cheap, and thus making his own burden too heavy.

Our Counselor said: "The books should be sold in such a way that the author will not be left barehanded and that the publishing house shall have a proper margin so that it will have means to carry on its work."

A PARABLE FOR OUR STUDY

"The kingdom of heaven is like unto a man that is an householder," Christ declared, "which went out early in the morning to hire laborers into his vineyard. And when he had agreed with the laborers for a penny a day, he sent them into his vineyard. And he went out about the third hour, and saw others standing idle in the market place, and said unto them; Go ye also into the vineyard, and whatsoever is right I will give you. And they went their way.

"Again he went out about the sixth and ninth hour, and did likewise. And about the eleventh hour he went out, and found others standing idle, and saith unto them, Why stand ye here all the day idle? They say unto him, Because no man hath hired us. He saith unto them, Go ye also into the vineyard; and whatsoever is right, that shall ye receive. So when even was come, the lord of the vineyard saith unto his steward, Call the laborers, and give them their hire, beginning from the last unto the first. And when they came that were hired about the eleventh hour, they received every man a penny.

"But when the first came, they supposed that they should have received more; and they likewise received every man a penny. And when they had received it, they murmured against the goodman of the house, saying, These last have wrought but one hour, and thou hast made them equal unto us, which have borne the burden and heat of the day. But he answered one of them, and said, Friend, I do thee no wrong: didst not thou agree with me for a penny? Take that thine is, and go thy way: I will give unto this last, even as unto thee. Is it not lawful for me to do what I will with mine own? Is thine eye evil, because I am good? So the last shall be first, and the first last: for many be called, but few chosen." Matthew 20:1-16.

Blessed will be the recompense of grace to those who have wrought for God in the simplicity of faith and love. The value of service to God is measured by the spirit in which it is rendered, rather than by the length of time spent in labor.

LIGHT FOR ALL

I am very desirous that the light contained in my books shall come to every soul possible, for God has sent the message for all. These books contain precious lessons in Christian experience. I would not dare forbid that these books be sold on special occasions at a low price, lest I should hinder the reading of the books, and thus withhold the light from some soul who might be converted to the truth. I have no forbiddings to place on the work of circulating our books. Let the light be placed on the candlestick, that it may give light to all that are in the house.

A LESSON IN COMMERCIALISM

"And Jesus went into the temple of God, and cast out all them that sold and bought in the temple, and overthrew the tables of the money-changers, and the seats of them that sold doves, and said unto them, It is written, My house shall be called the house of prayer; but ye have made it a den of thieves.

"And the blind and the lame came to Him in the temple; and He healed them. And when the chief priests and scribes saw the wonderful things that He did, and the children crying in the temple, and saying, Hosanna to the Son of David; they were sore displeased, and said unto Him, Hearest thou what these say? And Jesus saith unto them, Yea; have ye never read, Out of the mouth of babes and sucklings Thou hast perfected praise?" Matthew 21:12-16.

Sanitarium, California, May 4, 1908.

One point that should never be forgotten by our workers is that the Lord Jesus Christ is our chief director. He has outlined a plan by which the schools may be relieved of their indebtedness, and He will not vindicate the course of those who lay this plan aside for lack of confidence in its success. When His people will come up unitedly to the help of His cause in the earth, no good thing that God has promised will be withheld from them.

A BROADER VIEW

In carrying forward the Lord's work at home and abroad, those in positions of responsibility must plan wisely, so as to make the best possible use of men and of means. The burden of sustaining the work in many of the foreign fields must be largely borne by our conferences in the homeland. These conferences should have means with which to assist in opening new fields, where the testing truths of the third angel's message have never yet penetrated. Within the past few years, doors have been thrown open as if by magic; and men and women are needed to enter these doors and begin earnest work for the salvation of souls.

Our educational institutions can do much toward meeting the demand for trained workers for these mission fields. Wise plans should be laid to strengthen the work done in our training centers. Study should be given to the best methods for fitting consecrated young men and young women to bear responsibility and to win souls for Christ. They should be taught how to meet the people and how to present the third angel's message in an attractive manner. And in the management of financial matters they should be taught lessons that will help them when they are sent to isolated fields where they must suffer many privations and practice the strictest economy.

The Lord has instituted a plan whereby many of the students in our schools can learn practical lessons needful to success in afterlife. He has given them the privilege of handling precious books that have been dedicated for the advancement of our educational and sanitarium work. In the very handling of these books, the youth will meet with many experiences that will teach them how to cope with problems that await them in the regions beyond. During their school life, as they canvass for these books, many may learn how to approach people courteously and how to exercise tact in conversing with them on different points of present truth. And as they meet with a degree of success financially, some will learn lessons of thrift and economy, which will be of great advantage to them when they are sent out as missionaries.

The students who take up the work of selling *Christ's Object Lessons* and *Ministry of Healing* will need to study the book they expect to sell. As they familiarize their minds with the subject matter of the book in hand and endeavor to practice its teachings they will develop in knowledge and spiritual power. The messages in these books contain the light that God has revealed to me to give to the world. The teachers in our schools should encourage the students to make a careful study of every chapter. They should teach these truths to their students and seek to inspire the youth with a love for the precious thoughts the Lord has entrusted to us to communicate to the world.

Thus the preparation for handling these books, and the daily experiences gained while bringing them to the attention of the people, will prove an invaluable schooling to those who take part in this line of effort. Under the blessing of God the youth will obtain a fitting up for service in the Lord's vineyard.

There is a special work to be done for our young people by those bearing responsibility in local churches throughout the conferences. When the church officers see promising youth who are desirous of fitting themselves for usefulness in the Lord's service, but whose parents are unable to send them to school, they have a duty to perform in studying how to give help and encouragement. They should take counsel with parents and youth, and unite in planning wisely. Some youth may be best fitted to engage in home missionary work. There is a wide field of usefulness in the distribution of our literature and in bringing the third angels message to the attention of friends and neighbors. Other youth should be encouraged to enter the canvassing work to sell our larger books. Some may have qualifications that would make them valuable helpers in our institutions. And in many instances, if promising youth were wisely encouraged and properly directed, they could be led to earn their own schooling by taking up the sale of *Christ's Object Lessons* or *Ministry of Healing*.

In selling these books the youth would be acting as missionaries, for they would be bringing precious light to the notice of the people of the world. At the same time they would be earning money to enable them to attend school, where they could continue their preparation for wider usefulness in the Lord's cause. In the school they would receive encouragement and inspiration from teachers and students to continue their work of selling books; and when the time came for them to leave school, they would have received a practical training fitting them for the hard, earnest, self-sacrificing labor that has to be done in many foreign fields, where the third angel's message must be carried under difficult and trying circumstances.

How much better is this plan than for students to go through school without obtaining a practical education in field work, and, at the end of their course, leave under a burden of debt, with but little realization of the difficulties they will have to meet in new and untried fields!

How hard it will be for them to meet the financial problems that are connected with pioneer work in foreign lands! And what a burden someone will have to carry until the debts incurred by the student have been paid!

On the other hand, how much might be gained, if the self-supporting plan were followed! The student would often be enabled to leave the educational institution nearly or wholly free from personal indebtedness; the finances of the school would be in a more prosperous condition; and the lessons learned by the student while passing through these experiences in the home field would be of untold value to him in foreign fields.

Let wise plans be laid to help worthy students to earn their own schooling by handling these books, if they so desire. Those who earn sufficient means in this way to pay their way through a course at one of our training schools will gain a most valuable practical experience that will help fit them for pioneer missionary work in other fields.

A great work is to be done in our world in a short time, and we must study to understand and appreciate, more than we have in past years, the providence of God in placing in our hands the precious volumes, *Christ's Object Lessons* and *Ministry of Healing,* as a means of helping worthy students to meet their expenses while in training, as well as a means of liquidating the indebtedness on our educational and medical institutions.

Great blessings are in store for us as we wisely handle these precious books given us for the advancement of the cause of present truth. And as we labor in accordance with the Lord's plan we shall find that many consecrated youth will be fitted to enter the regions beyond as practical missionaries; and, at the same time, the conferences in the home field will have means with which to contribute liberally to the support of the work that shall be undertaken in new territory.

Sanitarium, California, April 17, 1908.

God desires that the sale of *Christ's Object Lessons* shall be recognized by all our people as His method of relieving our schools from debt. It is because this plan has been neglected that we now feel so keenly our lack of means for the advancing work. Had the schools availed themselves of the provision thus made for them, there would be more money in the school treasuries, and more money in the hands of God's servants, with which to relieve the necessities of other needy departments of the cause; and, best of all, teachers and students would have received the very lessons that they needed to learn in the Master's service.

In the cities within easy reach of our sanitariums and training schools a mission field is open to us that we have as yet only touched with the tips of our fingers. In some of these places, a good beginning has been made. But it was God's purpose that by the sale of *Ministry of Healing* and *Christ's Object Lessons* much means should be raised for the work of our sanitariums and schools, and that our people might thereby be left more free to donate of their means for the opening of the work in new missionary fields. If our people will now engage in the sale of these books as they ought, we shall have much more means than we now have to carry the work in the way the Lord designed that it should be carried.

CAMP MEETINGS AND OUR PUBLICATIONS

In connection with our camp meetings in past years, God's servants have improved many precious opportunities for instructing our people in practical methods of presenting the saving truths of the third angel's message to their friends and acquaintances. Many have been taught how to labor as self-supporting missionaries in their home communities. Many have returned home from these annual gatherings to labor with greater zeal and intelligence than hitherto.

It would be pleasing to God if far more of this practical instruction were given the church members who attend our camp meetings, than has usually been given in years past. Our general workers and our brethren and sisters in every conference should remember that one of the objects of our annual gatherings is that all may gain a knowledge of practical methods of personal missionary work. This phase of our camp meetings is outlined in *Testimonies for the Church,* volume 6, as follows:

"God has committed to our hands a most sacred work, and we need to meet together to receive instruction, that we may be fitted to perform this work. We need to understand what part we shall individually be called upon to act in building up the cause of God in the earth, in vindicating God's holy law, and in lifting up the Saviour as 'the Lamb of God, which taketh away the sin of the world.' John 1:29. We need to meet together and receive the divine touch, that we may understand our work in the home. Parents need to understand how they may send forth from the sanctuary of the home their sons and daughters so trained and educated that they will be fitted to shine as lights in the world. We need to understand in regard to the division of labor and how each part of the work is to be carried forward. Each one should understand the part he is to act, that there may be harmony of plan and of labor in the combined work of all."—Pages 32, 33.

"Properly conducted, the camp meeting is a school where pastors, elders, and deacons can learn to do more perfect work for the Master. It should be a school where the members of the church, old and young, are given opportunity to learn the way of the Lord more perfectly, a place where believers can receive an education that will help them to help others. . . .

"The best help that ministers can give the members of our churches is not sermonizing, but planning work for them. Give each one something to do for others. Help all to see that as receivers of the grace of Christ they are under obligation to work for Him. And let all be taught how to work. Especially should those who are newly come to the faith be educated to become laborers together with God. If set to work, the despondent will soon forget their despondency; the weak will become strong, the ignorant intelligent, and all will be prepared to present the truth as it is in Jesus. They will find an unfailing helper in Him who has promised to save all that come unto Him."—Pages 49, 50.

In some of our conferences the leaders have hesitated to introduce these practical methods of instruction. Some are naturally inclined to sermonize rather than to teach. But on such occasions as our annual camp meetings we must never lose sight of the opportunities afforded for teaching the believers how to do practical missionary work in the place where they may live. In many instances it would be well to set apart certain men to carry the burden of different lines of educational work at these meetings. Let some help the people to learn how to give Bible readings and to conduct cottage meetings. Let others bear the burden of teaching the people how to practice the principles of health and temperance, and how to give treatments to the sick. Still others may labor in the interests of our periodical and book work. And let chosen workers take a special interest in teaching many how to handle *Christ's Object Lessons* and *Ministry of Healing*.

Many have never learned how to sell the books dedicated to the advancement of our institutional work. But such should not excuse themselves. They should study diligently how they may do their part faithfully in connection with the circulation of these precious books. Our schools and sanitariums must be conducted on a high plane of efficiency, and a solemn responsibility rests upon us all to help place these institutions on vantage ground by giving the relief books a wide circulation. God will be glorified by everyone who takes an active interest in the work of placing these books in the hands of the multitudes who are in need of the saving truths of the gospel.

The opportunity we have of doing good by striving to carry out the Lord's plan for the relief of our schools and sanitariums has been presented to me over and over again in connection with the Southern California Conference. The conditions there are unusually favorable for a long-continued effort to push the sale of *Christ's Object Lessons* and *Ministry of Healing*. Our brethren and sisters in Southern California should never weary of this plan for raising money to meet the debts that have accumulated. The students of the Fernando school, and the nurses of the three sanitariums that have been established, can ill afford to lose the precious experiences in missionary work that come to those who handle the relief books. And the conference can ill afford to lose the results, spiritual as well as financial, that would accompany a continued effort of this sort.

But years have passed, and students who should have been gaining rich experiences in actual missionary work have not been encouraged to launch out heartily in the sale of *Christ's Object Lessons*. Church members in many places have daily met with strangers,—tourists, men and women of means and influence,—and yet such opportunities as these for circulating *Christ's Object Lessons* and *Ministry of Healing* have been allowed to pass by unimproved. Many honesthearted persons who could have been reached by diligent, wholehearted effort have not been given the light of the third angel's message.

Had the Lord's plan been followed, His name would have been glorified, and many spiritual victories would have been won. Those having means would have been more able and willing to come up to the help of the Lord when He was leading out in an extraordinary manner in the establishment of strong medical missionary centers in the vicinity of great thoroughfares of travel. Students would have received a training that would have greatly increased their efficiency as practical missionaries at home and abroad. Churches would have been revived with spiritual blessings. Many would have been won to the truth, and these would have brought into the cause their influence and their means.

In such places as Southern California, where thousands of tourists, many of them in search of health and strength, are constantly coming and going, special and continuous efforts should be put forth to scatter the bright rays of light and truth. The books *Ministry of*

Healing and *Christ's Object Lessons* are peculiarly adapted for use in tourist centers, and everything possible should be done to place copies of these works in the hands of those who have leisure and inclination to read. Especially do those who are seeking for restoration of health need the book *Ministry of Healing.* Every favorable opportunity for reaching this class is to be improved.

My heart has rejoiced as I have learned of a revival of the relief work in Southern California during the past few months. At Loma Linda some of the nurses have been given a special training for the work of selling *Ministry of Healing;* and as they have visited homes in the neighboring cities and villages, the blessing of heaven has rested richly upon them, and favorable impressions have been made in behalf of our people and their work.

At the Fernando school the teachers have recently led out in reviving an interest in the sale of *Christ's Object Lessons.* Bands of students, after prayerful study of the book, have visited Los Angeles in company with their teachers and have gained a sound, solid experience which they prize above silver and gold. This kind of work is, in fact, one of the means God has ordained for giving our youth a missionary training; and those who neglect to improve such opportunities lose out of their lives a chapter of experience of the highest value. By entering heartily into this work, students can learn how to approach with tact and discretion men and women in all walks of life, how to deal with them courteously, and how to lead them to give favorable consideration to the truths contained in the books that are sold.

Our greatest burden should be, not the raising of money, but the salvation of souls; and to this end we should do all in our power to teach students how to lead souls to a knowledge of the third angel's message. When we are successful in the work of soulsaving, those who are added to the faith will, in turn, use their ability in giving the truth to others. When we labor diligently for the salvation of our fellow men, God will prosper our every effort.

To the presidents of conferences, and to others in positions of leading responsibility, I would say: Let us do all in our power to impress upon the teachers connected with our educational institutions the great value of the blessings in store for those who seek diligently to make the best possible use of the gift, *Christ's Object Lessons*. Let us encourage the teachers to unite with many of their students in a prayerful study of this book, preparatory to going out with them into active field work. Let us help the educators to understand their responsibility in this matter. Let us do all we can to revive the *Christ's Object Lessons* work and to inaugurate plans for an active campaign with *Ministry of Healing*.

As teachers and students engage heartily in this line of work, they will gain an experience that will fit them to do valuable service in connection with our camp meetings. Through the instruction that they can give to the believers in attendance, and through the sale of many books in the places where such meetings are held, those who have been in the school will be able to do their part in reaching the multitudes who need to be given the third angel's message. Let teachers and students nobly bear their share of the burden of showing our own people how to communicate the message to their friends and neighbors.

When we follow plans of the Lord's devising "we are laborers together with God." Whatever our position,—whether presidents of conferences, ministers, teachers, students, or lay members,—we are held accountable by the Lord for making the most of our opportunities to enlighten those in need of present truth. And one of the principal agencies He has ordained for our use is the printed page. In our schools and sanitariums, in our home churches, and particularly in our annual camp meetings, we must learn to make a wise use of this precious agency. With patient diligence chosen workers must instruct our people how to approach unbelievers in a kindly, winning way and how to place in their hands literature in which the truth for this time is presented with clearness and power.

My brethren and sisters, let us not become weary in well-doing. During His earthly ministry, Christ traveled on foot from place to place. Wearied, as He offtimes was, His human nature taxed to the uttermost, yet He was ever ready to heal all who came unto Him, and to teach them the way of life eternal. Though often physically exhausted, He left not His work. There was a world to be saved. He made every sacrifice possible, in order that light and truth might shine forth.

The Lord God of Israel desires us to link up in holy union with Himself and exercise the living faith that works by love and purifies the soul. He desires that we shall be a working corps of laborers endowed with adaptability for His service, and to such He promises power to win a glorious victory for Him.

Sanitarium, California, July 10, 1908.

––––––––––

The men who stand as leaders in any part of the solemn work of the last gospel message must cultivate and cherish broad views and ideas. It is the privilege of all who bear responsibilities in the work of the gospel to be apt learners in the school of Christ. The professed follower of Christ must not be led by the dictates of his own will; his mind must be trained to think Christ's thoughts and enlightened to comprehend the will and way of God. Such a believer will be a follower of Christ's methods of work.

Our brethren should not forget that the wisdom of God has made provision for our schools in a way that will bring blessing to all who participate in the enterprise. The book *Christ's Object Lessons* was donated to the educational work, that the students and other friends of the schools might handle these books and by their sale raise much of the means needed to lift the school indebtedness. But this plan has not been presented to our schools as it should have been, the teachers and students have not been educated to take hold of this book and courageously push its sale for the benefit of the educational work.

Long ago the teachers and students in our schools should have learned to take advantage of the opportunity to raise means by the sale of *Christ's Object Lessons*. In selling these books the students will serve the cause of God, and, while doing this, by the dissemination of precious light, they will learn invaluable lessons in Christian experience. All our schools should now come into line and earnestly endeavor to carry out the plan presented to us for the education of workers, for the relief of the schools, and for the winning of souls to the cause of Christ.

THE WORK IN THE CITIES*

> "I heard the voice of the Lord saying, Whom shall I send and who will go for us? Then said I, Here am I; send me." Isaiah 6:8.

CONDITIONS IN THE CITIES

There is coming rapidly and surely an almost universal guilt upon the inhabitants of the cities because of the steady increase of determined wickedness. We are living in the midst of an "epidemic of crime" at which thoughtful, God-fearing men everywhere stand aghast. The corruption that prevails is beyond the power of the human pen to describe. Every day brings fresh revelations of political strife, bribery, and fraud; every day brings its heartsickening record of violence and lawlessness, of indifference to human suffering; of brutal, fiendish destruction of human life. Every day testifies to the increase of insanity, murder, and suicide.

The cities of today are fast becoming like Sodom and Gomorrah. Holidays are numerous; the whirl of excitement and pleasure attracts thousands from the sober duties of life. The exciting sports—theatergoing, horse racing, gambling, liquor drinking and reveling—stimulate every passion to activity.

---

* In the five articles in this section there have been gathered together and grouped in convenient order some of the many instructive, cheering, and inspiring testimonies regarding work in the cities. The statements included in this compilation have been found in special testimonies, in articles published in our periodicals, in the reports of sermons at the 1909 General Conference, and in letters to workers in the large cities.

The youth are swept away by the popular current. Those who learn to love amusement for its own sake open the door to a flood of temptations. They give themselves up to social gaiety and thoughtless mirth. They are led on from one form of dissipation to another, until they lose both the desire and the capacity for a life of usefulness. Their religious aspirations are chilled; their spiritual life is darkened. All the nobler faculties of the soul, all that link man with the spiritual world, are debased.

Through the working of trusts and the results of labor unions and strikes, the conditions of life in the cities are constantly becoming more and more difficult.

The intense passion for money getting, the thirst for display, the luxury and extravagance—all are forces that, with the great mass of mankind, are turning the mind from life's true purpose. They are opening the door to a thousand evils. Many, absorbed in their interest in worldly treasures, become insensible to the claims of God and the needs of their fellow men. They regard their wealth as a means of glorifying self. They add house to house and land to land; they fill their homes with luxury, while all about them are human beings in misery and crime, in disease and death.

By every species of oppression and extortion, men are piling up colossal fortunes, while the cries of starving humanity are coming up before God. There are multitudes struggling with poverty, compelled to labor hard for small wages, unable to secure the barest necessities of life. Toil and deprivation, with no hope of better things, make their burden heavy. When pain and sickness are added, the burden is almost unbearable. Care-worn and oppressed, they know not where to turn for relief.

The Scriptures describe the condition of the world just before Christ's second coming. James the apostle pictures the greed and oppression that will prevail. He says: "Go to now, ye rich men. . . . Ye have heaped treasure together for the last days. Behold, the hire of the laborers who have reaped down your fields, which is of you kept back by fraud, crieth: and the cries of them which have reaped are entered into the ears of the Lord of Sabaoth. Ye have lived in pleasure on the earth, and been wanton; ye have nourished your hearts, as in a day of slaughter. Ye have condemned and killed the just; and he doth not resist you." James 5:1-6.

This is a picture of what exists today. "Judgment is turned away backward, and justice standeth afar off: for truth is fallen in the street, and equity cannot enter. Yea, truth faileth; and he that departeth from evil maketh himself a prey." Isaiah 59:14, 15.

Even the church, which should be the pillar and ground of the truth, is found encouraging a selfish love of pleasure. When money is raised for religious purposes, to what means do many churches resort? To bazaars, suppers, fancy fairs, even to lotteries and like devices. Often the place set apart for God's worship is desecrated by feasting and drinking, buying, selling, and merrymaking. Respect for the house of God and reverence for His worship are lessened in the minds of the youth. The barriers of self-restraint are weakened. Selfishness, appetite, the love of display, are appealed to, and they strengthen as they are indulged.

From age to age the Lord has made known the manner of His working. When a crisis has come, He has revealed Himself and has interposed to hinder the working out of Satan's plans. With nations, with families, and with individuals He has often permitted matters to come to a crisis, that His interference might become marked. Then He has made it manifest that there is a God in Israel who will maintain His law and vindicate His people.

In the antediluvian world human agencies brought in all manner of devisings and ingenious practices to make of no effect the law of Jehovah. They cast aside His authority because it interfered with their schemes. As in the days before the Flood, so now the time is right upon us when the Lord must reveal His omnipotent power. In this time of prevailing iniquity we may know that the last great crisis is at hand. When defiance against God's law is almost universal, when His people are oppressed and afflicted by their fellow men, the Lord will interpose.

Satan is not asleep; he is wide awake to make of no effect the sure word of prophecy. With skill and deceptive power he is working to counterwork the expressed will of God, made plain in His word. For years Satan has been gaining control of human minds through subtle sophistries that he has devised to take the place of the truth. In this time of peril, rightdoers, in the fear of God, will glorify His name by repeating the words of David: "It is time for Thee, Lord, to work: for they have made void Thy law." Psalm 119:126.

THE JUDGMENTS OF GOD ON OUR CITIES

While at Loma Linda, California, April 16, 1906, there passed before me a most wonderful representation. During a vision of the night, I stood on an eminence, from which I could see houses shaken like a reed in the wind. Buildings, great and small, were falling to the ground. Pleasure resorts, theaters, hotels, and the homes of the wealthy were shaken and shattered. Many lives were blotted out of existence, and the air was filled with the shrieks of the injured and the terrified.

The destroying angels of God were at work. One touch, and buildings, so thoroughly constructed that men regarded them as secure against every danger, quickly became heaps of rubbish. There was no assurance of safety in any place. I did not feel in any special peril, but the awfulness of the scenes that passed before me I cannot find words to describe. It seemed that the forbearance of God was exhausted and that the Judgment day had come.

The angel that stood at my side then instructed me that but few have any conception of the wickedness existing in our world today, and especially the wickedness in the large cities. He declared that the Lord has appointed a time when He will visit transgressors in wrath for persistent disregard of His law.

Terrible as was the representation that passed before me, that which impressed itself most vividly upon my mind was the instruction given in connection with it. The angel that stood by my side declared that God's supreme rulership and the sacredness of His law must be revealed to those who persistently refused to render obedience to the King of kings. Those who choose to remain disloyal must be visited in mercy with judgments, in order that, if possible, they may be aroused to a realization of the sinfulness of their course.

Throughout the following day I pondered the scenes that had passed before me and the instruction that had been given. During the afternoon we journeyed to Glendale, near Los Angeles; and the following night I was again instructed regarding the holiness and binding claims of the Ten Commandments and the supremacy of God above all earthly rulers.

I seemed to be in an assembly, setting before the people the requirements of God's law. I read the scriptures regarding the institution of the Sabbath in Eden at the close of the creation week, and regarding the giving of the law at Sinai; and then declared that the Sabbath is to be observed "for a perpetual covenant" as a sign between God and His people forever, that they may know that they are sanctified by the Lord, their Creator.

Then I further dwelt upon the supreme rulership of God above all earthly rulers. His law is to be the standard of action. Men are forbidden to pervert their senses by intemperance or by yielding their minds to satanic influences, for this makes impossible the keeping of God's law. While the divine Ruler bears long with perversity, He is not deceived and will not always keep silence. His supremacy, His authority as Ruler of the universe, must finally be acknowledged and the just claims of His law vindicated.

Much more instruction regarding the long-sufferance of God and the necessity of arousing transgressors to a realization of their perilous position in His sight was repeated to the people, as received from my instructor.

On April 18, two days after the scene of falling buildings had passed before me, I went to fill an appointment in the Carr Street Church, Los Angeles. As we neared the church we heard the newsboys crying: "San Francisco destroyed by an earthquake!" With a heavy heart I read the first hastily printed news of the terrible disaster.

Two weeks later, on our homeward journey, we passed through San Francisco and, hiring a carriage, spent an hour and a half in viewing the destruction

A PRESENT-DAY WORK

More and more, as the days go by, it is becoming apparent that God's judgments are in the world. In fire and flood and earthquake He is warning the inhabitants of this earth of His near approach. The time is nearing when the great crisis in the history of the world will have come, when every movement in the government of God will be watched with intense interest and inexpressible apprehension. In quick succession the judgments of God will follow one another—fire and flood and earthquake, with war and bloodshed.

Oh, that the people might know the time of their visitation! There are many who have not yet heard the testing truth for this time. There are many with whom the Spirit of God is striving. The time of God's destructive judgments is the time of mercy for those who have had no opportunity to learn what is truth. Tenderly will the Lord look upon them. His heart of mercy is touched; His hand is still stretched out to save, while the door is closed to those who would not enter.

The mercy of God is shown in His long forbearance. He is holding back His judgments, waiting for the message of warning to be sounded to all. Oh, if our people would feel as they should the responsibility resting upon them to give the last message of mercy to the world, what a wonderful work would be done!

Behold the cities, and their need of the gospel! The need of earnest laborers among the multitudes of the cities has been kept before me for more than twenty years. Who are carrying a burden for the large cities? A few have felt the burden, but in comparison with the great need and the many opportunities but little attention has been given to this work.

IN THE CITIES OF THE EAST

Instruction has been given me that the message should go again with power in the cities in the Eastern States. In many of the large cities of the East the first and second angels' messages were proclaimed during the 1844 movement. To us, as God's servants, has been entrusted the third angel's message, the binding-off message, that is to prepare a people for the coming of the King. We are to make every effort to give a knowledge of the truth to all who will hear, and there are many who will listen. All through the large cities God has honest souls who are interested in what is truth.

Time is short; the Lord desires that everything connected with His cause shall be brought into order. He desires that the solemn message of warning and of invitation shall be proclaimed as widely as His messengers can carry it. Nothing that would hinder the advance of the message is to be allowed to come into our plans. "Repeat the message, repeat the message," were the words spoken to me over and over again. "Tell My people to repeat the message in the places where it was first preached, and where church after church took their position for the truth, the power of God witnessing to the message in a remarkable manner."

For years the pioneers of our work struggled against poverty and manifold hardships in order to place the cause of present truth on vantage ground. With meager facilities, they labored untiringly, and the Lord blessed their humble efforts. The message went with power in the East and extended westward until centers of influence had been established in many places. The laborers of today may not have to endure all the hardships of those early days. The changed conditions, however, should not lead to any slackening of effort. Now, when the Lord bids us proclaim the message once more with power in the East, when He bids us enter the cities of the East and of the South and of the West and of the North, shall we not respond as one man and do His bidding? Shall we not plan to send our messengers all through these fields and support them liberally? Shall not the ministers of God go into these crowded centers and there lift up their voices in warning the multitudes? What are our conferences for, if not for the carrying forward of this very work?

A beginning has been made in proclaiming the third angel's message in the city of Washington and in other cities of the South and the East; but in order to meet the mind of the Lord, we shall have to plan for the carrying forward of a far-reaching and systematic work. We must enter into this work with a perseverance that will not allow of any slackening of our efforts until we shall see of the salvation of God.

In Portland, Maine; in Boston and the towns round about; in New York and the populous cities close by; in Philadelphia and Baltimore and Washington, the Lord desires us to proclaim the third angel's message with power. We cannot exercise this power ourselves, but we can choose men of capability and urge them to go into these avenues of opportunity and there proclaim the message in the power of the Holy Spirit. We must plan to place in these cities capable men who can present the third angel's message in a manner so forcible that it will strike home to the heart. Men who can do this work we cannot afford to gather into one place to do a work that others might do.

As these workers talk the truth and live the truth, and pray for the advancement of the truth, God will move upon hearts. As they work with all the strength that God grants them, and in humility of heart put their entire trust in Him, their labors will not be without fruit. Their determined efforts to bring souls to a knowledge of the truth for this time will be seconded by holy angels, and many souls will be saved.

LIBERALITY IN MISSIONARY EFFORT

The Southern States are to have the light of present truth. Do not say: "Our printing offices and our churches need more help. We need all the means that we can get to carry on the work in hand." One after another has shut the door to certain lines of missionary effort for fear that this work would consume means which they desired for other enterprises. My brethren, you need more of the Spirit of Christ. Let your standard be raised higher; then those who are newly converted to the truth will understand that they have a work to do. In this way the means for the carrying on of the work will be always increasing.

Can we expect the inhabitants of the cities to come to us and say: "If you will come to us and preach, we will help you to do thus and so"? What do they know of our message? Let us do our part in warning these people who are ready to perish unwarned and unsaved. The Lord desires us to let our light so shine before men that His Holy Spirit can communicate the truth to the honest in heart who are seeking after Him.

As we do this work we shall find that means will flow

into our treasuries, and we shall have funds with which to carry on a still broader and more far-reaching work. Souls who have wealth will be brought into the truth and will give of their means to advance the work of God. I have been instructed that there is much means in the cities that are unworked. God has interested people there. Go to them; teach them as Christ taught; give them the truth. They will accept it. And as surely as honest souls will be converted, their means will be consecrated to the Lord's service, and we shall see an increase of resources.

Oh, that we might see the needs of these cities as God sees them! At such a time as this every hand is to be employed The Lord is coming; the end is near, yea, it hasteth greatly! In a little while we shall be unable to work with the freedom that we now enjoy. Terrible scenes are before us, and what we do we must do quickly.

A MOTIVE FOR SERVICE

Recently in the night season I was awakened from sleep and given a view of the sufferings of Christ for men. His sacrifice, the mockery and derision He received at the hands of wicked men, His agony in the Garden of Gethsemane, His betrayal and crucifixion—all were vividly portrayed before me.

I saw Christ in the midst of a large company of people. He was seeking to impress their minds with His teachings. But He was despised and rejected by them. Men were heaping upon Him abuse and shame. My distress was very great as I looked upon the scene. I pleaded with God: "What is to be done with this congregation? Will none give up their exalted opinions of self and seek the Lord as little children? Will none break their hearts before God in repentance and confession?"

There was presented to me Christ's agony in the Garden of Gethsemane, when the mysterious cup trembled in the Redeemer's hand. "Father, if it be possible," He prayed, "let this cup pass from Me: nevertheless not as I will, but as Thou wilt." Matthew 26:39. As He pleaded with the Father, great drops of blood fell from His face to the ground. The elements of darkness were gathered about the Saviour to discourage His soul.

Rising from the ground, Christ went to the place where He had left His disciples, bidding them watch and pray with Him lest they be overcome with temptation. He would see if they understood His agony; He needed their human sympathy. But He found them sleeping. Three times He went thus to them, and each time they were asleep.

Three times the Saviour prayed: "Father, if it be possible, let this cup pass from Me." It was here that the destiny of a lost world trembled in the balance. Should He refuse to drink the cup, the result would be eternal ruin to the human race. But an angel from heaven strengthened the Son of God to accept the cup and drink its bitter woe.

How few there are who realize that all this was borne for them individually! How few who say: "It was for *me*, that I might form a character for the future immortal life."

As these things were presented to me so vividly, I thought, "I shall never be able to present this subject before the people as it is;" and I have given you only a faint representation of what was shown me. As I have thought of that cup trembling in the hands of Christ;

as I have realized that He might have refused to drink, and left the world to perish in its sin, I have pledged that every energy of my life should be devoted to the work of winning souls to Him.

Christ came to the earth to suffer and die, that, through the exercise of faith in Him and the appropriation of His merits, we might become laborers together with God. It was the Saviour's purpose that after He ascended to heaven to become man's intercessor, His followers should carry on the work that He had begun. Shall the human agent show no special interest in giving the light of the gospel message to those who sit in darkness? There are some who are willing to go to the ends of the earth in order to carry the light of truth to men, but God demands that every soul who knows the truth shall seek to win others to the love of the truth. If we are not willing to make special sacrifices in order to save souls that are ready to perish, how can we be counted worthy to enter into the city of God?

There is an individual work to be done for each one of us. I know there are many who are placing themselves in right relation to Christ, whose one thought is to bring the message of present truth before the people of the world. They stand continually ready to offer their services. But my heart aches when I see so many who are satisfied with a cheap experience, an experience that costs them but little. Their lives say that for them Christ has died in vain.

If you do not feel that it is an honor to be a partaker of the sufferings of Christ; if you feel no burden of soul for those who are ready to perish; if you are unwilling to sacrifice that you may save means for the work that is to be done, there will be no room for you in the kingdom of God. We need to be partakers with Christ of His sufferings and self-denial at every step. We need to have the Spirit of God resting upon us, leading us to constant self-sacrifice.

GET READY

"Behold, I come quickly," Christ declares; "and My reward is with Me, to give every man according as his work shall be." Revelation 22: 12. The Lord at His coming will scrutinize every talent; He will demand interest on the capital He has entrusted. By His own humiliation and agony, by His life of toil and His death of shame, Christ has paid for the service of all who have taken His name and profess to be His servants. All are under deepest obligation to improve every capability for the work of winning souls to Him. "Ye are not your own," He says; "for ye are bought with a price;" therefore glorify God by a life of service that will win men and women from sin to righteousness. 1 Corinthians 6:19, 20. We are bought with the price of Christ's own life, bought that we may return to God His own in faithful service.

We have no time now to give our energies and talents to worldly enterprises. Shall we become absorbed in serving the world, serving ourselves, and lose eternal life and the everlasting bliss of heaven? Oh, we cannot afford to do this! Let every talent be employed in the work of God. Those who receive the truth are, by their efforts, to increase the number of men and women who shall be laborers together with God. Souls are to be enlightened and taught to serve God intelligently; they are to be continually increasing in the knowledge of righteousness.

All heaven is interested in the carrying forward of the work that Christ came to the world to do. Heavenly agencies are opening ways for the light of truth to shine to the dark places of the earth. Angels are waiting to communicate to those who will take hold of the work that has been pointed out to us for years. Shall we not manifest an interest to set in operation ways and means for the opening up of city work? Many opportunities have been lost through neglecting to do this work at once, through failing to go forward in faith. The Lord says: "Had you exercised faith in the messages I have sent, there would not be such a lack of workers and of means for their support."

The coming of Christ is near and hasteth greatly. The time in which to labor is short, and men and women are perishing. Said the angel: "Should not the men who have had great light co-operate with Him who sent His Son to the world to give light and salvation to men?" Shall men who have received the knowledge of the truth line upon line, precept upon precept, here a little and there a little, show but little appreciation of Him who came to the earth that His divine power might be the heritage of every believing soul? It was thus that the divinity of Christ was to become effectual in the salvation of the race, and the intercession of our great High Priest avail before the throne of God. The plan was devised in heaven. Shall those who have been bought with such a price fail of appreciating the great salvation?

The Lord cannot commend the people who, professing godliness, professing to believe in the soon coming of Christ, leave the cities unwarned of the judgments that are soon to fall on the land. Those who do this will be judged for their neglect. Christ gave His precious life to save the souls that are perishing in their sins. Shall we refuse to do the work assigned us, refuse to co-operate with God and heavenly agencies? There are thousands who are doing this, who are failing of becoming one with Christ, failing of letting the great sacrifice of Christ shine forth in the life, in saving grace that reveals the truth in works of righteousness. Yet this is the work given to men by the sacrifice of the Son of God. Knowing this, can we remain indifferent? I appeal to our brethren to wake up. The spiritual faculties will grow weak and die if they are not exercised in winning souls to Christ. What excuse can be offered for the neglect of the great, grand work that Christ gave His life to accomplish?

We cannot afford in the few days we have here on earth to spend our time in trifling and nothingness. We need to humble our souls before God, that every heart may drink in the truth, and let it work in the life a reformation that will convince the world that this is indeed the truth of God. Let the life be hid with Christ in God. Only when we seek the Lord as little children, when we cease picking flaws in our brethren and sisters, and in those who are seeking to carry faithfully the responsibilities of the work, and seek to get our own hearts right with God, can He use us to the glory of His name.

We all need to come into a self-sacrificing position before God if our work is to be accepted by Him. Let us remember that profession is nothing unless we have the truth in the heart. We need the converting power of God to take hold of us, that we may understand the needs of a perishing world. The burden of my message to you is: Get ready, get ready to meet the Lord. Trim your lamps, and let the light of truth shine forth into the byways and the hedges. There is a world to be warned of the near approach of the end of all things.

My brethren and sisters, seek the Lord while He may be found. There is a time coming when those who have wasted their time and opportunities will wish they had sought Him. God has given you reasoning faculties. He wants you to keep in the line of reason and in the line of labor. He wants you to go forth to our churches to labor earnestly for Him. He wants you to institute meetings for those outside the churches, that the people may learn the truths of this last message of warning. There are places where you will be gladly received, where souls will thank you for coming to their help. May the Lord help you to take hold of this work as you have never yet taken hold of it.

Let us begin to work for those who have not had the light. "All power is given unto Me in heaven and in earth," the Saviour declares, "and, lo, I am with you alway." Matthew 28:18, 20. What we need is a living faith, faith to proclaim over the rent sepulcher of Joseph that we have a living Saviour, one who will go before us and who will work with us. God will do the work if we will furnish Him the instruments. There needs to be among us a great deal more of prayer and much less of unbelief. We need to lift up the standard higher and still higher before the people. We need to remember that Christ is always at our right hand as we proclaim liberty to the captives and deal the bread of life to hungry souls. When we keep before our minds the urgency and importance of our work, the salvation of God will be revealed in a remarkable manner.

God help us to put on the armor and to act as if we were in earnest, as if the souls of men and women were worth saving. Let us seek a new conversion. We need the presence of the Holy Spirit of God with us, that our hearts may be softened and that we may not bring a harsh spirit into the work. I pray that the Holy Spirit may take full possession of our hearts. Let us act like children of God who are looking to Him for counsel, ready to work out His plans wherever presented. God will be glorified by such a people, and those who witness our zeal will say: Amen and amen.

"Awake, awake; put on thy strength, O Zion; put on thy beautiful garments, O Jerusalem, the Holy City. . . . How beautiful upon the mountains are the feet of him that bringeth good tidings, that publisheth peace; that bringeth good tidings of good, that publisheth salvation; that saith unto Zion, Thy God reigneth. Thy watchmen shall lift up the voice; with the voice together shall they sing: for they shall see eye to eye, when the Lord shall bring again Zion.

"Break forth into joy, sing together, ye waste places of Jerusalem: for the Lord hath comforted His people, He hath redeemed Jerusalem. The Lord hath made bare His holy arm in the eyes of all the nations; and all the ends of the earth shall see the salvation of our God." Isaiah 52:1-10.

METHODS OF LABOR

In connection with the proclamation of the message in large cities, there are many kinds of work to be done by laborers with varied gifts. Some are to labor in one way, some in another. The Lord desires that the cities shall be worked by the united efforts of laborers of different capabilities. All are to look to Jesus for direction, not depending on man for wisdom, lest they be led astray. As laborers together with God they should seek to be in harmony with one another. There should be frequent councils and earnest, wholehearted co-operation. Yet all are to look to Jesus for wisdom, not depending upon men alone for direction.

The Lord has given to some ministers the ability to gather and to hold large congregations. This calls for the exercise of tact and skill. In the cities of today, where there is so much to attract and please, the people can be interested by no ordinary efforts. Ministers of God's appointment will find it necessary to put forth extraordinary efforts in order to arrest the attention of the multitudes. And when they succeed in bringing together a large number of people they must bear messages of a character so out of the usual order that the people will be aroused and warned. They must make use of every means that can possibly be devised for causing the truth to stand out clearly and distinctly. The testing message for this time is to be borne so plainly and decidedly as to startle the hearers and lead them to desire to study the Scriptures.

Those who do the work of the Lord in the cities must put forth calm, steady, devoted effort for the education

(109)

of the people. While they are to labor earnestly to interest the hearers and to hold this interest, yet at the same time they must carefully guard against anything that borders on sensationalism. In this age of extravagance and outward show, when men think it is necessary to make a display in order to gain success, God's chosen messengers are to show the fallacy of spending means needlessly for effect. As they labor with simplicity, humility, and graceful dignity, avoiding everything of a theatrical nature, their work will make a lasting impression for good.

There is a necessity, it is true, for expending money judiciously in advertising the meetings and in carrying forward the work solidly. Yet the strength of every worker will be found to lie, not in these outward agencies, but in trustful dependence upon God, in earnest prayer to Him for help, in obedience to His word. Much more prayer, much more Christlikeness, much more conformity to God's will, is to be brought into the Lord's work. Outward show and extravagant outlay of means will not accomplish the work to be done.

God's work is to be carried forward with power. We need the baptism of the Holy Spirit. We need to understand that God will add to the ranks of His people men of ability and influence who are to act their part in warning the world. All in the world are not lawless and sinful. God has many thousands who have not bowed the knee to Baal. There are God-fearing men and women in the fallen churches. If this were not so, we would not be given the message to bear: "Babylon the great is fallen, is fallen. . . . Come out of her, My people." Revelation 18:2-4. Many of the honest in heart are gasping for a breath of life from heaven. They will recognize the gospel when it is brought to them in the beauty and simplicity with which it is presented in God's word.

THE NEED OF HOUSE-TO-HOUSE WORK

Of equal importance with special public efforts is house-to-house work in the homes of the people. In large cities there are certain classes that cannot be reached by public meetings. These must be searched out as the shepherd searches for his lost sheep. Diligent, personal effort must be put forth in their behalf. When personal work is neglected, many precious opportunities are lost, which, were they improved, would advance the work decidedly.

As the result of the presentation of the truth in large congregations, a spirit of inquiry is awakened, and it is especially important that this interest be followed up by personal labor. Those who desire to investigate the truth need to be taught to study diligently the word of God. Someone must help them to build on the sure foundation. At this critical time in their religious experience, how important it is that wisely directed Bible workers come to their help and open to their understanding the treasure house of God's word.

THE CITY MISSION A TRAINING SCHOOL

A well-balanced work can be carried on best when a training school for Bible workers is in progress. While the public meetings are being held, connected with this training school or city mission should be experienced laborers of deep spiritual understanding who can give the Bible workers daily instruction and who can also unite wholeheartedly in the general public effort being put forth. And as men and women are converted to the truth, those standing at the head of the city mission should with much prayer show these new converts how to experience the power of the truth in their lives. This united effort on the part of all the workers would be as a nail driven in a sure place

TEACHING THE PRINCIPLES OF HEALTH REFORM

As a people we have been given the work of making known the principles of health reform. There are some who think that the question of diet is not of sufficient importance to be included in their evangelistic work. But such make a great mistake. God's word declares: "Whether therefore ye eat, or drink, or whatsoever ye do, do all to the glory of God." 1 Corinthians 10:31. The subject of temperance, in all its bearings, has an important place in the work of salvation.

In connection with our city missions there should be suitable rooms where those in whom an interest has been awakened can be gathered for instruction. This necessary work is not to be carried on in such a meager way that an unfavorable impression will be made on the minds of the people. All that is done should bear favorable witness to the Author of truth and should properly represent the sacredness and importance of the truths of the third angel's message.

Cooking schools are to be held. The people are to be taught how to prepare wholesome food. They are to be shown the need of discarding unhealthful foods. But we should never advocate a starvation diet. It is possible to have a wholesome, nutritious diet without the use of tea, coffee, and flesh food. The work of teaching the people how to prepare a dietary that is at once wholesome and appetizing is of the utmost importance.

The work of health reforms the Lord's means for

lessening suffering in our world and for purifying His church. Teach the people that they can act as God's helping hand by co-operating with the Master Worker in restoring physical and spiritual health. This work bears the signature of heaven and will open doors for the entrance of other precious truths. There is room for all to labor who will take hold of this work intelligently.

Keep the work of health reform to the front is the message I am instructed to bear. Show so plainly its value that a widespread need for it will be felt. Abstinence from all hurtful food and drink is the fruit of true religion. He who is thoroughly converted will abandon every injurious habit and appetite. By total abstinence he will overcome his desire for health-destroying indulgences.

I am instructed to say to health reform educators: Go forward. The world needs every jot of the influence you can exert to press back the tide of moral woe. Let those who teach the third angel's message stand true to their colors. "I beseech you therefore, brethren, by the mercies of God, that ye present your bodies a living sacrifice, holy, acceptable unto God, which is your reasonable service. And be not conformed to this world: but be ye transformed by the renewing of your mind, that ye may prove what is that good, and acceptable, and perfect, will of God." Romans 12:1, 2. May the Lord arm those who labor in word and doctrine, with the clearest messages of truth. If His workers will give these messages with simplicity, assurance, and all authority, the Lord will work with them.

THE WEALTHY CLASSES NOT TO BE PASSED BY

The servants of Christ should labor faithfully for the rich men in our cities, as well as for the poor and lowly.

There are many wealthy men who are susceptible to the influences and impressions of the gospel message, and who, when the Bible, and the Bible alone, is presented to them as the expositor of Christian faith and practice, will be moved by the Spirit of God to open doors for the advancement of the gospel. They will reveal a living faith in the word of God and will use their entrusted means to prepare the way of the Lord, to make straight in the desert a highway for our God.

For years the perplexing question has been before us: How can we raise funds adequate for the support of the missions which the Lord has gone before us to open? We read the plain commands of the gospel; and the missions, in both home and foreign fields, present their necessities. The indications, yea, the positive revelations of Providence, unite in urging us to do quickly the work that is waiting to be done. The Lord desires that moneyed men shall be converted and act as His helping hand in reaching others. He desires that those who can help in the work of reform and restoration shall see the precious light of truth and be transformed in character and led to use their entrusted capital in His service. He would have them invest the means He has lent them, in doing good, in opening the way for the gospel to be preached to all classes nigh and afar off.

Will not heaven be appreciated by the worldly wise men? Oh, yes; there they will find rest and peace and repose from all trifling, all ambition, all self-serving. Urge them to seek for the peace and happiness and joy that Christ is longing to bestow upon them. Urge them to give their attention to securing the richest gift that can be given to mortal man—the robe of Christ's righteousness. Christ offers them a life that measures with the life of God, and a far more exceeding and eternal weight of glory. If they accept Christ they will have the highest honor, honor which the world can neither give nor take away. They will find that in the keeping of the commandments of God there is great reward.

The compassionate Redeemer bids His servants give to rich and poor the call to the supper. Go out into the highways and the hedges, and by your persevering, determined efforts, compel them to come in. Let ministers of the gospel take hold of these worldly moneyed men and bring them to the banquet of truth that Christ has prepared for them. He who gave His precious life for them says: "Bring them in, and seat them at My table, and I will serve them."

Ministers of Christ, link yourselves up with this class. Pass them not by as hopeless. Work with all the persuasion possible, and as the fruit of your faithful efforts you will see in the kingdom of heaven men and women who will be crowned as overcomers to sing the triumphant song of the conqueror. "They shall walk with Me in white," says the First and the Last; "for they are worthy." Revelation 3:4.

Altogether too little effort has been put forth for men in responsible places in the world. Many of them possess superior qualifications; they have means and influence. These are precious gifts, entrusted to them by the Lord to be increased and used for the good of others.

Seek to save men of wealth. Entreat them to return to the Lord the treasures He has lent them in trust, that in New York and other great cities there may be established centers of influence from which Bible truth in its simplicity shall go forth to the people. Persuade men to lay up their treasures beside the throne of God by returning to the Lord their substance, enabling His workers to do good and to advance His glory.

PLANS FOR ENLARGING OUR LABORING FORCES

The strength of an army is measured largely by the efficiency of the men in the ranks. A wise general instructs his officers to train every soldier for active service. He seeks to develop the highest efficiency on the part of all. If he were to depend on his officers alone he could never expect to conduct a successful campaign. He counts on loyal and untiring service from every man in his army. The responsibility rests largely upon the men in the ranks.

And so it is in the army of Prince Immanuel. Our General, who has never lost a battle, expects willing, faithful service from everyone who has enlisted under His banner. In the closing controversy now waging between the forces for good and the hosts of evil He expects all, laymen as well as ministers, to take part. All who have enlisted as His soldiers are to render faithful service as minutemen, with a keen sense of the responsibility resting upon them individually.

Those who have the spiritual oversight of the church should devise ways and means by which an opportunity may be given to every member of the church to act some part in God's work. Too often in the past this has not been done. Plans have not been clearly laid and fully carried out whereby the talents of all might be employed in active service. There are but few who realize how much has been lost because of this.

The leaders in God's cause, as wise generals, are to lay plans for advance moves all along the line. In their planning they are to give special study to the work that can be done by the laity for their friends and neighbors. The work of God in this earth can never be finished until the men and women comprising our church membership rally to the work and unite their efforts with those of ministers and church officers.

The salvation of sinners requires earnest, personal labor. We are to bear to them the word of life, not to wait for them to come to us. Oh, that I could speak words to men and women that would arouse them to diligent action! The moments now granted to us are few. We are standing upon the very borders of the eternal world. We have no time to lose. Every moment is golden and altogether too precious to be devoted merely to self-serving. Who will seek God earnestly and from Him draw strength and grace to be His faithful workers in the missionary field?

DEVELOPMENT OF TALENT IN THE CHURCHES

In every church there is talent, which, with the right kind of labor, might be developed to become a great help in this work. That which is needed now for the upbuilding of our churches is the nice work of wise laborers to discern and develop talent in the church—talent that can be educated for the Master's use. There should be a well-organized plan for the employment of workers to go into all our churches, large and small, to instruct the members how to labor for the upbuilding of the church and also for unbelievers. It is training, education, that is needed. Those who labor in visiting the churches should give the brethren and sisters instruction in practical methods of doing missionary work.

All the preaching in the world will not make men feel deeply the need of perishing souls around them.

Nothing will so arouse in men and women a self-sacrificing zeal as to send them forth into new fields to work for those in darkness. Prepare workers to go out into the highways and hedges. We need wise nurserymen who will transplant trees to different localities and give them advantages, that they may grow. It is the positive duty of God's people to go into the regions beyond. Let forces be set at work to clear new ground, to establish new centers of influence wherever an opening can be found. Rally workers who possess true missionary zeal, and let them go forth to diffuse light and knowledge far and near. Let them take the living principles of health reform into the communities that to a large degree are ignorant of these principles.

Men in humble walks of life are to be encouraged to take up the work of God. As they labor they will gain a precious experience. There is a dearth of laborers, and we have not one to spare. Instead of discouraging those who are trying to serve the Master, we should encourage many more laborers to enter the field.

JOYOUS SERVICE

All who commune with God will find abundance of work to do for Him. Those who go forth in the spirit of the Master, seeking to reach souls with the truth, will not find the work of drawing souls to Christ a dull, uninteresting drudgery. They are charged with a work as God's husbandmen, and they will become more and more vitalized as they give themselves to the service of God. It is a joyous work to open the Scriptures to others.

Young men and women should be educated to become workers in their own neighborhoods and in other places. Let all set their hearts and minds to become intelligent in regard to the work for this time, qualifying themselves to do that for which they are best adapted.

Many young men who have had the right kind of education at home are to be trained for service and encouraged to lift the standard of truth in new places by well-planned and faithful work. By associating with our ministers and experienced workers in city work, they will gain the best kind of training. Acting under divine guidance and sustained by the prayers of their more experienced fellow workers, they may do a good and blessed work. As they unite their labors with those of the older workers, using their youthful energies to the very best account, they will have the companionship of heavenly angels; and as workers together with God, it is their privilege to sing and pray and believe, and work with courage and freedom. The confidence and trust that the presence of heavenly agencies will bring to them and to their fellow workers will lead to prayer and praise and the simplicity of true faith.

There should be no delay in this well-planned effort to educate the church members. Persons should be chosen to labor in the large cities who are fully consecrated and who understand the sacredness and importance of the work. Do not send those who are not qualified in these respects. Men are needed who will push the triumphs of the cross, who will persevere under discouragements and privations, who will have the zeal and resolution and faith that are indispensable to the missionary field. And to those who do not engage personally in the work I would say: Do not hinder those who are willing to work, but give them encouragement and support.

All this work of training should be accompanied with earnest seeking of the Lord for His Holy Spirit. Let this be urged home upon those who are willing to give themselves to the Master's service. Our conduct is watched by the world. Every act is scrutinized and commented upon. There must be diligent cultivation of the Christian graces, that those who profess the truth may be able to teach it to others as it is in Jesus, that they themselves may be ensamples, and that our enemies may be able to say no evil of them truthfully. God calls for greater piety, for holiness of life and purity of conduct, in accordance with the elevating, sanctifying principles that we profess. The lives of the workers for Christ should be such that unbelievers, seeing their godly walk and circumspect conversation, may be charmed by the faith that produces such results.

PERSONAL EFFORT IN CONNECTION
WITH CAMP MEETINGS

The work at our camp meetings should be conducted, not according to man's devising, but after the manner of Christ's working. The church members should be drawn out to labor. Angels of God will direct in the opening of fields nigh and afar off, that the work of warning the world may be quickly accomplished. God calls upon believers to obtain an experience in missionary work by branching out into new territory and working intelligently for the people in the byways. To those who will do this, openings for labor will come.

In following up the interests after a camp meeting, helpers are needed in various lines, and these occasions should be as training schools for workers. Let young men work in connection with experienced laborers who will pray with them and patiently instruct them. Consecrated women should engage in Bible work from house to house. Some of the workers should act as colporteurs, selling our literature and giving judiciously to those who cannot buy.

Those who are truly converted must become more and more intelligent in their understanding of the Scriptures, that they may be able to speak words of light and salvation to those who are in darkness and perishing in their sins. As workers together with Him we are to expect special blessings and definite results as we strive to save souls from the snares of Satan that they may become the children of light.

TOURIST CENTERS AND CENTERS OF COMMERCE

Those who in response to the call of the hour have entered the service of the Master Workman may well study His methods of labor. During His earthly ministry the Saviour took advantage of the opportunities to be found along the great thoroughfares of travel. It was at Capernaum that Jesus dwelt at the intervals of His journeys to and fro, and it came to be known as "His own city." This city was well adapted to be the center of the Saviour's work. Being on the highway from Damascus to Jerusalem and Egypt, and to the Mediterranean Sea, it was a great thoroughfare of travel. People from many lands passed through the city or tarried for rest on their journeyings to and fro. Here Jesus could meet all nations and all ranks, the rich and great, as well as the poor and lowly; and His lessons would be carried to other countries and into many households. Investigation of the prophecies would thus be excited; attention would be directed to the Saviour, and His mission would be brought before the world.

In these days of travel the opportunities for coming

in contact with men and women of all classes and of many nationalities are much greater than in the days of Israel. The thoroughfares of travel have multiplied a thousandfold. God has wonderfully prepared the way. The agency of the printing press, with its manifold facilities, is at our command. Bibles, and publications in many languages, setting forth the truth for this time, are at our hand and can be swiftly carried to every part of the world.

Christians who are living in the great centers of commerce and travel have special opportunities. Believers in these cities can work for God in the neighborhood of their homes.

In the world-renowned health resorts and centers of tourist traffic, crowded with many thousands of seekers after health and pleasure, there should be stationed ministers and canvassers capable of arresting the attention of the multitudes. Let these workers watch their chance for presenting the message for this time, and hold meetings as they have opportunity. Let them be quick to seize opportunities to speak to the people. Accompanied by the power of the Holy Spirit, let them meet the people with the message borne by John the Baptist: "Repent ye: for the kingdom of heaven is at hand." Matthew 3:2. The word of God is to be presented with clearness and power, that those who have ears to hear may hear the truth. Thus the gospel of present truth will be placed in the way of those who know it not, and it will be accepted by not a few and carried by them to their own homes in all parts of the world.

WITH UNFLAGGING ZEAL

We are to give the last warning of God to men, and what should be our earnestness in studying the Bible and our zeal in spreading the light! Let every soul who has received the divine illumination seek to impart it. Let the workers go from house to house, opening the Bible to the people, circulating the publications, telling others of the light that has blessed their own souls. Let literature be distributed judiciously, on the trains, in the street, on the great ships that ply the sea, and through the mails.

A great work is to be done, and those who know the truth should make mighty intercession for help. The love of Christ must fill their own hearts. The Spirit of Christ must be poured out upon them, and they must be making ready to stand in the judgment. As they consecrate themselves to God, a convincing power will attend their efforts to present the truth to others. We must no longer sleep on Satan's enchanted ground, but call into requisition all our resources, availing ourselves of every facility with which Providence has furnished us. The last warning is to be proclaimed before "many peoples, and nations, and tongues, and kings," and the promise is given, "Lo, I am with you alway, even unto the end of the world." Revelation 10:11; Matthew 28:20.

I am instructed to point our ministers to the unworked cities and to urge them by every possible means to open the way for the presentation of the truth. In some of the cities where the message of the second coming of the Lord was first given, we are compelled to take up the work as if it were a new field. How much longer will these barren fields, these unworked cities, be passed by? Without delay the sowing of the seed should begin in many, many places.

The Lord demands that in His servants shall be found a spirit that is quick to feel the value of souls, quick to discern the duties to be done, quick to respond to the obligations that the Lord lays upon them. There must be a devotion that will regard no earthly interest of sufficient value to take the place of the work to be done in winning souls to a knowledge of the truth.

Ministers, preach the truths that will lead to personal labor for those who are out of Christ. Encourage personal effort in every possible way. Remember that a minister's work does not consist merely in preaching. He is to visit families in their homes, to pray with them, and to open to them the Scriptures. He who does faithful work outside of the pulpit will accomplish tenfold more than he who confines his labors to the desk. Let our ministers carry their load of responsibility with fear and trembling, looking to the Lord for wisdom and asking constantly for His grace. Let them make Jesus their pattern, diligently studying His life and bringing into the daily practice the principles that actuated Him in His service while upon the earth.

———

"Come unto Me, all ye that labor and are heavy-laden, and I will give you rest." This is a prescription for the healing of all mental and physical and spiritual ills. It is Christ's gift to those who seek Him in sincerity and in truth. He is the Mighty Healer. Then comes another invitation: "Take My yoke upon *you,* and learn of *Me;* for I am meek and lowly in heart: and ye shall find rest unto your souls. For My yoke is easy, and My burden is light." Matthew 11:28-30. Wearing Christ's yoke and learning of Him the lesson of meekness and lowliness, we find rest in faith, and confidence and trust. We find that Christ's yoke is easy and His burden light.

AN APPEAL TO LAYMEN

When a special effort is put forth by laborers of experience in a community where our own people live, here rests upon the believers in that field a most solemn obligation to do all in their power to open the way for the Lord to work. They should search their hearts prayerfully, and clear the King's highway by putting away every sin that would hinder them from co-operating with God and with their brethren.

This has not always been fully understood. Satan has often brought in a spirit that has made it impossible for church members to discern opportunities for service. Believers have not infrequently allowed the enemy to work through them at the very time when they should have been wholly consecrated to God and to the advancement of His work. Unconsciously they have wandered far from the way of righteousness. Cherishing a spirit of criticism and faultfinding, of pharisaical piety and pride, they have grieved away the Spirit of God and have greatly retarded the work of God's messengers.

This evil has been pointed out many times and in many places. Sometimes those who have indulged in a censorious, condemnatory spirit have repented and been converted. Then God has been able to use them to His name's honor and glory.

We are living in a special period of this earth's history. A great work must be done in a very short time, and every Christian is to act a part in sustaining this work. God is calling for men who will consecrate themselves to the work of soulsaving. When we begin to comprehend what a sacrifice Christ made in order to save a perishing world, there will be seen a mighty wrestling to save souls. Oh, that all our churches might see and realize the infinite sacrifice of Christ!

A REFORMATORY MOVEMENT

In visions of the night, representations passed before me of a great reformatory movement among God's people. Many were praising God. The sick were healed, and other miracles were wrought. A spirit of intercession was seen, even as was manifested before the great Day of Pentecost. Hundreds and thousands were seen visiting families and opening before them the word of God. Hearts were convicted by the power of the Holy Spirit, and a spirit of genuine conversion was manifest. On every side doors were thrown open to the proclamation of the truth. The world seemed to be lightened with the heavenly influence. Great blessings were received by the true and humble people of God. I heard voices of thanksgiving and praise, and there seemed to be a reformation such as we witnessed in 1844.

Yet some refused to be converted. They were not willing to walk in God's way, and when, in order that the work of God might be advanced, calls were made for freewill offerings, some clung selfishly to their earthly possessions. These covetous ones became separated from the company of believers.

LABORING WHILE PROBATION LINGERS

The judgments of God are in the earth, and, under the influence of the Holy Spirit, we must give the message of warning that He has entrusted to us. We must give this message quickly, line upon line, precept upon precept. Men will soon be forced to great decisions, and it is our duty to see that they are given an opportunity to understand the truth, that they may take their stand intelligently on the right side. The Lord calls upon His people to labor—labor earnestly and wisely—while probation lingers.

THE IMPORTANCE OF PERSONAL LABOR

Among the members of our churches there should be more house-to-house labor in giving Bible readings and distributing literature. A Christian character can be symmetrically and completely formed only when the human agent regards it as a privilege to work disinterestedly in the proclamation of the truth and to sustain the cause of God with means. We must sow beside all waters, keeping our souls in the love of God, working while it is day, and using the means the Lord has given us to do whatever duty comes next. Whatever our hands find to do, we are to do it with faithfulness; whatever sacrifice we are called upon to make, we are to make it cheerfully. As we sow beside all waters we shall realize that "he which soweth bountifully shall reap also bountifully." 2 Corinthians 9:6.

Christ's example must be followed by those who claim to be His children. Relieve the physical necessities of your fellow men, and their gratitude will break down the barriers and enable you to reach their hearts. Consider this matter earnestly. As churches you have had opportunity to work as laborers together with God. Had you obeyed the word of God, had you entered upon this work, you would have been blessed and encouraged, and would have obtained a rich experience. You would have found yourselves, as the human agencies of God, earnestly advocating a scheme of saving, of restoration, of salvation. This scheme would not be fixed, but progressive, moving on from grace to grace and from strength to strength.

The Lord has presented before me the work that is to be done in our cities. The believers in these cities are to work for God in the neighborhood of their homes. They are to labor quietly and in humility, carrying with them wherever they go the atmosphere of heaven. If they keep self out of sight, pointing always to Christ, the power of their influence will be felt.

It is not the Lord's purpose that ministers should be left to do the greatest part of the work of sowing the seeds of truth. Men who are not called to the ministry are to labor for their Master according to their several ability. As a worker gives himself unreservedly to the service of the Lord, he gains an experience that enables him to work more and more successfully for the Master. The influence that drew him to Christ helps him to draw others to Christ. The work of a public speaker may never be laid upon him, but he is nonetheless a minister for God, and his work testifies that he is born of God.

Women as well as men can engage in the work of hiding the truth where it can work out and be made manifest. They can take their place in the work at this crisis, and the Lord will work through them. If they are imbued with a sense of their duty, and labor under the influence of the Spirit of God, they will have just the self-possession required for this time. The Saviour will reflect upon these self-sacrificing women the light of His countenance, and this will give them a power that will exceed that of men. They can do in families a work that men cannot do, a work that reaches the inner life. They can come close to the hearts of those whom men cannot reach. Their work is needed. Discreet and humble women can do a good work in explaining the truth to the people in their homes. The word of God thus explained will do its leavening work, and through its influence whole families will be converted.

My brethren and sisters, study your plans; grasp every opportunity of speaking to your neighbors and associates or of reading something to them from books that contain present truth. Show that you regard as of first importance the salvation of the souls for whom Christ has made so great a sacrifice.

In working for perishing souls, you have the companionship of angels. Thousands upon thousands, and ten thousand times ten thousand angels are waiting to cooperate with members of our churches in communicating the light that God has generously given, that a people may be prepared for the coming of Christ. "Now is the accepted time; behold, now is the day of salvation." Let every family seek the Lord in earnest prayer for help to do the work of God.

Do not pass by the little things, and look for a large work. You might do successfully the small work, but fail utterly in attempting a large work and fall into discouragement. Take hold wherever you see that there is work to be done. Whether you are rich or poor, great or humble, God calls you into active service for Him. It will be by doing with your might what your hands find to do that you will develop talent and aptitude for the work. And it is by neglecting your daily opportunities that you become fruitless and withered. This is why there are so many fruitless trees in the garden of the Lord.

In the home circle, at your neighbor's fireside, at the bedside of the sick, in a quiet way you may read the Scriptures and speak a word for Jesus and the truth.

Precious seed may thus be sown that will spring up and bring forth fruit after many days.

There is missionary work to be done in many unpromising places. The missionary spirit needs to take hold of our souls, inspiring us to reach classes for whom we had not planned to labor and in ways and places that we had no idea of working. The Lord has His plan for the sowing of the gospel seed. In sowing according to His will, we shall so multiply the seed that His word may reach thousands who have never heard the truth.

Opportunities are opening on every side. Press into every providential opening. Eyes need to be anointed with the heavenly eyesalve to see and sense their opportunities. God calls now for wide-awake missionaries. There are ways that will be presented before us. We are to see and understand these providential openings.

God's messengers are commissioned to take up the very work that Christ did while on this earth. They are to give themselves to every line of ministry that He carried on. With earnestness and sincerity they are to tell men of the unsearchable riches and the immortal treasure of heaven. They are to be filled with the Holy Spirit. They are to repeat Heaven's offers of peace and pardon. They are to point to the gates of the city of God, saying: "Blessed are they that do His commandments, that they may have right to the tree of life, and may enter in through the gates into the city." Revelation 22:14.

CHERISHING A SPIRIT OF SELF-DENIAL

Every church member should cherish a spirit of sacrifice. In every home there should be taught lessons of self-denial. Fathers and mothers, teach your children to economize. Encourage them to save their pennies for missionary work. Christ is our example. For our sakes He became poor, that we through His poverty might be made rich. He taught that all should come together in love and unity, to work as He worked, to sacrifice as He sacrificed, to love as the children of God.

My brethren and sisters, you must be willing to be converted yourselves in order to practice the self-denial of Christ. Dress plainly but neatly. Spend as little as possible upon yourselves. Keep in your homes a self-denial box into which you can put the money saved by little acts of self-denial. Day by day gain a clearer understanding of the word of God, and improve every opportunity to impart the knowledge you have gained. Do not become weary in well-doing, for God is constantly imparting to you the great blessing of His Gift to the world. Co-operate with the Lord Jesus, and He will teach you the priceless lessons of His love. Time is short; in due season when time shall be no longer, you will receive your reward.

To those who love God sincerely and have means, I am bidden to say: Now is the time for you to invest your means in sustaining the work of the Lord. Now is the time to uphold the hands of the ministers in their self-denying efforts to save perishing souls. When you meet in the heavenly courts the souls you have helped to save, will you not have a glorious reward?

Let none withhold their mites, and let those who have much rejoice that they can lay up in heaven a treasure that faileth not. The money that we refuse to invest in the work of the Lord, will perish. On it no interest will accumulate in the bank of heaven.

In the following words the apostle Paul describes those who withhold from God His own: "They that will be rich fall into temptation and a snare, and into many foolish and hurtful lusts, which drown men in destruction and perdition. For the love of money is the root of all evil: which while some coveted after, they have erred from the faith, and pierced themselves through with many sorrows." 1 Timothy 6:9, 10.

It means much to sow beside all waters. It means a continual imparting of gifts and offerings. God will furnish facilities so that the faithful steward of His entrusted means shall be supplied with a sufficiency in all things, and be enabled to abound to every good work. "As it is written, He hath dispersed abroad; he hath given to the poor: his righteousness remaineth forever. Now he that ministereth seed to the sower both minister bread for your food, and multiply your seed sown, and increase the fruits of your righteousness." 2 Corinthians 9:9, 10. The seed sown with full, liberal hand is taken charge of by the Lord. He who ministers seed to the sower gives His worker that which enables him to co-operate with the Giver of the seed.

The Lord now calls upon Seventh-day Adventists in every locality to consecrate themselves to Him and to do their very best, according to their circumstances, to assist in His work. By their liberality in making gifts and offerings, He desires them to reveal their appreciation of His blessings and their gratitude for His mercy.

My dear brethren and sisters, all the money we have is the Lord's. I now appeal to you in the name of the Lord to unite in carrying to successful completion the enterprises that have been undertaken in the counsels of God. Let not the work of establishing memorials for

God in many places be made difficult and burdensome because the necessary means is withheld. Let not those who are struggling to build up important enterprises, great and small, become disheartened because we are slow to unite in placing these enterprises in a position to do efficient service. Let all our people arise and see what they can do. Let them show that there is unity and strength among Seventh-day Adventists.

CONDITIONS OF ACCEPTABLE SERVICE

As a people we must come into a sacred nearness to God. We need the light of heaven to shine into our hearts and into the chambers of our mind; we need the wisdom that God alone can give, if we carry the message to these cities with success. Let our churches everywhere come into line. Let none who have pledged themselves by baptism to live for the service and glory of God take back their pledge. There is a world to be saved; let this thought urge us on to greater sacrifices and more earnest labor for those who are out of the way.

When you follow out the principles of the word of God, your influence will be of value to any church, any organization. You are to come up to the help of the Lord, to the help of the Lord against the mighty. All frivolous words, all lightness and trifling, are enticements of the enemy to deprive you of spiritual strength. Brace yourselves against this evil, in the name of the God of Israel. If you will humble yourselves before God, He will give you a message for those in the highways and the hedges, and for those in foreign countries who need your help. Trim your lamps, and keep them burning, that wherever you may go you may reveal in speech and action precious rays of light.

If we will give ourselves for service to the Lord, He will instruct us what to do. If we will come into close relation with God, He will work with us. Let us not become so absorbed in self and self-interests that we shall forget those who are climbing the ladder of Christian experience and who need our help. We must stand ready to use our God-given capabilities in the work of the Lord, ready to speak words in season and out of season—words that will help and bless.

My brethren and sisters, do we take into consideration the needs of the large cities of the East? Do we not know that they must be warned of Christ's near approach? The work we have to do is a wonderfully great work. There is a world to be saved; there are souls to be labored for in the cities of the East, in the states where the message of the coming of our Lord was first preached. Who will give themselves to do this line of missionary work? There are hundreds of our people who ought to be out in the field who are doing little or nothing for the advancement of the message. Those who have had every advantage of knowing the truth, who have received instruction line upon line, precept upon precept, here a little and there a little, have a great responsibility resting upon them in these souls who have never heard the last gospel message.

If in this opportune time the members of the churches will come humbly before God, putting out of their hearts all that is wrong and consulting Him at every step, He will manifest Himself to them and will give them courage in Him. And as the church members do their part faithfully, the Lord will lead and guide His chosen ministers, and strengthen them for their important work. In much prayer let us all unite in holding up their hands and in drawing bright beams from the heavenly sanctuary.

The end is near, stealing upon us stealthily, imperceptibly, like the noiseless approach of a thief in the night. May the Lord grant that we shall no longer sleep as do others, but that we shall watch and be sober. The truth is soon to triumph gloriously, and all who now choose to be laborers together with God will triumph with it. The time is short; the night soon cometh when no man can work. Let those who are rejoicing in the light of present truth now make haste to impart the truth to others. The Lord is inquiring: "Whom shall I send?" Those who wish to sacrifice for the truth's sake are now to respond: "Here am I; send me." Isaiah 6:8.

Let those who bear responsibilities remember that it is the Holy Spirit who is to do the fashioning. It is the Lord who controls. We are not to try to mold, according to our own ideas, those for whom we work, but to let Christ do the molding. He follows no human pattern. He works according to His own mind and Spirit. It is man's work to reveal to the world that which *Christ* has placed in his heart; through His grace man becomes a partaker of the divine nature, having escaped the corruption that is in the world through lust. The higher powers of the one who receives Christ are strengthened and ennobled, and he receives a fitness for God's service.

Many of the world's learned men have received so high an education that they cannot touch the common people. Their knowledge is intricate. It soars high, but rests nowhere. The most intelligent businessmen desire simple truth such as Christ gave to the people when He was on this earth—the truth that He declares to be spirit and life. His words are as the leaves of the tree of life. What the world needs today is the light of Christ's example, reflected from the lives of Christlike men and women. The intellect most powerful in behalf of truth is the intellect that Christ controls, ennobling and purifying it by the sanctification of the Holy Spirit.

Christ has given His commission: "Go ye into all the world." Mark 16:15. All must hear the message of warning. A prize of richest value is held up before those who are running the Christian race. Those who run with patience will receive a crown of life that fadeth not away.

Cultivate restfulness, and commit the keeping of your souls unto God as unto a faithful Creator. He will keep that which is committed to His trust. He is not pleased to have us cover His altar with our tears and complaints. You have enough to praise God for already, if you do not see another soul converted. But the good work will go on if you will only go forward and not be trying to adjust everything to your own ideas. Let the peace of God rule in your hearts, and be ye thankful. Let the Lord have room to work. Do not block His way. He can and will work if we will let Him.

While extensive plans should be laid, great care must be taken that the work in each branch of the cause be harmoniously united with that in every other branch, thus making a perfect whole.

WORDS OF COUNSEL TO MINISTERS

Sanitarium, California, November 3, 1901.

To a Worker of Long Experience
in New York City—

As I have considered the situation in New York, a great burden has come upon my soul. In the night season matters have been presented to me in this light: New York will be worked; openings will be found in parts of the city in which there are no churches, where the truth will find standing room. There is a vast amount of work to be done in proclaiming the truth for this time to those who are dead in trespasses and sins. Most startling messages will be borne by men of God's appointment, messages of a character to warn the people, to arouse them. And while some will be provoked by the warning and led to resist light and evidence, we are to see from this that we are giving the testing message for this time.

Messages will be given out of the usual order. The judgments of God are in the land. While city missions must be established where colporteurs, Bible workers, and practical medical missionaries may be trained to reach certain classes, we must also have, in our cities, consecrated evangelists through whom a message is to be borne so decidedly as to startle the hearers.

"Bring forth the blind people that have eyes, and the deaf that have ears. Let all the nations be gathered together, and let the people be assembled: who among them can declare this, and show us former things? Let them bring forth their witnesses, that they may be justified: or let them hear, and say, It is truth. Ye are My witnesses, saith the Lord, and My servant whom I have chosen: that ye may know and believe Me, and understand that I am He: before Me there was no God formed, neither shall there be after Me. I, even I, am the Lord; and beside Me there is no savior. I have declared, and have saved, and I have showed, when there was no strange god among you: therefore ye are My witnesses, saith the Lord, that I am God. Yea, before the day was I am He; and there is none that can deliver out of My hand: I will work, and who shall let it?" Isaiah 43:8-13.

"I will bring the blind by a way that they knew not; I will lead them in paths that they have not known: I will make darkness light before them, and crooked things straight. These things will I do unto them, and not forsake them. They shall be turned back, they shall be greatly ashamed, that trust in graven images, that say to the molten images, Ye are our gods. Hear, ye deaf; and look, ye blind, that ye may see. Who is blind, but My servant? or deaf, as My messenger that I sent? who is blind as he that is perfect, and blind as the Lord's servant? Seeing many things, but thou observest not; opening the ears, but he heareth not. The Lord is well pleased for His righteousness' sake; He will magnify the law, and make it honorable." Isaiah 42:16-21.

The work outlined in these scriptures is the work before us. The terms "My servant," "Israel," "the Lord's servant," mean anyone that the Lord may select and appoint to do a certain work. He makes them ministers of His will, though some who are selected may be as ignorant of His will as was Nebuchadnezzar.

God will work for those of His people who will submit themselves to the working of the Holy Spirit. He pledges His glory for the success of the Messiah and His kingdom. "Thus saith God the Lord, He that created the heavens, and stretched them out; He that spread forth the earth, and that which cometh out of it; He that giveth breath unto the people upon it, and spirit to them that walk therein: I the Lord have called thee in righteousness, and will hold thine hand, and will keep thee, and give thee for a covenant of the people, for a light of the Gentiles; to open the blind eyes, to bring out the prisoners from the prison, and them that sit in darkness out of the prison house."

"Who among you will give ear to this? who will hearken and hear for the time to come?" Verses 5-7, 23.

The people of God who have had light and knowledge have not carried out the high and holy purposes of God. They have not advanced from victory to victory, adding new territory, lifting up the standard in the cities and their suburbs. Great spiritual blindness has been shown by those who have had great light flashed upon them by the Lord, but who have not advanced in the light to greater and still greater light. Church members have not been encouraged to use spiritual nerve and muscle in the work of advancement. They should be made to understand that ministers cannot work out their salvation by hovering over them. It is thus that they are made weaklings when they ought to be strong men.

In every church young men and young women should be selected to bear responsibilities. Let them make every effort to qualify themselves to help those who know not the truth. God calls for earnest, whole-souled workers. The humble and contrite will learn by personal experience that *beside Him* there is no savior.

Bible truth must be preached and practiced. Every ray of light given is to shine forth with clear, distinct brightness. The truth is to go forth as a lamp that burneth. *There are hundreds of God's servants who must respond to this call and take the field as earnest, soul-saving workers,* coming up to the help of the Lord, to the help of the Lord against the mighty. God calls for *live men,* men who are filled with the vivifying influence of His Spirit, men who see God as the Supreme Ruler and receive from Him abundant proof of the fulfillment of His promises, men who are not lukewarm, but hot and fervent with His love.

Should all the labor that has been expended on the churches during the past twenty years be again expended upon them, it would fail, as it has failed in the past, of making the members self-denying, cross-bearing followers of Christ. Many have been overfed with spiritual food, while in the world thousands are perishing for the bread of life. Church members must work; they must educate themselves, striving to reach the high standard set before them. This the Lord will help them to reach if they will co-operate with Him. If they keep their own souls in the love of the truth they will not hold the ministers back from presenting the truth in new fields.

The large cities should have been worked just as soon as the churches received the light, but many have carried no burden for souls, and Satan, finding them susceptible to his temptations, has spoiled their experience. God asks His people to repent, to be converted, and to return to their first love, which they have lost by their failure to follow in the footsteps of the self-sacrificing Redeemer.

IN COURAGE AND SIMPLICITY

The time has come to make decided efforts in places where the truth has not yet been proclaimed. How shall the Lord's work be done? In every place that is entered, a solid foundation is to be laid for permanent work. The Lord's methods are to be followed. It is not for you to be intimidated by outward appearances, however forbidding they may be. It is for you to carry forward the work as the Lord has said it should be carried. Preach the word, and the Lord by His Holy Spirit will send conviction to the minds of the hearers. The word is: "And they went forth, and preached everywhere, the Lord working with them, and confirming the word with signs following." Mark 16:20.

Many workers are to act their part, doing house-to-house work and giving Bible readings in families. They are to show their growth in grace by submission to the will of Christ. Thus they will gain a rich experience. As in faith they receive, believe, and obey Christ's word, the efficiency of the Holy Spirit will be seen in their life-work. There will be seen an intensity of earnest effort. There will be cherished a faith that works by love and purifies the soul. The fruits of the Spirit will be seen in the life.

Christ is the Light of the world. Those who follow Him do not walk in darkness, but have the light of life. John declares of Christ: "As many as received Him, to them gave He power to become the sons of God, even to them that believe on His name." John 1:12. Behold Christ. Beholding Him brings heart and mind and character into conformity to the will of God.

There is need of all the instruction that our missions

can give. Continue in your work in the power of the same Spirit that led in its establishment. By opening the Scriptures, by praying, by exercising faith, educate the people in the way of the Lord; and there will be built up a church founded on the Rock, Christ Jesus.

The work must be carried forward in the simplicity of truth. God says: "I have words of encouragement for you." The Lord has in our large cities many precious souls who have not bowed the knee to Baal, and He has those who have worshiped Baal ignorantly. On these the light of truth is to shine, that they may see Christ as the way, the truth, and the life.

Carry forward your work in humility. Never rise above the simplicity of the gospel of Christ. Not in the art of display, but in lifting up Christ, the sin-pardoning Redeemer, will you find success in winning souls. As you work for God in humility and lowliness of heart, He will manifest Himself to you.

By the use of charts, symbols, and representations of various kinds the minister can make the truth stand out clearly and distinctly. This is a help, and in harmony with the word of God; but when the worker makes his labors so expensive that others are unable to secure from the treasury sufficient means to support them in the field, he is not working in harmony with God's plan. The work in the large cities is to be done after Christ's order, not after the order of a theatrical performance. It is not a theatrical performance that glorifies God, but the presentation of the truth in the love of Christ.

Do not divest the truth of its dignity and impressiveness by preliminaries that are more after the order of the world than after the order of heaven. Let your hearers understand that you hold meetings, not to charm their senses with music and other things, but to preach the truth in all its solemnity, that it may come to them as a warning, arousing them from their deathlike sleep of self-indulgence. It is the naked truth that like a sharp, two-edged sword cuts both ways. It is this that will arouse those who are dead in trespasses and sins.

He who gave His life to save men and women from idolatry and self-indulgence left an example to be followed by all who take up the work of presenting the gospel to others. God's servants in this age have been given most solemn truths to proclaim, and their actions and methods and plans must correspond to the importance of their message. If you are presenting the word in Christ's way, your audience will be deeply impressed with the truths you teach. The conviction will come to them that this is the word of the living God.

FORMALITY IN WORSHIP

In their efforts to reach the people, the Lord's messengers are not to follow the ways of the world. In the meetings that are held, they are not to depend on worldly singers and theatrical display to awaken an interest. How can those who have no interest in the word of God, who have never read His word with a sincere desire to understand its truths, be expected to sing with the spirit and the understanding? How can their hearts be in harmony with the words of sacred song? How can the heavenly choir join in music that is only a form?

The evil of formal worship cannot be too strongly depicted, but no words can properly set forth the deep blessedness of genuine worship. When human beings sing with the spirit and the understanding, heavenly musicians take up the strain and join in the song of thanksgiving He who has bestowed upon us all the gifts that enable us to be workers together with God, expects His servants to cultivate their voices so that they can speak and sing in a way that all can understand. It is not *loud* singing that is needed, but clear intonation, correct pronunciation, and distinct utterance. Let all take time to cultivate the voice so that God's praise can be sung in clear, soft tones, not with harshness and shrillness that offend the ear. The ability to sing is the gift of God; let it be used to His glory.

In the meetings held let a number be chosen to take part in the song service. And let the singing be accompanied with musical instruments skillfully handled. We are not to oppose the use of instrumental music in our work. This part of the service is to be carefully conducted, for it is the praise of God in song.

The singing is not always to be done by a few. As often as possible, let the entire congregation join.

UNITY IN DIVERSITY

In our efforts in behalf of the multitudes dwelling in cities, we must try to do thorough service. The work in a large center of population is greater than one man can successfully handle. God has different ways of working, and He has different workmen to whom He entrusts varied gifts.

One worker may be a ready speaker; another a ready writer; another may have the gift of sincere, earnest, fervent prayer; another the gift of singing; another may have special power to explain the word of God with clearness. And each gift is to become a power for God because He works with the laborer. To one God gives the word of wisdom, to another knowledge, to another faith; but all are to work under the same Head. The diversity of gifts leads to a diversity of operations, but "it is the same God which worketh all in all." 1 Corinthians 12:6.

The Lord desires His chosen servants to learn how to unite together in harmonious effort. It may seem to some that the contrast between their gifts and the gifts of a fellow laborer is too great to allow them to unite in harmonious effort; but when they remember that there are varied minds to be reached, and that some will reject the truth as it is presented by one laborer, only to open their hearts to God's truth as it is presented in a different manner by another laborer, they will hopefully endeavor to labor together in unity. Their talents, however diverse, may all be under the control of the same Spirit. In every word and act, kindness and love will be revealed; and as each worker fills his appointed place faithfully, the prayer of Christ for the unity of His followers will be answered, and the world will know that these are His disciples.

In loving sympathy and confidence God's workers are to unite with one another. He who says or does anything that tends to separate the members of Christ's church is counterworking the Lord's purpose. Wrangling and dissension in the church, the encouragement of suspicion and unbelief, are dishonoring to Christ. God desires His servants to cultivate Christian affection for one another. True religion unites hearts not only with Christ, but with one another in a most tender union. When we know what it means to be thus united with Christ and with our brethren, a fragrant influence will attend our work wherever we go.

The workers in the large cities must act their several parts, making every effort to bring about the best results. They are to talk faith and to act in such a way as to impress the people. They are not to narrow the work down to their own particular ideas. In the past too much of this has been done by us as a people, and it has been a drawback to the success of the work. Let us remember that the Lord has different ways of working, that He has different workmen to whom He entrusts different gifts. We are to see His purpose in the sending of certain men to certain places.

A little longer will the voice of mercy be heard; a little longer will be given the gracious invitation: "If any man thirst, let him come unto Me, and drink." John 7:37. God sends His warning message to the cities everywhere. Let the messengers whom He sends work so harmoniously that all will take knowledge that they have learned of Jesus.

IN THE MEEKNESS OF CHRIST

No human being is to seek to bind other human beings to himself as if he were to control them, telling them to do this and forbidding them to do that, commanding, dictating, acting like an officer over a company of soldiers. This is the way the priests and rulers did in Christ's day, but it is not the right way. After the truth has made the impression upon hearts, and men and women have accepted its teachings, they are to be treated as the property of Christ, not as the property of man. In fastening minds to yourself, you lead them to disconnect from the source of their wisdom and sufficiency. Their dependence must be wholly in God; only thus can they grow in grace.

However large may be a man's claim to knowledge and wisdom, unless he is under the teaching of the Holy Spirit he is exceedingly ignorant of spiritual things. He needs to realize his danger and his inefficiency, and to place entire dependence upon the One who alone is able to keep the souls committed to His trust, able to imbue them with His Spirit, and to fill them with unselfish love for one another, thus enabling them to bear witness that God has sent His Son into the world to save sinners. Those who are truly converted will press together in Christian unity. Let there be no division in the church of God, no unwise authority exerciscd over those who accept the truth. The meekness of Christ is to appear in all that is said and done.

Christ is the foundation of every true church. We have His unalterable promise that His presence and protection will be given to His faithful ones who walk in His counsel. To the end of time Christ is to be first. He is the source of life and strength, of righteousness and holiness. And He is all this to those who wear His yoke and learn of Him how to be meek and lowly.

The duty and delight of all service is to uplift Christ before the people. This is the end of all true labor. Let Christ appear; let self be hidden behind Him. This is self-sacrifice that is of worth. Such self-sacrifice God accepts. "Thus saith the high and lofty One that inhabiteth eternity, whose name is Holy; I dwell in the high and holy place, with him also that is of a contrite and humble spirit, to revive the spirit of the humble, and to revive the heart of the contrite ones." Isaiah 57:15.

MEETING OPPOSITION

Often, as you seek to present the truth, opposition will be aroused; but if you seek to meet the opposition with argument you will only multiply it, and that you cannot afford to do. Hold to the affirmative. Angels of God are watching you, and they understand how to impress those whose opposition you refuse to meet with argument. Dwell not on the negative points of questions that arise, but gather to your minds affirmative truths, and fasten them there by much study and earnest prayer and heart consecration. Keep your lamps trimmed and burning, and let bright rays shine forth, that men, beholding your good works, may be led to glorify your Father which is in heaven.

If Christ had not held to the affirmative in the wilderness of temptation, He would have lost all that He desired to gain. Christ's way is the best way to meet our opponents. We strengthen their arguments when we repeat what they say. Keep always to the affirmative. It may be that the very man who is opposing you will carry your words home and be converted to the sensible truth that has reached his understanding.

I have often said to our brethren: "Your opponents will make statements about your work that are false. Do not repeat their statements; but hold to your assertions of the living truth, and angels of God will open the way before you. We have a great work to carry forward, and we must carry it in a sensible way. Let us never get excited or allow evil feelings to arise. Christ did not do this, and He is our example in all things. For the work given us to do we need much more of heavenly, sanctified, humble wisdom, and much less of self. We need to lay hold firmly on divine power."

Those who have departed from the faith will come to our congregations to divert our attention from the work that God would have done. You cannot afford to turn your ears from the truth to fables. Do not stop to try to convert the one who is speaking words of reproach against your work; but let it be seen that you are inspired by the Spirit of Jesus Christ, and angels of God will put into your lips words that will reach the hearts of the opposers. If these men persist in pressing their way in, those who are of a sensible mind in the congregation will understand that yours is the higher standard. So speak that it will be known that Jesus Christ is speaking through you.

THE NEED OF EARNEST, WHOLE-SOULED LABOR

If our ministers realized how soon the inhabitants of the world are to be arraigned before the judgment seat of God, to answer for the deeds done in the body, how earnestly they would work together with God to present the truth! How untiringly they would labor to advance God's cause in the world, proclaiming in word and deed: "The end of all things is at hand." 1 Peter 4:7.

"Prepare to meet thy God" is the message we are everywhere to proclaim. The trumpet is to give a certain sound. Clearly and distinctly the warning is to ring out: "Babylon the great is fallen, is fallen. . . . Come out of her, My people, that ye be not partakers of her sins, and that ye receive not of her plagues." Revelation 18:2-4. The words of this scripture are to be fulfilled. Soon the last test is to come to all the inhabitants of the earth. At that time prompt decisions will be made. Those who have been convicted under the presentation of the word will range themselves under the blood-stained banner of Prince Immanuel. They will see and understand as never before they have missed many opportunities for doing the good they ought to have done. They will realize that they have not worked as zealously as they should, to seek and save the lost, to snatch them, as it were, out of the fire.

God's servants are to be "not slothful in business; fervent in spirit; serving the Lord." Listlessness and inefficiency are not piety. When we realize that we are working for God we shall have a higher sense than we have ever had before of the sacredness of spiritual service. This realization will put life and vigilance and persevering energy into the discharge of every duty.

Religion, pure, undefiled religion, is intensely practical. Nothing but earnest, wholehearted labor will avail in the saving of souls. We are to make our everyday duties acts of devotion, constantly increasing in usefulness, because we see our work in the light of eternity.

Our work has been marked out for us by our heavenly Father. We are to take our Bibles and go forth to warn the world. We are to be God's helping hands in saving souls—channels through which His love is day by day to flow to the perishing. The realization of the great work in which he has the privilege of taking part, ennobles and sanctifies the true worker. He is filled with the faith that works by love and purifies the soul. Nothing is drudgery to the one who submits to the will of God. "Doing it unto the Lord" is a thought that throws a charm over whatever work God gives him to do.

Carry on all your work on strictly religious principles. Let your earnest inquiry be: "What can I do to please the Master?" Visit places where the believers need encouragement and help. At every step ask: "Is this the way of the Lord? Am I, in spirit, in word, in action, in harmony with His will?" If you labor for God with an eye single to His glory, your work will bear the divine mold, and you will be carrying out the Lord's purposes.

In your study of the word of God, penetrate deeper and still deeper beneath the surface. Lay hold by faith on divine power and sound the depths of inspiration. Bring into your ministry the power of God, remembering that the Lord is behind you. Let His love shine through all you do and say. Let the truth, the precious, simple truth of the word of God, shine out in full brightness. Humble self before God. Christ will be your efficiency. He has appointed you as rulers over His household, to give meat in due season. Christ's laborers are very near His heart of love. He desires to perfect His household through the perfection of His ministers.

Christ is the sympathetic, compassionate Redeemer. In His sustaining power, men and women become strong to resist evil. As the convicted sinner looks at sin, it becomes to him exceeding sinful. He wonders that he did not come to Christ before. He sees that his faults must be overcome and that his appetites and passions must be subjected to God's will, that he must be a partaker of the divine nature, having overcome the corruption that is in the world through lust. Having repented of his transgression of God's law, he strives earnestly to overcome sin. He seeks to reveal the power of Christ's grace, and he is brought into personal touch with the Saviour. Constantly he keeps Christ before him. Praying, believing, receiving the blessings he needs, he comes nearer and nearer to God's standard for him.

New virtues are revealed in his character as he denies self and lifts the cross, following where Christ leads the way. He loves the Lord Jesus with his whole heart, and

Christ becomes his wisdom, his righteousness, his sanctification, and his redemption.

Christ is our example, our inspiration, our exceeding great reward. "Ye are God's husbandry, ye are God's building." 1 Corinthians 3:9. God is the Master Builder, but man has a part to act. He is to co-operate with God. "We are laborers together with God." Verse 9. Never forget the words: *"together with God."* "Work out your own salvation with fear and trembling. For it is God which worketh in you both to will and to do of His good pleasure." Philippians 2:12, 13. The miracle-working power of Christ's grace is revealed in the creation in man of a new heart, a higher life, a holier enthusiasm. God says: "A new heart also will I give you." Ezekiel 36:26. Is not this, the renewal of man, the greatest miracle that can be performed? What cannot the human agent do who by faith takes hold of the divine power?

Remember that in working with Christ as your personal Saviour lies your strength and your victory. This is the part all are to act. Christ is the way, the truth, and the life. He declares: "Without Me ye can do nothing." John 15:5. And the repentant, believing soul responds: "I can do *all things* through Christ which strengtheneth me." Philippians 4:13. To those who do this comes the assurance: "As many as received Him, to them gave He power to become the sons of God." John 1:12.

THE HEALTH WORK

"Beloved, I wish above all
things that thou mayest prosper
and be in health." 3 John 2.

FAITHFULNESS IN HEALTH REFORM*

I am instructed to bear a message to all our people on the subject of health reform, for many have backslidden from their former loyalty to health reform principles.

God's purpose for His children is that they shall grow up to the full stature of men and women in Christ. In order to do this, they must use aright every power of mind, soul, and body. They cannot afford to waste any mental or physical strength.

The question of how to preserve the health is one of primary importance. When we study this question in the fear of God we shall learn that it is best, for both our physical and our spiritual advancement, to observe simplicity in diet. Let us patiently study this question. We need knowledge and judgment in order to move wisely in this matter. Nature's laws are not to be resisted, but obeyed.

Those who have received instruction regarding the evils of the use of flesh foods, tea and coffee, and rich and unhealthful food preparations, and who are determined to make a covenant with God by sacrifice, will not continue to indulge their appetite for food that they know to be unhealthful. God demands that the appetites be cleansed, and that self-denial be practiced in regard

---

* Manuscript read before the delegates at the General Conference, Washington, D. C., May 31, 1909.

(153)

to those things which are not good. This is a work that will have to be done before His people can stand before Him a perfected people.

PERSONAL RESPONSIBILITY

The remnant people of God must be a converted people. The presentation of this message is to result in the conversion and sanctification of souls. We are to feel the power of the Spirit of God in this movement. This is a wonderful, definite message; it means everything to the receiver, and it is to be proclaimed with a loud cry. We must have a true, abiding faith that this message will go forth with increasing importance till the close of time.

There are some professed believers who accept certain portions of the *Testimonies* as the message of God, while they reject those portions that condemn their favorite indulgences. Such persons are working contrary to their own welfare and the welfare of the church. It is essential that we walk in the light while we have the light. Those who claim to believe in health reform, and yet work counter to its principles in the daily life practice, are hurting their own souls and are leaving wrong impressions upon the minds of believers and unbelievers.

STRENGTH THROUGH OBEDIENCE

A solemn responsibility rests upon those who know the truth, that all their works shall correspond with their faith, and that their lives shall be refined and sanctified, and they be prepared for the work that must rapidly be done in these closing days of the message. They have no time or strength to spend in the indulgence of appetite. The words should come to us now with impelling earnestness: "Repent ye therefore, and be converted, that your sins may be blotted out, when the times of refreshing shall come from the presence of the Lord." Acts 3:19. There are many among us who are deficient in spirituality and who, unless they are wholly converted, will certainly be lost. Can you afford to run the risk?

Pride and weakness of faith are depriving many of the rich blessings of God. There are many who, unless they humble their hearts before the Lord, will be surprised and disappointed when the cry is heard: "Behold, the Bridegroom cometh." Matthew 25:6. They have the theory of the truth, but they have no oil in their vessels with their lamps. Our faith at this time must not stop with an assent to, or belief in, the theory of the third angel's message. We must have the oil of the grace of Christ that will feed the lamp and cause the light of life to shine forth, showing the way to those who are in darkness.

If we would escape having a sickly experience, we must begin in earnest without delay to work out our own salvation with fear and trembling. There are many who give no decided evidence that they are true to their baptismal vows. Their zeal is chilled by formality, worldly ambition, pride, and love of self. Occasionally their feelings are stirred, but they do not fall on the Rock, Christ Jesus. They do not come to God with hearts that are broken in repentance and confession. Those who experience the work of true conversion in their hearts will reveal the fruits of the Spirit in their lives. Oh, that those who have so little spiritual life would realize that eternal life can be granted only to those who become partakers of the divine nature and escape the corruption that is in the world through lust!

The power of Christ alone can work the transformation in heart and mind that all must experience who would partake with Him of the new life in the kingdom of heaven. "Except a man be born again," the Saviour has said, "he cannot see the kingdom of God." John 3:3. The religion that comes from God is the only religion that can lead to God. In order to serve Him aright, we must be born of the divine Spirit. This will lead to watchfulness. It will purify the heart and renew the mind, and give us a new capacity for knowing and loving God. It will give us willing obedience to all His requirements. This is true worship.

God requires of His people continual advancement. We need to learn that indulged appetite is the greatest hindrance to mental improvement and soul sanctification. With all our profession of health reform, many of us eat improperly. Indulgence of appetite is the greatest cause of physical and mental debility, and lies largely at the foundation of feebleness and premature death. Let the individual who is seeking to possess purity of spirit bear in mind that in Christ there is power to control the appetite.

FLESH FOODS

If we could be benefited by indulging the desire for flesh foods, I would not make this appeal to you; but I know we cannot. Flesh foods are injurious to the physical well-being, and we should learn to do without them. Those who are in a position where it is possible to secure a vegetarian diet, but who choose to follow their own preferences in this matter, eating and drinking as they please, will gradually grow careless of the instruction the Lord has given regarding other phases of the present truth and will lose their perception of what is truth; they will surely reap as they have sown.

I have been instructed that the students in our schools are not to be served with flesh foods or with food preparations that are known to be unhealthful. Nothing that will serve to encourage a desire for stimulants should be placed on the tables. I appeal to old and young and to middle-aged. Deny your appetite of those things that are doing you injury. Serve the Lord by sacrifice.

Let the children have an intelligent part in this work. We are all members of the Lord's family, and the Lord would have His children, young and old, determine to deny appetite and to save the means needed for the building of meetinghouses and the support of missionaries.

I am instructed to say to parents: Place yourselves, soul and spirit, on the Lord's side of this question. We need ever to bear in mind that in these days of probation we are on trial before the Lord of the universe. Will you not give up indulgences that are doing you injury? Words of profession are cheap; let your acts of self-denial testify that you will be obedient to the demands that God makes of His peculiar people. Then put into the treasury a portion of the means you save by your acts of self-denial, and there will be that with which to carry on the work of God.

There are many who feel that they cannot get along without flesh food; but if these would place themselves on the Lord's side, resolutely resolved to walk in the way of His guidance, they would receive strength and wisdom as did Daniel and his fellows. They would find that the Lord would give them sound judgment. Many would be surprised to see how much could be saved for the cause of God by acts of self-denial. The small sums saved by deeds of sacrifice will do more for the up-building of the cause of God than larger gifts will accomplish that have not called for denial of self.

Seventh-day Adventists are handling momentous truths. More than forty years ago the Lord gave us special light on health reform, but how are we walking in that light? How many have refused to live in harmony with the counsels of God! As a people, we should make advancement proportionate to the light received. It is our duty to understand and respect the principles of health reform. On the subject of temperance we should be in advance of all other people; and yet there are among us well-instructed members of the church, and even ministers of the gospel, who have little respect for the light that God has given upon this subject. They eat as they please and work as they please.

Let those who are teachers and leaders in our cause take their stand firmly on Bible ground in regard to health reform, and give a straight testimony to those who believe we are living in the last days of this earth's history. A line of distinction must be drawn between those who serve God and those who serve themselves.

I have been shown that the principles that were given us in the early days of the message are as important and should be regarded just as conscientiously today as they were then. There are some who have never followed the light given on the question of diet. It is now time to take the light from under the bushel and let it shine forth in clear, bright rays.

The principles of healthful living mean a great deal to us individually and as a people. When the message of health reform first came to me, I was weak and feeble, subject to frequent fainting spells. I was pleading with God for help, and He opened before me the great subject of health reform. He instructed me that those who are keeping His commandments must be brought into sacred relation to Himself, and that by temperance in eating and drinking they must keep mind and body in the most favorable condition for service. This light has been a great blessing to me. I took my stand as a health reformer, knowing that the Lord would strengthen me. I have better health today, notwithstanding my age, than I had in my younger days.

It is reported by some that I have not followed the principles of health reform as I have advocated them with my pen; but I can say that I have been a faithful health reformer. Those who have been members of my family know that this is true.

"TO THE GLORY OF GOD"

We do not mark out any precise line to be followed in diet; but we do say that in countries where there are fruits, grains, and nuts in abundance, flesh food is not the right food for God's people. I have been instructed that flesh food has a tendency to animalize the nature, to rob men and women of that love and sympathy which they should feel for everyone, and to give the lower passions control over the higher powers of the being. If meat eating was ever healthful, it is not safe now. Cancers, tumors, and pulmonary diseases are largely caused by meat eating.

We are not to make the use of flesh food a test of fellowship, but we should consider the influence that professed believers who use flesh foods have over others. As God's messengers, shall we not say to the people: "Whether therefore ye eat, or drink, or whatsoever ye do, do all to the glory of God"? 1 Corinthians 10:31. Shall we not bear a decided testimony against the indulgence of perverted appetite? Will any who are ministers of the gospel, proclaiming the most solemn truth ever given to mortals, set an example in returning to the flesh-pots of Egypt? Will those who are supported by the tithe from God's storehouse permit themselves by self-indulgence to poison the life-giving current flowing through their veins? Will they disregard the light and warnings that God has given them? The health of the body is to be regarded as essential for growth in grace and the acquirement of an even temper. If the stomach is not properly cared for, the formation of an upright, moral character will be hindered. The brain and nerves are in sympathy with the stomach. Erroneous eating and drinking result in erroneous thinking and acting.

All are now being tested and proved. We have been baptized into Christ, and if we will act our part by separating from everything that would drag us down and make us what we ought not to be, there will be given us strength to grow up into Christ, who is our living head, and we shall see the salvation of God.

Only when we are intelligent in regard to the principles of healthful living can we be fully aroused to see the evils resulting from improper diet. Those who, after seeing their mistakes, have courage to change their habits, will find that the reformatory process requires a struggle and much perseverance; but when correct tastes are once formed, they will realize that the use of the food which they formerly regarded as harmless was slowly but surely laying the foundation for dyspepsia and other diseases.

Fathers and mothers, watch unto prayer. Guard strictly against intemperance in every form. Teach your children the principles of true health reform. Teach them what things to avoid in order to preserve health. Already the wrath of God has begun to be visited upon the children of disobedience. What crimes, what sins, what iniquitous practices, are being revealed on every hand! As a people we are to exercise great care in guarding our children against depraved associates.

TEACHING HEALTH PRINCIPLES

Greater efforts should be put forth to educate the people in the principles of health reform. Cooking schools should be established, and house-to-house instruction should be given in the art of cooking wholesome food. Old and young should learn how to cook more simply. Wherever the truth is presented, the people are to be taught how to prepare food in a simple, yet appetizing way. They are to be shown that a nourishing diet can be provided without the use of flesh foods.

Teach the people that it is better to know how to keep well than how to cure disease. Our physicians should be wise educators, warning all against self-indulgence and showing that abstinence from the things that God has prohibited is the only way to prevent ruin of body and mind.

Much tact and discretion should be employed in preparing nourishing food to take the place of that which has formerly constituted the diet of those who are learning to be health reformers. Faith in God, earnestness of purpose, and a willingness to help one another will be required. A diet lacking in the proper elements of nutrition brings reproach upon the cause of health reform. We are mortal and must supply ourselves with food that will give proper nourishment to the body.

EXTREMES IN DIET

Some of our people, while conscientiously abstaining from eating improper foods, neglect to supply themselves with the elements necessary for the sustenance of the body. Those who take an extreme view of health reform are in danger of preparing tasteless dishes, making them so insipid that they are not satisfying. Food should be prepared in such a way that it will be appetizing as well as nourishing. It should not be robbed of that which the system needs. I use some salt, and always have, because salt, instead of being deleterious, is actually essential for the blood. Vegetables should be made palatable with a little milk or cream, or something equivalent.

While warnings have been given regarding the dangers of disease through butter, and the evil of the free use of eggs by small children, yet we should not consider it a violation of principle to use eggs from hens that are well cared for and suitably fed. Eggs contain properties that are remedial agencies in counteracting certain poisons.

Some, in abstaining from milk, eggs, and butter, have failed to supply the system with proper nourishment, and as a consequence have become weak and unable to work. Thus health reform is brought into disrepute. The work that we have tried to build up solidly is confused with strange things that God has not required, and the energies of the church are crippled. But God will interfere to prevent the results of these too strenuous ideas. The gospel is to harmonize the sinful race. It is to bring the rich and poor together at the feet of Jesus.

The time will come when we may have to discard some of the articles of diet we now use, such as milk and cream and eggs; but it is not necessary to bring upon ourselves perplexity by premature and extreme restrictions. Wait until the circumstances demand it and the Lord prepares the way for it.

Those who would be successful in proclaiming the principles of health reform must make the word of God their guide and counselor. Only as the teachers of health reform principles do this can they stand on vantage ground. Let us never bear a testimony against health reform by failing to use wholesome, palatable food in place of the harmful articles of diet that we have discarded. Do not in any way encourage an appetite for stimulants. Eat only plain, simple, wholesome food, and thank God constantly for the principles of health reform. In all things be true and upright, and you will gain precious victories.

DIET IN DIFFERENT COUNTRIES

While working against gluttony and intemperance, we must recognize the condition to which the human family is subjected. God has made provision for those who live in the different countries of the world. Those who desire to be co-workers with God must consider carefully before they specify just what foods should and should not be eaten. We are to be brought into connection with the masses. Should health reform in its most extreme form be taught to those whose circumstances forbid its adoption, more harm than good would be done. As I preach the gospel to the poor, I am instructed to tell them to eat that food which is most nourishing. I cannot say to them "You must not eat eggs, or milk, or cream. You must use no butter in the preparation of food." The gospel must be preached to the poor, but the time has not yet come to prescribe the strictest diet.

A WORD TO THE WAVERING

Those ministers who feel at liberty to indulge the appetite are falling far short of the mark. God wants them to be health reformers. He wants them to live up to the light that has been given on this subject. I feel sad when

I see those who ought to be zealous for our health principles, not yet converted to the right way of living. I pray that the Lord may impress their minds that they are meeting with great loss. If things were as they should be in the households that make up our churches, we might do double work for the Lord.

CONDITIONS OF ANSWERED PRAYER

In order to be purified and to remain pure, Seventh-day Adventists must have the Holy Spirit in their hearts and in their homes. The Lord has given me light that when the Israel of today humble themselves before Him, and cleanse the soul-temple from all defilement, He will hear their prayers in behalf of the sick and will bless in the use of His remedies for disease. When in faith the human agent does all he can to combat disease, using the simple methods of treatment that God has provided, his efforts will be blessed of God.

If, after so much light has been given, God's people will cherish wrong habits, indulging self and refusing to reform, they will suffer the sure consequences of transgression. If they are determined to gratify perverted appetite at any cost, God will not miraculously save them from the consequences of their indulgence. They "shall lie down in sorrow." Isaiah 50:11.

Those who choose to be presumptuous, saying, "The Lord has healed me, and I need not restrict my diet; I can eat and drink as I please," will erelong need, in body and soul, the restoring power of God. Because the Lord has graciously healed you, you must not think you can link yourselves up with the self-indulgent practices of the world. Do as Christ commanded after His work of healing—"go, and sin no more." John 8:11. Appetite must not be your god.

The Lord gave His word to ancient Israel, that if they would cleave strictly to Him and do all His requirements, He would keep them from all the diseases such as He had brought upon the Eygptians; but this promise was given on the condition of obedience. Had the Israelites obeyed the instruction they received, and profited by their advantages, they would have been the world's object lesson of health and prosperity. The Israelites failed of fulfilling God's purpose, and thus failed of receiving the blessings that might have been theirs. But in Joseph and Daniel, in Moses and Elijah, and many others, we have noble examples of the results of the true plan of living. Like faithfulness today will produce like results. To us it is written: "Ye are a chosen generation, a royal priesthood, an holy nation, a peculiar people; that ye should show forth the praises of Him who hath called you out of darkness into His marvelous light." 1 Peter 2:9.

SELF-SURRENDER AND REST

Oh, how many lose the richest blessings that God has in store for them in health and spiritual endowments! There are many souls who wrestle for special victories and special blessings that they may do some great thing. To this end they are always feeling that they must make an agonizing struggle in prayer and tears. When these persons search the Scriptures with prayer to know the expressed will of God, and then do His will from the heart without one reservation or self-indulgence, they will find rest. All the agonizing, all the tears and struggles, will not bring them the blessing they long for. Self must be entirely surrendered. They must do the work that presents itself, appropriating the abundance of the grace of God which is promised to all who ask in faith.

"If any man will come after Me," said Jesus, "let him

deny himself, and take up his cross daily, and follow Me." Luke 9:23. Let us follow the Saviour in His simplicity and self-denial. Let us lift up the Man of Calvary by word and by holy living. The Saviour comes very near to those who consecrate themselves to God. If ever there was a time when we needed the working of the Spirit of God upon our hearts and lives, it is now. Let us lay hold of this divine power for strength to live a life of holiness and self-surrender.

The word of God is to be our lessonbook. The Lord is our helper and our God. Let us look to Him to open the way for the carrying out of our plans.

A PLEA FOR MEDICAL MISSIONARY EVANGELISTS*

We are living in the last days. The end of all things is at hand. The signs foretold by Christ are fast fulfilling. There are stormy times before us, but let us not utter one word of unbelief or discouragement. He who understands the necessities of the situation arranges that advantages should be brought to the workers in various places to enable them more effectively to arouse the attention of the people. He knows the needs and the necessities of the feeblest of His flock, and He sends His own message into the highways and the byways. He loves us with an everlasting love. Let us remember that we bear a message of healing to a world filled with sin-sick souls. May the Lord increase our faith and help us to see that He desires us all to become acquainted with His ministry of healing and with the mercy seat. He desires the light of His grace to shine forth from many places.

SANITARIUMS AS MISSIONARY AGENCIES

There are souls in many places who have not yet heard the message. Henceforth medical missionary work is to be carried forward with an earnestness with which it has never yet been carried. This work is the door through which the truth is to find entrance to the large cities, and sanitariums are to be established in many places.

Sanitarium work is one of the most successful means of reaching all classes of people. Our sanitariums are the right hand of the gospel, opening ways whereby suffering humanity may be reached with the glad tidings of heal-

---

* Manuscript read before the delegates at the General Conference, Washington, D. C., June 1, 1909.

ing through Christ. In these institutions the sick may be taught to commit their cases to the Great Physician, who will co-operate with their earnest efforts to regain health, bringing to them healing of soul as well as healing of body.

Christ is no longer in this world in person, to go through our cities and towns and villages, healing the sick; but He has commissioned us to carry forward the medical missionary work that He began. In this work we are to do our very best. Institutions for the care of the sick are to be established, where men and women suffering from disease may be placed under the care of God-fearing physicians and nurses, and be treated without drugs.

I have been instructed that we are not to delay to do the work that needs to be done in health reform lines. Through this work we are to reach souls in the highways and byways. I have been given special light that in our sanitariums many souls will receive and obey present truth. In these institutions men and women are to be taught how to care for their own bodies and at the same time how to become sound in the faith. They are to be taught what is meant by eating the flesh and drinking the blood of the Son of God. Said Christ: "The words that I speak unto you, they are spirit, and they are life." John 6:63.

Our sanitariums are to be schools in which instruction shall be given in medical missionary lines. They are to bring to sin-sick souls the leaves of the tree of life, which will restore to them peace and hope and faith in Christ Jesus.

Let the Lord's work go forward. Let the medical missionary and the educational work go forward. I am sure that this is our great lack—earnest, devoted, intelligent, capable workers. In every large city there should be a representation of true medical missionary work. Let many now ask: "Lord, what wilt Thou have me to do?" Acts 9:6. It is the Lord's purpose that His method of healing without drugs shall be brought into prominence in every large city through our medical institutions. God invests with holy dignity those who go forth farther and still farther, in every place to which it is possible to obtain entrance. Satan will make the work as difficult as possible, but divine power will attend all truehearted workers. Guided by our heavenly Father's hand, let us go forward, improving every opportunity to extend the work of God.

The Lord speaks to all medical missionaries, saying: Go, work today in My vineyard to save souls. God hears the prayers of all who seek Him in truth. He has the power that we all need. He fills the heart with love, and joy, and peace, and holiness. Character is constantly being developed. We cannot afford to spend the time working at cross-purposes with God.

There are physicians who, because of a past connection with our sanitariums, find it profitable to locate close to these institutions; and they close their eyes to the great field, neglected and unworked, in which unselfish labor would be a blessing to many. Missionary physicians can exert an uplifting, refining, sanctifying influence. Physicians who do not do this abuse their power and do a work that the Lord repudiates.

THE TRAINING OF WORKERS

If ever the Lord has spoken by me, He speaks when I say that the workers engaged in educational lines, in ministerial lines, and in medical missionary lines must stand as a unit, all laboring under the supervision of God, one helping the other, each blessing each.

Those connected with our schools and sanitariums are to labor with earnest alacrity. The work that is done under the ministration of the Holy Spirit, out of love for God and for humanity, will bear the divine signature and will make its impression on human minds.

The Lord calls upon our young people to enter our schools and quickly fit themselves for service. In various places outside of cities, schools are to be established where our youth can receive an education that will prepare them to go forth to do evangelical work and medical missionary work.

The Lord must be given an opportunity to show men their duty and to work upon their minds. No one is to bind himself to serve for a term of years under the direction of one group of men or in one specified branch of the Master's work; for the Lord Himself will call men, as of old He called the humble fishermen, and will Himself give them instruction regarding their field of labor and the methods they should follow. He will call men from the plow and from other occupations to give the last note of warning to perishing souls. There are many ways in which to work for the Master, and the Great Teacher will open the understanding of these workers, enabling them to see wondrous things in His word.

NURSES AS EVANGELISTS

Christ, the great Medical Missionary, is our example. Of Him it is written that He "went about all Galilee, teaching in their synagogues, and preaching the gospel of the kingdom, and healing all manner of sickness and all manner of disease among the people." Matthew 4:23. He healed the sick and preached the gospel. In His service, healing and teaching were linked closely together. Today they are not to be separated.

The nurses who are trained in our institutions are to be fitted up to go out as medical missionary evangelists, uniting the ministry of the word with that of physical healing.

We must let our light shine amid the moral darkness. Many who are now in darkness, as they see a reflection of the Light of the world, will realize that they have a hope of salvation. Your light may be small, but remember that it is what God has given you, and that He holds you responsible to let it shine forth. Someone may light his taper from yours, and his light may be the means of leading others out from the darkness.

All around us are doors open for service. We should become acquainted with our neighbors and seek to draw them to Christ. As we do this, He will approve and cooperate with us.

Often the inhabitants of a city where Christ labored wished Him to stay with them and continue to work among them. But He would tell them that He must go to cities that had not heard the truths that He had to present. After He had given the truth to those in one place He left them to build upon what He had given them, while He went to another place. His methods of labor are to be followed today by those to whom He has left His work. We are to go from place to place, carrying the message. As soon as the truth has been proclaimed in one place, we are to go to warn others.

There should be companies organized and educated most thoroughly to work as nurses, as evangelists, as ministers, as canvassers, as gospel students, to perfect a character after the divine similitude. To prepare to receive the higher education in the school above is now to be our purpose.

From the instruction that the Lord has given me from time to time, I know that there should be workers who make medical evangelistic tours among the towns and villages. Those who do this work will gather a rich harvest of souls from both the higher and lower classes. The way for this work is best prepared by the efforts of the faithful canvasser.

Many will be called into the field to labor from house to house, giving Bible readings and praying with those who are interested.

Let our ministers, who have gained an experience in preaching the word, learn how to give simple treatments and then labor intelligently as medical missionary evangelists.

Workers—gospel medical missionaries—are needed now. You cannot afford to spend years in preparation. Soon doors now open to the truth will be forever closed. Carry the message now. Do not wait, allowing the enemy to take possession of the fields now open before you. Let little companies go forth to do the work to which Christ appointed His disciples. Let them labor as evangelists, scattering our publications and talking of the truth to those they meet. Let them pray for the sick, ministering to their necessities, not with drugs, but with nature's remedies, and teaching them how to regain health and avoid disease.

THE LOMA LINDA COLLEGE OF EVANGELISTS*

While attending the General Conference of 1905, at Washington, D. C., I received a letter from J. A. Burden describing a property he had found about four miles from Redlands. As I read his letter I was impressed that this was one of the places I had seen in vision, and I immediately telegraphed him to secure the property without delay. Later, when I visited the property, I recognized it as one of the places I had seen nearly two years before in vision. How thankful I am to the Lord our God for this place!

One of the chief advantages of Loma Linda is the pleasing variety of charming scenery on every side. The extensive view of valley and mountain is magnificent. But more important than magnificent scenery and beautiful buildings and spacious grounds is the close proximity of this institution to a densely populated district and the opportunity thus afforded of communicating to many, many people a knowledge of the third angel's message. We are to have clear spiritual discernment, else we shall fail of discerning the opening providences of God that are preparing the way for us to enlighten the world.

With the possession of this place comes the weighty responsibility of making the work of the institution educational in character. Loma Linda is to be not only a sanitarium, but an educational center. A school is to be established here for the training of gospel medical missionary evangelists. Much is involved in this work, and it is very essential that a right beginning be made. The

---

* Manuscript read before the delegates at the General Conference, Washington, D. C., June 1, 1909.

Lord has a special work to be done in this field. He instructed me to call on Elder and Mrs. Haskell to help us in getting properly started a work similar to that which they had carried on at Avondale. Laborers of experience have consented to unite with the forces at Loma Linda to develop the school that must be carried on there. As they go forward in faith, the Lord will go before them, preparing the way.

In regard to the school I would say: Make it especially strong in the education of nurses and physicians. In medical missionary schools many workers are to be qualified with the ability of physicians to labor as medical missionary evangelists. This training, the Lord has specified, is in harmony with the principles underlying true higher education. We hear a great deal about the higher education. The highest education is to follow in the footsteps of Christ, patterning after the example He gave when He was in the world. We cannot gain an education higher than this, for this class of training will make men laborers together with God.

To have the higher education is to have a living connection with Christ. The Saviour took the unlearned fishermen from their boats and their fishing nets and connected them with Himself as He traveled from place to place, teaching the people and ministering to their needs. Sitting down on a rock or on some elevated place, He would gather His disciples about Him and give them instruction, and, before long, hundreds of people would be listening to His words. There are many men and women who suppose that they know all that is worth knowing, when they greatly need to sit humbly at the feet of Jesus and learn of Him who gave His life that He might redeem a fallen world. We all need Christ—the One who left the royal courts, laying off His kingly robe and crown and His majesty in the heavens, and clothing Himself with humanity. The Son of God came as a little babe, that He might understand the experiences of humanity and know how to deal with them. He knows the wants of the children. In the days of His earthly ministry He would not allow them to be forbidden to come to Him. Send them not away, He said to His disciples, "for of such is the kingdom of heaven."

In the work of the school maintain simplicity. No argument is so powerful as is success founded on simplicity. You may attain success in the education of students as medical missionaries without a medical school that can qualify physicians to compete with the physicians of the world. Let the students be given a practical education. The less dependent you are upon worldly methods of education, the better it will be for the students. Special instruction should be given in the art of treating the sick without the use of poisonous drugs and in harmony with the light that God has given. In the treatment of the sick, poisonous drugs need not be used. Students should come forth from the school without having sacrificed the principles of health reform or their love for God and righteousness.

The education that meets the world's standard is to be less and less valued by those who are seeking for efficiency in carrying the medical missionary work in connection with the work of the third angel's message. They are to be educated from the standpoint of conscience, and, as they conscientiously and faithfully follow right methods in their treatment of the sick, these methods will come to be recognized as preferable to the methods to which many have become accustomed, which demand the use of poisonous drugs.

We should not at this time seek to compete with

worldly medical schools. Should we do this, our chances of success would be small. We are not now prepared to carry out successfully the work of establishing large medical institutions of learning. Moreover, should we follow the world's methods of medical practice, exacting the large fees that worldly physicians demand for their services, we would work away from Christ's plan for our ministry to the sick.

There should be at our sanitariums intelligent men and women who can instruct in Christ's methods of ministry. Under the instruction of competent, consecrated teachers the youth may become partakers of the divine nature and learn how to escape the corruption that is in the world through lust. I have been instructed that we should have many more women who can deal especially with the diseases of women, many more lady nurses who will treat the sick in a simple way without the use of drugs.

It is not in harmony with the instruction given at Sinai that gentlemen physicians should do the work of midwives. The Bible speaks of women at childbirth being attended by women, and thus it ought always to be. Women should be educated and trained to act skillfully as midwives and physicians to their sex. This is the Lord's plan. Let us educate ladies to become intelligent in the work of treating the diseases of their sex. We ought to have a school where women can be educated by women physicians to do the best possible work in treating the diseases of women. Among us as a people the medical work should stand at its highest.

In Loma Linda we have an advantageous center for the carrying on of various missionary enterprises. We can see that it was in the providence of God that this sanitarium was placed in the possession of our people. We should appreciate Loma Linda as a place which the Lord foresaw we should need and which He gave us. There is a very precious work to be done in connection with the interests of the sanitarium and the school at Loma Linda, and this will be done, when we all work to that end, moving unitedly in God's order.

At Loma Linda many can be educated to work as missionaries in the cause of health and temperance. Teachers are to be prepared for many lines of work. Schools are to be established in places where as yet no efforts have been made. Missionaries are to go to other states where little work has been done. The work of promulgating the principles of health reform must be accomplished. God help us as a people to be wise.

I feel a deep interest that careful study shall be given to the needs of our institutions at Loma Linda and that right moves shall be made. In the carrying forward of the work at this place, men of talent and decided spirituality are needed. The best teachers are to be employed in the educational work, men and women who will walk circumspectly, depending wholly upon the Lord. If the teachers in medical lines will stand in their place in the fear of God, we shall see a good work done. With Christ as our educator we may reach a high standard in the knowledge of the true science of healing.

That which is of the most importance is that the students be taught how to represent aright the principles of health reform. Teach them to pursue this line of study faithfully, combined with other essential lines of education. The grace of Jesus Christ will give wisdom to all who follow the Lord's plan of true education. Let the students follow closely the example of the One who purchased the human race with the costly price of His own life. Let them appeal to the Saviour and depend upon Him as the One who heals all manner of diseases. The Lord would have the workers make special efforts to point the sick and suffering to the Great Physician who made the human body.

It is well that our training schools for Christian workers should be established near to our health institutions, that the students may be educated in the principles of healthful living. Institutions that send forth workers who are able to give a reason for their faith, and who have a faith which works by love and purifies the soul, are of great value. I have clear instruction that, wherever it is possible, schools should be established near to our sanitariums, that each institution may be a help and strength to the other. He who created man has an interest in those who suffer. He has directed in the establishment of our sanitariums and in the building up of our schools close to our sanitariums, that they may become efficient mediums in training men and women for the work of ministering to suffering humanity.

Let Seventh-day Adventist medical workers remember that the Lord God omnipotent reigneth. Christ was the greatest physician that ever trod this sin-cursed earth. The Lord would have His people come to Him for their power of healing. He will baptize them with His Holy Spirit and fit them for a service that will make them a blessing in restoring the spiritual and physical health of those who need healing.

THE SPIRIT OF UNITY*

"That they all may be one."
John 17:21.

UNITY AMONG DIFFERENT NATIONALITIES†

"If any man thirst, let him come unto Me, and drink." "Whosoever drinketh of the water that I shall give him shall never thirst; but the water that I shall give him shall be in him a well of water springing up into everlasting life." John 7:37; 4:14.

If, with these promises before us, we choose to remain parched and withered for want of the water of life, it is our own fault. If we would come to Christ with the simplicity of a child coming to its earthly parents, and ask for the things that He has promised, believing that we receive them, we should have them. If all of us had exercised the faith we should we would have been blessed with far more of the Spirit of God in our meetings than we have yet received. I am glad that a few days of the meeting still remain. Now the question is: Will we come to the fountain and drink? Will the teachers of truth set the example? God will do great things for us if we by faith take Him at His word. Oh, that we might see here a general humbling of the heart before God!

Since these meetings began, I have felt urged to dwell much upon love and faith. This is because you need this

---

* Portions of the tract, *Special Testimonies,* Series B, No. 4, are included in this section.

† Address delivered at the European Union Council, Basel, Switzerland, September 24, 1885.

testimony. Some who have entered these missionary fields have said: "You do not understand the French people; you do not understand the Germans. They have to be met in just such a way."

But I inquire: Does not God understand them? Is it not He who gives His servants a message for the people? He knows just what they need; and if the message comes directly from Him through His servants to the people, it will accomplish the work whereunto it is sent; it will make all one in Christ. Though some are decidedly French, others decidedly German, and others decidedly American, they will be just as decidedly Christlike.

The Jewish temple was built of hewn stones quarried out of the mountains; and every stone was fitted for its place in the temple, hewed, polished, and tested before it was brought to Jerusalem. And when all were brought to the ground, the building went together without the sound of ax or hammer. This building represents God's spiritual temple, which is composed of material gathered out of every nation, and tongue, and people, of all grades, high and low, rich and poor, learned and unlearned. These are not dead substances to be fitted by hammer and chisel. They are living stones, quarried out from the world by the truth; and the great Master Builder, the Lord of the temple, is now hewing and polishing them, and fitting them for their respective places in the spiritual temple. When completed, this temple will be perfect in all its parts, the admiration of angels and of men; for its Builder and Maker is God.

Let no one think that there need not be a stroke placed upon him. There is no person, no nation, that is perfect in every habit and thought. One must learn of another. Therefore God wants the different nationalities to mingle together, to be one in judgment, one in purpose. Then the union that there is in Christ will be exemplified.

I was almost afraid to come to this country because I heard so many say that the different nationalities of Europe were peculiar and had to be reached in a certain way. But the wisdom of God is promised to those who feel their need and who ask for it. God can bring the people where they will receive the truth. Let the Lord take possession of the mind and mold it as the clay is molded in the hands of the potter, and these differences will not exist. Look to Jesus, brethren; copy His manners and spirit, and you will have no trouble in reaching these different classes. We have not six patterns to follow nor five; we have only one, and that is Christ Jesus. If the Italian brethren, the French brethren, and the German brethren try to be like Him, they will plant their feet upon the same foundation of truth; the same spirit that dwells in one will dwell in the other—Christ in them, the hope of glory. I warn you, brethren and sisters, not to build up a wall of partition between different nationalities. On the contrary, seek to break it down wherever it exists. We should endeavor to bring all into the harmony that there is in Jesus, laboring for the one object, the salvation of our fellow men.

Will you, my ministering brethren, grasp the rich promises of God? Will you put self out of sight and let Jesus appear? Self must die before God can work through you. I feel alarmed as I see self cropping out in one and another here and there. I tell you, in the name of Jesus of Nazareth, your wills must die; they must become as God's will. He wants to melt you over and to cleanse you from every defilement. There is a great work to be done for you before you can be filled with the power of God. I beseech you to draw nigh to Him, that you may realize His rich blessing before this meeting closes.

There are those here upon whom great light in warnings and reproofs has shone. Whenever reproofs are given, the enemy seeks to create in those reproved a desire for human sympathy. Therefore I would warn you to beware lest in appealing to the sympathy of others and going back over your past trials, you again err on the same points in seeking to build yourselves up. The Lord brings His erring children over the same ground again and again; but if they continually fail to heed the admonitions of His Spirit, if they fail to reform on every point where they have erred, He will finally leave them to their own weakness.

I entreat you, brethren, to come to Christ and drink; drink freely of the water of salvation. Do not appeal to your own feelings. Do not think that sentimentalism is religion. Shake yourself from every human prop and lean heavily upon Christ. You need a new fitting up before you are prepared to engage in the work of saving souls. Your words, your actions, have an influence upon others, and you must meet that influence in the day of God. Jesus says: "Behold, I have set before thee an open door, and no man can shut it." Revelation 3:8. Light is shining from that door, and it is our privilege to receive it if we will. Let us direct our eyes within that open door and try to receive all that Christ is willing to bestow.

Each one will have a close struggle to overcome sin in his own heart. This is at times a very painful and discouraging work; because, as we see the deformities in our character, we keep looking at them, when we should look to Jesus and put on the robe of His righteousness. Everyone who enters the pearly gates of the city of God will enter there as a conqueror, and his greatest conquest will have been the conquest of self.

"For this cause I bow my knees unto the Father of our Lord Jesus Christ, of whom the whole family in heaven and earth is named, that He would grant you, according to the riches of His glory, to be strengthened with might by His Spirit in the inner man; that Christ may dwell in your hearts by faith; that ye, being rooted and grounded in love, may be able to comprehend with all saints what is the breadth, and length, and depth, and height; and to know the love of Christ, which passeth knowledge, that ye might be filled with all the fullness of God." Ephesians 3:14-19.

As workers together for God, brethren and sisters, lean heavily upon the arm of the Mighty One. Labor for unity, labor for love, and you will become a power in the world.

UNITY IN CHRIST JESUS

Loma Linda, California, August 24, 1905.

To Our Brethren Connected With the Publishing Work at College View—

While attending the council meeting of the General Conference Committee, held in September, 1904, my mind was deeply exercised regarding the unity that should attend our work. I was not able to attend all the meetings, but in the night season scene after scene passed before me, and I felt that I had a message to bear to our people in many places.

My heart is pained as I see that, with such wonderful incentives to bring our powers and capabilities to the very highest state of development, we are content to be dwarfs in the work of Christ. God's desire is that all His workers shall grow to the full stature of men and women in Christ. Where there is vitality, there is growth; the growth testifies to the vitality. The words and works bear living testimony to the world of what Christianity does for the followers of Christ.

When you do your appointed work without contention or criticism of others, a freedom, a light, and a power will attend it that will give character and influence to the institutions and enterprises with which you are connected.

Remember that you are never on vantage ground when you are ruffled and when you carry the burden of setting right every soul who comes near you. If you yield to the temptation to criticize others, to point out their faults, to tear down what they are doing, you may be sure that you will fail to act your own part nobly and well.

This is a time when every man in a responsible position, and every member of the church, should bring every feature of his work into close accord with the teachings of the word of God. By untiring vigilance, by fervent prayer, by Christlike words and deeds, we are to show the world what God desires His church to be.

From His high position, Christ, the King of glory, the Majesty of heaven, saw the condition of men. He pitied human beings in their weakness and sinfulness, and came to this earth to reveal what God is to men. Leaving the royal courts, and clothing His divinity with humanity, He came to the world Himself, in our behalf to work out a perfect character. He did not choose His dwelling among the rich of the earth. He was born in poverty, of lowly parentage, and lived in the despised village of Nazareth. As soon as He was old enough to handle tools, He shared the burden of caring for the family.

Christ humbled Himself to stand at the head of humanity, to meet the temptations and endure the trials that humanity must meet and endure. He must know what humanity has to meet from the fallen foe, that He might know how to succor those who are tempted.

And Christ has been made our Judge. The Father is not the Judge. The angels are not. He who took humanity upon Himself, and in this world lived a perfect life, is to judge us. He only can be our Judge. Will you remember this, brethren? Will you remember it, ministers? Will you remember it, fathers and mothers? Christ took humanity that He might be our Judge. No one of you has been appointed to be a judge of others. It is all that you can do to discipline yourselves. In the name of Christ I entreat you to heed the injunction that He gives you never to place yourselves on the judgment seat. From day to day this message has been sounded in my ears: "Come down from the judgment seat. Come down in humility."

Never was there a time when it was more important that we should deny ourselves and take up the cross daily than now. How much self-denial are we willing to practice?

A LIFE OF GRACE AND PEACE

In the first chapter of the second epistle of Peter you will find the promise that grace and peace will be multiplied unto you, if you will "add to your faith virtue; and to virtue knowledge; and to knowledge temperance; and to temperance patience; and to patience godliness; and to godliness brotherly kindness; and to brotherly kindness charity." 2 Peter 1:5-7. These virtues are wonderful treasures. They "make a man more precious than fine gold; even a man than the golden wedge of Ophir." Isaiah 13:12.

"If these things be in you, and abound, they make you that ye shall neither be barren nor unfruitful in the knowledge of our Lord Jesus Christ." 2 Peter 1:8.

Shall we not strive to use to the very best of our ability the little time that is left us in this life, adding grace to grace, power to power, making it manifest that we have a source of power in the heavens above? Christ says: "All power is given unto Me in heaven and in earth." Matthew 28:18. What is this power given to Him for? For us. He desires us to realize that He has returned to heaven as our Elder Brother and that the measureless power given Him has been placed at our disposal.

Those who will carry out in their lives the instruction

given to the church through the apostle Peter will receive power from above. We are to live upon the plan of addition, giving all diligence to make our calling and election sure. We are to represent Christ in all that we say and do. We are to live His life. The principles by which He was guided are to shape our course of action toward those with whom we are associated.

When we are securely anchored in Christ, we have a power that no human being can take from us. Why is this? Because we are partakers of the divine nature, having escaped the corruption that is in the world through lust, partakers of the nature of Him who came to this earth clothed with the habiliments of humanity, that He might stand at the head of the human race and develop a character that was without spot or stain of sin.

Why are many of us so weak and inefficient? It is because we look to self, studying our own temperaments and wondering how we can make a place for ourselves, our individuality, and our peculiarities, in the place of studying Christ and His character.

Brethren who could work together in harmony if they would learn of Christ, forgetting that they are Americans or Europeans, Germans or Frenchmen, Swedes, Danes, or Norwegians, seem to feel that if they should blend with those of other nationalities, something of that which is peculiar to their own country and nation would be lost and something else would take its place.

My brethren, let us put all this aside. We have no right to keep our minds stayed on ourselves, our preferences, and our fancies. We are not to seek to maintain a peculiar identity of our own, a personality, an individuality, which will separate us from our fellow laborers. We have a character to maintain, but it is the character of Christ. Having the character of Christ, we can carry on the work of God together. The Christ in us will meet the Christ in our brethren, and the Holy Spirit will give that union of heart and action which testifies to the world that we are children of God. May the Lord help us to die to self and be born again, that Christ may live in us, a living, active principle, a power that will keep us holy.

Strive earnestly for unity. Pray for it, work for it. It will bring spiritual health, elevation of thought, nobility of character, heavenly-mindedness, enabling you to overcome selfishness and evil surmisings, and to be more than conquerors through Him that loved you and gave Himself for you. Crucify self; esteem others better than yourselves. Thus you will be brought into oneness with Christ. Before the heavenly universe, and before the church and the world, you will bear unmistakable evidence that you are God's sons and daughters. God will be glorified in the example that you set.

The world needs to see worked out before it the miracle that binds the hearts of God's people together in Christian love. It needs to see the Lord's people sitting together in heavenly places in Christ. Will you not give in your lives an evidence of what the truth of God can do for those who love and serve Him? God knows what you can be. He knows what divine grace can do for you if you will be partakers of the divine nature.

THE PUBLISHING WORK AT COLLEGE VIEW

Loma Linda, California, August 24, 1905.

I approve of the efforts that have been made to establish our German and Scandinavian publishing work at College View. I hope that plans will be devised for the encouragement and strengthening of this work.

The whole burden of the work must not be left with our foreign brethren. Nor should our brethren throughout the field leave too heavy a load on the conferences near College View. The members of these conferences should lead out and do their best, and all should come to their assistance. The truth is to be proclaimed to all nations and kindreds and tongues and peoples.

Our German and Danish and Swedish brethren have no good reason for not being able to act in harmony in the publishing work. Those who believe the truth should remember that they are God's little children, that they are under His training. Let them be thankful to God for His manifold mercies and be kind to one another. They have one God and one Saviour; and one Spirit—the Spirit of Christ—is to bring unity into their ranks.

After His resurrection, Christ ascended to heaven, and He is today presenting our needs to the Father. "I have graven thee upon the palms of My hands," He says. Isaiah 49:16. It cost something to engrave them there. It cost untold agony. If we would humble ourselves before God, and be kind and courteous and tenderhearted and pitiful, there would be one hundred conversions to the truth where now there is only one. But, though professing to be converted, we carry around with us a bundle of self that we regard as altogether too precious to be given up. It is our privilege to lay this burden at the feet of Christ and in its place take the character and similitude of Christ. The Saviour is waiting for us to do this.

Christ laid aside His royal robe, His kingly crown, and His high command, and stepped down, down, down, to the lowest depths of humiliation. Bearing human nature, He met all the temptations of humanity and in our behalf defeated the enemy on every point.

All this He did that He might bring men power by which they might be overcomers. "All power," He says, "is given unto Me." Matthew 28:18. And this He gives to all who will follow Him. They may demonstrate to the world the power that there is in the religion of Christ for the conquest of self.

"Learn of Me," Christ says, "and ye shall find rest unto your souls." Matthew 11:29. Why do we not learn of the Saviour every day? Why do we not live in constant communion with Him, so that in our connection with one another we can speak and act kindly and courteously? Why do we not honor the Lord by manifesting tenderness and love for one another? If we speak and act in harmony with the principles of heaven, unbelievers will be drawn to Christ by their association with us.

CHRIST'S RELATION TO NATIONALITY

Christ recognized no distinction of nationality or rank or creed. The scribes and Pharisees desired to make a local and a national benefit of all the gifts of heaven and to exclude the rest of God's family in the world. But Christ came to break down every wall of partition. He came to show that His gift of mercy and love is as unconfined as the air, the light, or the showers of rain that refresh the earth.

The life of Christ established a religion in which there is no caste, a religion by which Jew and Gentile, free and bond, are linked in a common brotherhood, equal before God. No question of policy influenced His movements. He made no difference between neighbors and strangers, friends and enemies. That which appealed to His heart was a soul thirsting for the waters of life.

He passed no human being by as worthless, but sought to apply the healing remedy to every soul. In whatever company He found Himself, He presented a lesson appropriate to the time and the circumstances. Every neglect or insult shown by men to their fellow men only made Him more conscious of their need of His divine-human sympathy. He sought to inspire with hope the roughest and most unpromising, setting before them the assurance that they might become blameless and harmless, attaining such a character as would make them the children of God.

A SURE FOUNDATION

"Wherefore the rather, brethren," says the apostle Peter, "give diligence to make your calling and election sure: for if ye do these things, ye shall never fall: for so an entrance shall be ministered unto you abundantly into the everlasting kingdom of our Lord and Saviour Jesus Christ." 2 Peter 1:10, 11.

Years ago, when the company of believers in the soon coming of Christ was very small, the Sabbathkeepers at Topsham, Maine, met for worship in the large kitchen in the home of Brother Stockbridge Howland. One Sabbath morning Brother Howland was absent. We were surprised at this, because he was always so punctual. Soon he came in, his face aglow, shining with the glory of God. "Brethren," he said, "I have found it. I have found that we can pursue a course of action regarding which the guarantee of God's word is: 'Ye shall never fall.' I am going to tell you about it."

He then told us that he had noticed that one brother, a poor fisherman, had been feeling that he was not as highly respected as he ought to be and that Brother Howland and others thought themselves above him. This was not true, but it seemed true to him; and for several weeks he had not attended the meetings. So Brother Howland went to his house and knelt before him, saying: "My brother, forgive me. What is it that I have done?" The man took him by the arm and tried to raise him to his feet. "No," said Brother Howland, "what have you against me?" "I have nothing against you." "But you must have," said Brother Howland, "because once we could speak to one another, but now you do not speak to me at all, and I want to know what is the matter."

"Get up, Brother Howland," he said. "No," said Brother Howland, "I will not." "Then I must get down," he said, and he fell on his knees, and confessed how childish he had been and how many evil surmisings he had cherished. "And now," he said, "I will put them all away."

As Brother Howland told this story, his face shone with the glory of the Lord. Just as he had finished, the fisherman and his family came in, and we had an excellent meeting.

Suppose that some of us should follow the course pursued by Brother Howland. If when our brethren surmise evil, we would go to them, saying, "Forgive me if I have done anything to harm you," we might break the spell of Satan and set our brethren free from their temptations. Do not let anything interpose between you and your brethren. If there is anything that you can do by sacrifice to clear away the rubbish of suspicion, do it. God wants us to love one another as brethren. He wants us to be pitiful and courteous. He wants us to educate ourselves to believe that our brethren love us, and to believe that Christ loves us. Love begets love.

Do we expect to meet our brethren in heaven? If we can live with them here in peace and harmony we could live with them there. But how could we live with them in heaven if we cannot live with them here without continued contention and strife? Those who are following a course of action that separates them from their brethren and brings in discord and dissension, need a thorough conversion. Our hearts must be melted and subdued by the love of Christ. We must cherish the love that He showed in dying for us on the cross of Calvary. We need to draw closer and closer to the Saviour. We should be much in prayer, and we must learn to exercise faith. We must be more tenderhearted, more pitiful and courteous. We shall pass through this world but once. Shall we not strive to leave on those with whom we associate the impress of the character of Christ?

Our hard hearts need to be broken. We need to come together in perfect unity, and we need to realize that we are the purchase of the blood of Jesus Christ of Nazareth. Let each one say: "He gave His life for me, and He wants me, as I go through this world, to reveal the love that He revealed in giving Himself for me." Christ bore our sins in His own body on the cross, that God might be just and yet the justifier of those who believe in Him. There is life, eternal life, for all who will surrender to Christ.

I want to see the King in His beauty. I want to behold

His matchless charms. I want you to behold Him, too. Christ will lead His redeemed ones beside the river of life and will explain to them all that perplexed them in this world. The mysteries of grace will unfold before them. Where their finite minds discerned only confusion and broken purposes, they will see the most perfect and beautiful harmony.

Let us serve God with all our capabilities, with all our intelligence. Our intelligence will increase as we make use of that which we have. Our religious experience will strengthen as we bring it into the daily life. Thus we shall climb round after round of the ladder reaching to heaven, until at last we step from off the topmost round into the kingdom of God. Let us be Christians in this world. Then we shall have eternal life in the kingdom of glory.

Unity existing among the followers of Christ is an evidence that the Father has sent His Son to save sinners. It is a witness to His power; for nothing short of the miraculous power of God can bring human beings with their different temperaments together in harmonious action, their one aim being to speak the truth in love.

God's warnings and counsels are plain and decided. As we read the Scriptures and see the power for good that there is in unity and the power for evil that there is in disunion, how can we fail to receive the word of God into our hearts? Suspicion and distrust are as evil leaven. Unity bears witness to the power of the truth.

GERMAN AND SCANDINAVIAN CONFERENCES

Loma Linda, California, September 1, 1905.

Dear Brethren: Some of our ministers have written to me, asking if the work among the Germans and Scandinavians should not be carried forward under separate organizations. This matter has been presented to me several times. When I was in College View, the Lord gave me a straight testimony to bear, and since that time the matter has been presented to me again.

At one time I seemed to be in a council meeting where these matters were being considered. One of authority stood in the midst of those assembled and opened before them principles that should be followed in the work of God. The instruction given was that should such separation take place, it would not tend to advance the interests of the work among the various nationalities. It would not lead to the highest spiritual development. Walls would be built up that would have to be removed in the near future.

According to the light given me of God, separate organizations, instead of bringing about unity, will create discord. If our brethren will seek the Lord together in humility of mind, those who now think it necessary to organize separate German and Scandinavian conferences will see that the Lord desires them to work together as brethren.

Were those who seek to disintegrate the work of God, to carry out their purpose, some would magnify themselves to do a work that should not be done. Such an arrangement would greatly retard the cause of God. If we are to carry on the work most successfully, the talents

(195)

to be found among the English and Americans should be united with the talents of those of every other nationality. And each nationality should labor earnestly for every other nationality. There is but one Lord, one faith. Our effort should be to answer Christ's prayer for His disciples, that they should be one.

"Sanctify them through Thy truth: Thy word is truth. As Thou hast sent Me into the world, even so have I also sent them into the world. And for their sakes I sanctify Myself, that they also might be sanctified through the truth.

"Neither pray I for these alone, but for them also which shall believe on Me through their word, that they all may be one; as Thou, Father, art in Me, and I in Thee, that they also may be one in Us: that the world may believe that Thou hast sent Me." John 17:17-21.

It should be understood that perfect unity among the laborers is necessary to the successful accomplishment of the work of God. In order to preserve peace, all must seek wisdom from the Great Teacher. Let all be careful how they introduce ambitious propositions that will create dissension.

We are to be subject one to another. No man, in himself, is a complete whole. Through submission of the mind and will to the Holy Spirit we are ever to be learners of the Great Teacher.

Study the second chapter of Acts. In the early church the Spirit of God wrought mightily through those who were harmoniously united. On the Day of Pentecost they were all with one accord in one place.

We are to demonstrate to the world that men of every nationality are one in Christ Jesus. Then let us remove every barrier and come into unity in the service of the Master.

In the erection of national barriers you present to the world a plan of human invention that God can never endorse. To those who would do this, the apostle Paul says: "Ye are yet carnal: for whereas there is among you envying, and strife, and divisions, are ye not carnal? . . . Who then is Paul, and who is Apollos, but ministers by whom ye believed, even as the Lord gave to every man? I have planted, Apollos watered; but God gave the increase. So then neither is he that planteth anything, neither he that watereth; but God that giveth the increase. Now he that planteth and he that watereth are one: and every man shall receive his own reward according to his own labor. For we are laborers together with God: ye are God's husbandry, ye are God's building." 1 Corinthians 3:3-9.

AN EXAMPLE OF BROTHERLY KINDNESS

When our brethren in Scandinavia faced a financial crisis, the testimony was given that we must not permit our brethren to stand as bankrupt before the world. That would have been dishonoring to God. And the prompt and liberal action of our American brethren was an acknowledgment that the difference in nationality could not release them from their duty to assist one another in the work of God. "All ye are brethren." Matthew 23:8. We are one in the unity of the truth.

We must now, by diligent, self-sacrificing effort, endeavor to walk in the love of Christ, in the unity of the Spirit, through sanctification of the truth. No halfway work will suffice to fulfill the representation given in the prayer of Christ. We are to practice the principles of heaven here below. In heaven there is one grand meeting place.

I must write plainly regarding the building up of partition walls in the work of God. Such an action has been revealed to me as a fallacy of human invention. It is not the Lord's plan for His people to separate themselves into separate companies, because of differences in nationality and language. Did they do this, their ideas would become narrow, and their influence would be greatly lessened. God calls for a harmonious blending of a variety of talents.

I again repeat the words of Christ. I would impress them deeply upon your minds. "Neither pray I for these alone, but for them also which shall believe on Me through their word; *that they all may be one;* as Thou, Father, art in Me, and I in Thee, *that they also may be one in Us:* that the world may believe that Thou hast sent Me. And the glory which Thou gavest Me I have given them; that they may be one, even as We are one: I in them, and Thou in Me, that they may be made perfect in one; and that the world may know that Thou hast sent Me, and hast loved them, as Thou hast loved Me."

Christ has hedged in His people from the world, but those who would build up national separation, would do a work for which the Lord Jesus Christ has given no encouragement.

Brethren, unify; draw close together, laying aside every human invention and following closely in the footsteps of Jesus, your great Example.

AMONG THE COLORED PEOPLE

> "Pray ye therefore the Lord of the harvest that He will send forth laborers into His harvest." Matthew 9:38.

A CALL FOR COLORED LABORERS

Most decided efforts should be made to educate and train colored men and women to labor as missionaries in the Southern States of America. Christian colored students should be preparing to give the truth to their own race. Those who make the fear of the Lord the beginning of their wisdom and give heed to the counsel of men of experience can be a great blessing to the Negro race by carrying to their own people the light of present truth. Every worker laboring in humility and in harmony with his brethren will be a channel of light to many who are now in the darkness of ignorance and superstition.

Instead of wondering whether they are not fitted to labor for white people, let our colored brethren and sisters devote themselves to missionary work among the colored people. There is an abundance of room for intelligent colored men and women to labor for their own people. Much work remains to be done in the Southern field. Special efforts are to be made in the large cities. In each of these cities there are thousands of colored people, to whom the last warning message of mercy must be given. Let the missionary spirit be awakened in the hearts of our colored church members. Let earnest work be done for those who know not the truth.

To every colored brother and sister I would say: Look at the situation as it is. Ask yourself: "In view of the opportunities and advantages granted me, how much do I owe to my Lord? How can I best glorify Him and promote the interests of my people? How can I use to the best advantage the knowledge God has been pleased to give me? Should I not open my Bible and teach the truth to my people? Are there not thousands perishing for lack of knowledge, whom I can help if I submit myself to God so that He can use me as His instrument? Have I not a work to do for my oppressed, discouraged fellows?"

The Southern field is suffering for workers. Will you pass by your people, making no effort to help them, or will you with a humble heart work to save the perishing? There is a work you can do if you will humble yourself before God. Trusting in Him, you will find peace and comfort, but following your own way and your own will, you will find thorns and thistles, and you will lose the reward.

Time is short, and what you do must be done quickly. Resolve to redeem the time. Seek not your own pleasure. Rouse yourself! Take hold of the work with a new purpose of heart. The Lord will open the way before you. Make every possible effort to work in Christ's lines, in meekness and lowliness, relying upon Him for strength. Understand the work the Lord gives you to do, and, trusting in God, you will be enabled to go on from strength to strength, from grace to grace. You will be enabled to work diligently, perseveringly, for your people while the day lasts; for the night cometh in which no man shall work.

There is the greatest need for all kinds of missionary work in the South. Without delay, workers must be prepared for this field. Our people should provide a fund for the education of men and women in the Southern States who, being accustomed to the climate, can work there without endangering their health.

Promising young men and young women should be educated to become teachers. They should have the very best advantages. Schoolhouses and meetinghouses should be built in different places, and teachers employed.

Those who for years have been working to help the colored people are well fitted to give counsel in regard to the opening of such schools. So far as possible these schools should be established outside the cities. But in the cities there are many children who could not attend schools away from the cities; and for the benefit of these, schools should be opened in the cities as well as in the country.

The children and youth in these schools are to be taught something more than merely how to read. Industrial lines of work are to be carried forward. The students are to be provided with facilities for learning trades that will enable them to support themselves.

Our churches in the North, as well as in the South, should do what they can to help support the school work for the colored children. The schools already established should be faithfully maintained. The establishment of new schools will require additional funds. Let all our brethren and sisters do their part wholeheartedly to place these schools on vantage ground.

In addition to engaging in this line of school work, our colored brethren may do a good work by establishing mission Sunday schools and Sabbath schools among their own people—schools in which the youth may be taught by teachers whose hearts are filled with love for souls.

Opportunities are continually presenting themselves in the Southern States, and many wise, Christian colored men will be called to the work. But for several reasons white men must be chosen as leaders. We are all members of one body and are complete only in Christ Jesus, who will uplift His people from the low level to which sin has degraded them and will place them where they shall be acknowledged in the heavenly courts as laborers together with God.

There is work to be done in many hard places, and out of these hard places bright laborers are to come. Let the work be managed so that colored laborers will be educated to work for their own race. Among the Negro race there are many who have talent and ability. Let us search out these men and women, and teach them how to engage in the work of saving souls. God will co-operate with them and give them the victory.

"LABORERS TOGETHER WITH GOD"

The ear of the Lord is open to the cries of those who are in His service. He has promised: "I will guide thee with Mine eye." Psalm 32:8. Walk humbly with God, and ask Him to make your course of duty plain. When He speaks to His representatives and asks them to be laborers together with Him, they will do the same kind of work that Jesus announced as His work when He stood up to read in the synagogue at Nazareth. He opened the book of the prophet Esaias and read: "The Spirit of the Lord God is upon Me; because the Lord hath anointed Me to preach good tidings unto the meek; He hath sent Me to bind up the brokenhearted, to proclaim liberty to the captives, and the opening of the prison to them that are bound." Isaiah 61:1.

The truth is now overcast in the world by clouds of error that prevail. He who can influence even the most lowly, and can win them to Christ, is co-operating with divine agencies in seeking to save that which is lost. In presenting to the sinner a personal, sin-pardoning Saviour, we reach a hand of sympathy and Christlike love to grasp the hand of one fallen, and, laying hold of the hand of Christ by faith, we form a link of union between the sinner and the Saviour.

The end is near, and every soul is now to walk carefully, humbly, meekly with Christ Jesus. Our precious Saviour, from whom all the rays of truth radiate to the world, wants us to put not our trust in princes, nor in the son of man, in whom there is no help; but to lean wholly upon Him. He says: "Without Me ye can do nothing." John 15:5. We need to look to Jesus constantly in order that He may impress upon us His own lovely image. We are to behold the Lamb of God, which taketh away the sin of the world. Then we shall reveal Christ to our fellow men.

PROCLAIMING THE TRUTH WHERE THERE IS RACE ANTAGONISM

I am burdened, heavily burdened, for the work among the colored people. The gospel is to be presented to the downtrodden Negro race. But great caution will have to be shown in the efforts put forth for the uplifting of this people. Among the white people in many places there exists a strong prejudice against the Negro race. We may desire to ignore this prejudice, but we cannot do it. If we were to act as if this prejudice did not exist we could not get the light before the white people. We must meet the situation as it is and deal with it wisely and intelligently.

For many years I have borne a heavy burden in behalf of the Negro race. My heart has ached as I have seen the feeling against this race growing stronger and still stronger, and as I have seen that many Seventh-day Adventists are apparently unable to understand the necessity for an earnest work being done quickly. Years are passing into eternity with apparently little done to help those who were recently a race of slaves.

One of the difficulties attending the work is that many of the white people living where the colored people are numerous are not willing that special efforts should be put forth to uplift them. When they see schools established for them, when they see them being taught to be self-supporting, to follow trades, to provide themselves with comfortable homes instead of continuing to live in hovels, they see the possibility that selfish plans will be interfered with—that they will no longer be able to hire the Negro for a mere pittance; and their enmity is aroused. They feel that they are injured and abused.

Some act as if slavery had never been abolished. This spirit is growing stronger as the Spirit of God is being withdrawn from the world, and in many places it is impossible now to do that work which could have been done for the colored people in past years.

Much might have been accomplished by the people of America if adequate efforts in behalf of the freed men had been put forth by the Government and by the Christian churches immediately after the emancipation of the slaves. Money should have been used freely to care for and educate them at the time they were so greatly in need of help. But the Government, after a little effort, left the Negro to struggle, unaided, with his burden of difficulties. Some of the strong Christian churches began a good work, but sadly failed to reach more than a comparatively few; and the Seventh-day Adventist Church has failed to act its part. Some persevering efforts have been put forth by individuals and by societies to uplift the colored people, and a noble work has been done. But how few have had a part in this work which should have had the sympathy and help of all!

Noble efforts have been put forth by some Seventh-day Adventists to do the work that needed to be done for the colored people. Had those who were engaged in this work received the co-operation of all their ministering brethren, the result of their work would now be altogether different from what it is. But the great majority of our ministers did not co-operate, as they should have done, with the few who were struggling to carry forward a much-needed work in a difficult field.

As time advances, and opposition strengthens, circumstances warn us that discretion is the better part of valor. If unwise moves have been made in the work done for the colored people, it is not because warnings have not been given. From Australia, across the broad waters of the Pacific, cautions were sent that every movement must be guarded, that the workers were to make no political speeches, and that the mingling of whites and blacks in social equality was by no means to be encouraged.

In a council meeting held in 1895 at Armadale, a suburb of Melbourne, Victoria, I spoke of these matters, in answer to the inquiries of my brethren, and urged the necessity of caution. I said that perilous times were coming, and that the sentiments that could then be expressed in regard to what should be done along missionary lines for the colored people could not be expressed in the future without imperiling lives. I said plainly that the work done for the colored people would have to be carried on along lines different from those followed in some sections of the country in former years.

Let as little as possible be said about the color line, and let the colored people work chiefly for those of their own race.

In regard to white and colored people worshiping in the same building, this cannot be followed as a general custom with profit to either party—especially in the South. The best thing will be to provide the colored people who accept the truth, with places of worship of their own, in which they can carry on their services by themselves. This is particularly necessary in the South in order that the work for the white people may be carried on without serious hindrance.

Let the colored believers be provided with neat, tasteful houses of worship. Let them be shown that this is done not to exclude them from worshiping with white people, because they are black, but in order that the progress of the truth may be advanced. Let them understand that this plan is to be followed until the Lord shows us a better way.

The colored members of ability and experience should be encouraged to lead the services of their own people; and their voices are to be heard in the representative assemblies.

Among the colored believers there are many who can labor to advantage for their own people—workers to whom the Lord has given light and knowledge and who possess capabilities of no mean order. These are to labor perseveringly and in every effective way. They are to use our literature and hold tent meetings and meetings in halls. And sometimes (where it is permissible) white ministers should help them. Special efforts should be made to increase the force of colored workers. Colored men are to be thoroughly educated and trained to give Bible readings and hold tent meetings among their own people. There are many having capability, who should be prepared for this work.

We should be deeply interested in the establishment of schools for the colored people. And we must not overlook the importance of placing the present truth before the teachers and students in the large colleges for colored people that have been established by men of the world.

Schools and sanitariums for colored people should be established, and in these the colored youth should be taught and trained for service by the very best teachers that can be employed.

The colored ministers should make every effort possible to help their own people to understand the truth for this time. As time advances, and race prejudices increase, it will become almost impossible, in many places, for

white workers to labor for the colored people. Sometimes the white people who are not in sympathy with
our work will unite with colored people to oppose it,
claiming that our teaching is an effort to break up
churches and bring in trouble over the Sabbath question. White ministers and colored ministers will make
false statements, arousing in the minds of the people
such a feeling of antagonism that they will be ready to
destroy and to kill.

The powers of hell are working with all their ingenuity
to prevent the proclamation of the last message of mercy
among the colored people. Satan is working to make it
most difficult for the gospel minister and teacher to ignore the prejudice that exists between the white and the
colored people.

Let us follow the course of wisdom. Let us do nothing
that will unnecessarily arouse opposition—nothing that
will hinder the proclamation of the gospel message.
Where demanded by custom or where greater efficiency
is to be gained, let the white believers and the colored
believers assemble in separate places of worship. Let us
cultivate the meekness of Christ. He was the Majesty of
heaven, the only-begotten Son of God. Yet "God so
loved the world, that He gave His only-begotten Son, that
whosoever believeth in Him should not perish, but have
everlasting life." John 3:16.

If, to save a perishing world, God condescended to
give up His Son to a painful, ignominious death, should
not the Lord's missionaries be willing to make every
effort in their power to win and help those who are in
the depths of sin, and to flash the light upon those who
are in darkness as to what is truth? Christ clothed His
divinity with humanity, that He might reach down and

uplift fallen human beings. Shall not His followers, for His sake, be willing to submit to many things unjust and grievous to be borne, in order to help the very ones who need help? Let the work be done in a way that will not arouse prejudice which would close doors now open for the entrance of the truth.

The men of talent among the colored believers are to be laborers together with God for their own people. And yet there will sometimes be opportunities for them to bear a testimony in tent meetings and in large assemblies, which will reach many, many souls. These opportunities will appear as the Southern field is worked and the loud cry is given. When the Holy Spirit is poured out, there will be a triumph of humanity over prejudice in seeking the salvation of the souls of human beings. God will control minds. Human hearts will love as Christ loved. And the color line will be regarded by many very differently from the way in which it is now regarded. To love as Christ loves, lifts the mind into a pure, heavenly, unselfish atmosphere.

He who is closely connected with Christ is lifted above the prejudice of color or caste. His faith takes hold of eternal realities. The divine Author of truth is to be uplifted. Our hearts are to be filled with the faith that works by love and purifies the soul. The work of the good Samaritan is the example that we are to follow.

We are not to agitate the color line question, and thus arouse prejudice and bring about a crisis. The light of the third angel's message is to be given to those who need light. We are to labor calmly, quietly, faithfully, trusting in our Elder Brother. We are not to be in haste to define the exact course to be pursued in the future regarding the relation to be maintained between white and colored people. The truth for this time is to be proclaimed before the thousands of people in the Southern States. The way is to be cleared, as far as possible, of all obstruction. Let the gospel message be given to the people. Let white and colored people be labored for in separate, distinct lines, and let the Lord take care of the rest. The truth must come before the white men and women of the Southern States. Then there will be a work done in their families that will lead to the salvation of many souls.

"IN ALL WISDOM AND PRUDENCE"

While men are trying to settle the question of the color line, time rolls on, and souls go down into the grave, unwarned and unsaved. Let this condition of things continue no longer. Let men and women go to work, and let them labor as the Spirit of God shall impress their minds. We need the talent of the colored believers, every jot of it, in this work. Let colored workers labor for their own people, assisted by white workers as occasion demands. They will often need counsel and advice. Let the colored believers have their place of worship and the white believers their place of worship. Let each company be zealous to do genuine missionary work for its own people and for the colored people wherever and whenever they can.

When the truth has been presented in a place, and as many white people as will hear and believe have accepted the truth, opportunities will sometimes appear for efforts to be made, in a quiet, unobtrusive manner, by white laborers for the colored people. Such opportunities should not be overlooked.

But we must not unnecessarily arouse prejudice that would close the way against the proclamation of the third angel's message to the white people. They need this message; for a time of trouble is before us, such as never was since there was a nation.

Great care must be exercised that nothing be said or done to inflame the feelings of the colored people against the whites. Let us not aggravate the difficulties that already exist. However wisely the workers labor, they will have opposition to meet, without creating an agitation over the color line. Let us clear the King's highway. Let God have a chance to work. Let men keep out of His way. He will plan and manage better than human beings possibly can. Let us remember that our first great work is to preach the word of God, to give the warnings of the Bible.

The Lord calls upon all to take up the work in humility of mind. The ministers are not all sanctified through the truth. The Lord calls upon all to lay down their controversies. Let men beware of doing that which would cut off our last hope of entering difficult fields where there is race prejudice and antagonism.

As a means of overcoming prejudice and gaining access to minds, medical missionary work must be done, not in one or two places only, but in many places where the truth has not yet been proclaimed. We are to work as gospel medical missionaries, to heal the sin-sick souls by giving them the message of salvation. This work will break down prejudice as nothing else can.

THE SABBATH

The Sabbath question is one that will demand great care and wisdom in its presentation. Much of the grace and power of God will be needed to cast down the idol that has been erected in the shape of a false sabbath. Lift up the standard, lift it up, *higher and still higher.* Point the people to the twentieth chapter of Exodus, in which the law of God is recorded. The first four of the Ten Commandments outline our duty to our Maker. He who is false to his God cannot be true to his neighbor. He who loves God supremely will love his neighbor as himself. Pride lifts itself up unto vanity, leading the human agent to make a god of himself. The gospel of Christ sanctifies the soul, expelling self-love.

"Remember the Sabbath day, to keep it holy." Exodus 20:8. The Sabbath was instituted in Eden, after God had created the world. "Thus the heavens and the earth were finished, and all the host of them. And on the seventh day God ended His work which He had made; and He rested on the seventh day from all His work which He had made. And God blessed the seventh day, and sanctified it: because that in it He had rested from all His work which God created and made." Genesis 2:1-3.

"And the Lord spake unto Moses, saying, Speak thou also unto the children of Israel, saying, Verily My Sabbaths ye shall keep: for it is a *sign* between Me and you throughout your generations; that ye may know that I am the Lord that doth sanctify you. Ye shall keep the Sabbath therefore; for it is holy unto you: everyone that defileth it shall surely be put to death: for whosoever doeth any work therein, that soul shall be cut off from among his people. Six days may work be done; but in the seventh is the Sabbath of rest, holy to the Lord: whosoever doeth any work in the Sabbath day, he shall surely be put to death. Wherefore the children of Israel shall keep the Sabbath, to observe the Sabbath throughout their generations, for a perpetual covenant." Exodus 31:12-16.

October 19, 1908.

THE COLOR LINE

I have some things to say in regard to the colored people of the Southern States of America and the relation that we should sustain to them. So long were they under the curse of slavery that it is a difficult problem to know how they should now be treated.

When God's workers allow His Spirit to work upon their minds, much will be accomplished in the saving of souls. The Lord is our helper. He will guide us in all matters if we will trust in Him. One thing is certain: We must have faith in God—faith that He will arrange matters in a way that will enable us to work successfully. No one ever trusted God in vain. He will never disappoint those who put their trust in Him.

We are to avoid entering into contention over the problem of the color line. If this question is much agitated, difficulties will arise that will consume much precious time to adjust. We cannot lay down a definite line to be followed in dealing with this subject. In different places and under varying circumstances, the subject will need to be handled differently. In the South, where race prejudice is so strong, we could do nothing in presenting the truth were we to deal with the color line question as we can deal with it in some places in the North. The white workers in the South will have to move in a way that will enable them to gain access to the white people.

It is Satan's plan to call minds to the study of the color line. If his suggestions are heeded, there will be diversity of opinion and great confusion. No one is capable of clearly defining the proper position of the colored people. Men may advance theories, but I assure you that it will not do for us to follow human theories. So far as possible the color line question should be allowed to rest.

The cities of the South are to be worked, and for this work the best talent is to be secured, and that without delay. Let white workers labor for the white people, proclaiming the message of present truth in its simplicity. They will find openings through which they may reach the higher class. Every opportunity for reaching this class is to be improved.

Let colored laborers do what they can to keep abreast, working earnestly for their own people. I thank God that among the colored believers there are men of talent who can work efficiently for their own people, presenting the truth in clear lines. There are many colored people of precious talent who will be converted to the truth if our colored ministers are wise in devising ways of training teachers for the schools and other laborers for the field.

The colored people should not urge that they be placed on an equality with white people. The relation of the two races has been a matter hard to deal with, and I fear that it will ever remain a most perplexing problem. So far as possible, everything that would stir up the race prejudice of the white people should be avoided. There is danger of closing the door so that our white laborers will not be able to work in some places in the South.

I know that if we attempt to meet the ideas and preferences of some of the colored people, we shall find our way blocked completely. The work of proclaiming the truth for this time is not to be hindered by an effort to adjust the position of the Negro race. Should we attempt to do this we should find that barriers like mountains would be raised to hinder the work that God desires to have done. If we move quietly and judiciously, laboring in the way that God has marked out, both white and colored people will be benefited by our labors.

The time has not come for us to work as if there were no prejudice. Christ said: "Be ye therefore wise as serpents, and harmless as doves." Matthew 10:16. If you see that by doing certain things which you have a perfect right to do, you hinder the advancement of God's work, refrain from doing those things. Do nothing that will close the minds of others against the truth. There is a world to save, and we shall gain nothing by cutting loose from those we are trying to help. All things may be lawful, but all things are not expedient.

The wise course is the best. As laborers together with God, we are to work in the way that will enable us to accomplish the most for Him. Let none go to extremes. We need wisdom from above; for we have a difficult problem to solve. If rash moves are made now, great mischief will be done. The matter is to be presented in such a way that the truly converted colored people will cling to the truth for Christ's sake, refusing to renounce one principle of sound Bible doctrine because they may think that the very best course is not being pursued toward the Negro race.

We must sit as learners at the feet of Christ, that He may teach us the will of God and that we may know how to work for the white people and the colored people in the Southern field. We are to do as the Spirit of the Lord shall dictate, and agitate the subject of the color line as little as possible. We must use every energy to present the closing gospel message to all classes in the South. As we are led and controlled by the Spirit of God we shall find that this question will adjust itself in the minds of our people.

Let us individually seek the Lord. Let those whose religious experience in the past has been only a surface work, draw near to God. Repent, repent, and be converted, that your sins may be blotted out.

When we are prepared to take hold of the work in earnest we shall be better able than we are now to deal with the questions involved in this work. Let every believer do his best to prepare the way for the gospel missionary work that is to be done. But let no one enter into controversy. It is Satan's object to keep Christians occupied in controversies among themselves. He knows that if they do not watch, the day of the Lord will come on them as a thief in the night. We have no time now to give place to the spirit of the enemy and to cherish prejudices that confuse the judgment and lead us away from Christ.

It will take money and earnest, persevering effort to do that which needs to be done among the colored people. Every man needs now to stand in his lot and place, confessing and forsaking his sins, and working in harmony with his brethren. God's workers are to be of one mind and one heart, praying for the impartation of the Spirit and believing that God will fulfill His word.

A LESSON FROM CHRIST'S LABORS

On one occasion, while Christ was in the midst of His work of teaching and healing, one of the company assembled about Him said: "Master, speak to my brother, that he divide the inheritance with me." Luke 12:13.

This man had witnessed Christ's wonderful works. He had been astonished at the clearness of His comprehension, His superior judgment, and the fairness with which He viewed the cases brought to Him. He heard Christ's stirring appeals and His solemn denunciations of the scribes and Pharisees. If words of such command could be spoken to this brother, he would not dare to refuse the aggrieved man his portion. He solicited Christ's influence on his side. "Speak to my brother," he said, "that he divide the inheritance with me."

The Holy Spirit was pleading with this man to become an heir of the inheritance that is incorruptible and undefiled, and that fadeth not away. He had seen evidence of the power of Christ. Now the opportunity was his to speak to the Great Teacher, to express the desire uppermost in his heart. But like the man with the muckrake in Bunyan's allegory, his eyes were fixed on the earth. He saw not the crown above his head. Like Simon Magus he valued the gift of God as a means of worldly gain.

The Saviour's mission on earth was fast drawing to a close. Only a few months remained for Him to complete what He came to do in establishing the kingdom of His grace. Yet human greed would have turned Him from His work to take up the dispute over a piece of land. But Jesus was not to be diverted from His mission. His answer was: "Man, who made Me a judge or a divider over you?" Luke 12:14.

Christ gave the man plainly to understand that this was not His work. He was striving to save souls. He was not to be turned aside from this to take up the duties of a civil magistrate.

How often today labor is forced upon the church that should never be allowed to enter the work of the gospel ministry!

Again and again Christ had been asked to decide legal and political questions. But He refused to interfere in temporal matters. He knew that in the political world there were iniquitous proceedings and great tyranny. But His only exposure of these was the proclamation of Bible truth. To the great multitudes that thronged His steps He presented the pure, holy principles of the law of God and spoke of the blessing found in obeying these principles. With authority from on high He enforced the importance of justice and mercy. But He refused to become entangled in personal disputes.

Christ stood in our world as the Head of the great spiritual kingdom that He came to our world to establish— the kingdom of righteousness. His teaching made plain the ennobling, sanctifying principles that govern this kingdom. He showed that justice and mercy and love are the controlling powers in Jehovah's kingdom.

A TIME OF PREPARATION

We are living in the great antitypical day of atonement. We must individually seek God. This is a personal work. Let us draw near to God, allowing nothing to come into our efforts that would misrepresent the truth for this time. Let everyone confess, not his brother's sin, but his own sin. Let him humble his heart before God and become so filled with the Holy Spirit that his life will show that he has been born again. We read: "As many as received Him, to them gave He power to become the sons of God, even to them that believe on His name." John 1:12.

The gospel of Christ is to be lived, practiced in the daily life. The servants of God are to be cleansed from all coldness, all selfishness. Simplicity, meekness, lowliness, are of great value in the work of God. Try to unite the workers in confidence and love. If you cannot do this, be right yourselves, and leave the rest with God. Labor in faith and prayer. Select Christian youth, and train them to be, not workers with hearts like iron, but workers who are willing to harmonize.

I pray that the Lord will change the hearts of those who, unless they receive more grace, will enter into temptation. I pray that He will soften and subdue every heart. We need to live in close fellowship with God, that we may love one another as Christ has loved us. It is by this that the world is to know that we are His disciples. Let there be no self-exaltation. If the workers will humble their hearts before God, the blessing will come. They will all the while be receiving fresh, new ideas, and there will be a wonderful revival of gospel medical missionary work.

The great work before us all, as Christians, is to extend Christ's kingdom as rapidly as possible, in accordance with the divine commission. The gospel is to advance from conquest to conquest, from victory to victory. The greatness of the kingdom under the whole heaven shall be given to the people of the saints of the Most High, and they shall take the kingdom and possess the kingdom for ever and ever.

THE WARFARE BEFORE US

God's servants are to put on every piece of the Christian armor. We are not wrestling simply with human foes. God calls upon every Christian to enter the warfare and fight under His leadership, depending for success on the grace and help of Heaven.

We are to go forward in the strength of the Mighty

One. Never are we to yield to Satan's attacks. Why should not we, as Christian warriors, stand against principalities and powers, and against the rulers of the darkness of this world? God calls upon us to press forward, using the gifts entrusted to us. Satan will place temptation before us. He will try to overcome us by stratagem. But in the strength of God we are to stand firm as a rock to principle.

In this warfare there is no release. Satan's agents never pause in their work of destruction. Those who are in Christ's service must watch every outpost. Our object is to save perishing souls from ruin. This is a work of infinite greatness, and man cannot hope to obtain success in it unless he unites with the divine Worker.

From eternity Christ has been man's Redeemer. Ever since the Fall there has come to those uniting with Him in His great work the word: "Be not weary in well-doing." 2 Thessalonians 3:13. "Be ye steadfast, unmovable, always abounding in the work of the Lord." 1 Corinthians 15:58.

The Christian is encouraged to show patient perseverance in carrying forward the work of the gospel ministry in connection with the medical missionary work. As he gains an experience in genuine religion, he obtains a spiritual knowledge that makes character.

The life of a true Christian is one continuous round of service. "We are laborers together with God." Every day brings to the one in God's service duties proportionate to his powers. His usefulness increases as, under the guidance of a supreme Power, he performs these duties. The fulfillment of one duty makes us better prepared to take up another. Those who have a true sense of what is to be done will place themselves in the direct light of the word of God, in union with His other working forces. Every day, clothed with the whole armor, he will go forth into the battle. With prayer and watchfulness and perseverance he will labor, determined that the close of his lifework shall not find him unprepared, not having done all that he could for the salvation of perishing souls.

If Christians were to act in concert, moving forward as one, under the direction of one Power, for the accomplishment of one purpose, they would move the world.

The principles that should actuate us as workers in God's cause are laid down by the apostle Paul. He says: "We are laborers together with God." 1 Corinthians 3:9. "Whatsoever ye do, do it heartily, *as to the Lord,* and not unto men." Colossians 3:23. And Peter exhorts the believers: "As every man hath received the gift, even so minister the same one to another, as good stewards of the manifold grace of God. If any man speak, let him speak as the oracles of God; if any man minister, let him do it as of the ability which God giveth: that God in all things may be glorified through Jesus Christ." 1 Peter 4:10, 11.

There are great laws that govern the world of nature, and spiritual things are controlled by principles equally certain. The means for an end must be employed, if the desired results are to be attained. God has appointed to every man his work according to his ability. It is by education and practice that persons are to be qualified to meet any emergency which may arise; and wise planning is needed to place each one in his proper sphere, that he may obtain an experience that will fit him to bear responsibility.

God wants us to help one another by a manifestation of sympathy and unselfish love. There are those who have inherited peculiar tempers and dispositions. They may be hard to deal with; but are we faultless? They are not to be discouraged. Their errors are not to be made common property. Christ pities and helps those who err in judgment. He has suffered death for every man, and because of this He has a touching and profound interest in every man.

A man may be trying to serve God, but temptations from within and from without assail him. Satan and his angels urge and coax him to transgress. Perhaps he falls a prey to their temptings. How then do his brethren treat him? Do they speak harsh, cutting words, driving him further from the Saviour? What a sad sight for Christ and the angels to behold!

Let us remember that we are struggling and falling, failing in speech and action to represent Christ, falling and rising again, despairing and hoping. Let us beware of dealing unkindly with those who, like ourselves, are subjects of temptation and who, like ourselves also, are the objects of Christ's unfailing love.

God deals with men as responsible beings. He will work by His Spirit through the mind He has put in man if man will only give Him a chance to work and will recognize His dealings. He designs that each shall use his mind and conscience for himself. He does not intend that one man shall become the shadow of another, uttering only another's sentiments.

CONSIDERATION FOR COLORED LABORERS

The religion of the Bible recognizes no caste or color. It ignores rank, wealth, worldly honor. God estimates men as men. With Him, character decides their worth. And we are to recognize the Spirit of Christ in whomsoever it is revealed. No one need be ashamed to speak with an honest black man in any place or to shake him by the hand. He who is living in the atmosphere in which Christ lives will be taught of God and will learn to put His estimate on men.

Our colored ministers are to be treated with consideration. This has not always been done. These men are to be encouraged to obtain a thorough knowledge of the truth. They are to learn how to be efficient in teaching the truth to others. And when they are faithfully engaged in work they should receive their hire. Remember that they must have bread.

The Lord desires His people in the North to maintain a kindly attitude toward the colored brethren and sisters. We should not be hasty in finding fault with them. We cannot expect them to be in all respects like those who have enjoyed greater advantages. We should remember the disadvantages under which the colored people have lived. Far different from the surroundings of the white race have been their surroundings. The Northern people have lived in a clearer, purer moral atmosphere than have the colored people of the South. We cannot expect that, in all things, they will be as firm and clear in their ideas of morality. Were Christ on earth today, He would teach the Negro race in a way that would surprise us. He calls upon us to remember that even those who have had great advantages in many things often feel hurt

(223)

if their errors are unduly noticed and if words of counsel and admonition are spoken in an unsympathetic manner.

When things of an objectionable nature take place among the colored people, remember that the Lord desires you to act with the wisdom of a faithful shepherd. Remember that kindness will accomplish more than censure. Let the colored brethren and sisters see that their brethren want them to reach the highest standard and that they are willing to help them. And if in some things the colored people fail, do not be quick to condemn them and separate them from the work.

Exact and impartial justice is to be shown to the Negro race. Christ demands from His servants tender compassion for the suffering, sympathy for the unfortunate, and a generous consideration for misdemeanors.

_____

The poor are not excluded from the privilege of giving. They, as well as the wealthy, may act a part in this work. The lesson that Christ gave in regard to the widow's two mites shows us that the smallest willing offerings of the poor, if given from a heart of love, are as acceptable as the largest donations of the rich. In the balances of the sanctuary, the gifts of the poor, made from love to Christ, are not estimated according to the amount given, but according to the love which prompts the sacrifice.

THE NEEDS OF A MISSION FIELD

For many years the Lord has been keeping before His people the needs of the work among the colored people in the Southern States of America. The moral darkness of this field is, in itself, a powerful plea for the exercise of liberality. In the past some have done what they could to support this branch of our work, and their beneficence has borne fruit in the conversion of many souls.

Although much remains to be done for the colored people, we have cause for rejoicing over the good beginning that has been made. In a recent number of *The Gospel Herald* [1907] it is reported that "fifteen years ago there were not over twenty colored Seventh-day Adventists south of Mason and Dixon's line; but today there are seven hundred. Twelve years ago there was only one colored Seventh-day Adventist church; today there are fifty, not counting those in Africa and the West Indies. . . . The tithe of the colored people last year in the United States amounted to five thousand dollars; fifteen years ago it was not over fifty dollars."

Let us thank God, dear brethren and sisters, and take courage! God is laying bare His arm to do a mighty work in this mission field within the borders of our own land. He is now giving His people unusual opportunities to extend the message rapidly in the South. Especially should we reveal a spirit of beneficence at the time the yearly offering for the support of the colored work is taken up. God has reposed confidence in us by making us stewards of means and of His rich grace; and He now points us to the poor and suffering and oppressed, to souls bound in chains of superstition and error, and assures us that if we do good to these, He will accept the deed as though done to Himself. "Inasmuch as ye have done it unto one of the least of these My brethren," He declares, "ye have done it unto Me." Matthew 25:40.

Thousands of colored people in the South may now be uplifted, and become human agents to help their own race, if they can receive the help God is calling upon us to give them. Multitudes of men and women in this field feel their deep poverty and their need of uplifting. And when faithful teachers shall come in to open to them the Scriptures just as they read, presenting truth in its native purity, the darkness will disappear. Bright beams of light will shine upon the soul searching for truth. And with those who have had advantages, a close and intelligent investigation will take place upon the subjects of truth revealed in the Scriptures. Many will be taught of God. They will learn aright from the Great Teacher, and will accept with joy the truths that will sanctify and uplift. The moral image of God will be restored in the soul, and many will be eternally saved.

My dear brethren and sisters, Christ is now saying to you: "Lift up your eyes and look on this Southern field; for it needs workers—sowers of the seed, and reapers. It needs your means for the maintenance of these workers." The grace of Christ is unlimited, it is God's free gift. Then why should not this neglected people have some hope and courage and faith brought into their lives? There is sunshine in the heart for all who will accept Christ.

September, 1907.

THE RELIGIOUS LIBERTY WORK *

> "Proclaim liberty throughout all the
> land unto all the inhabitants thereof."
> "Be ye therefore wise as serpents, and
> harmless as doves." Leviticus 25:10;
> Matthew 10:16.

A TIME OF TRIAL BEFORE US

A season of great trial is before us. It becomes us now to use all our capabilities and gifts in advancing the work of God. The powers the Lord has given us are to be used to build up, not to tear down. Those who are ignorantly deceived are not to remain in this condition. The Lord says to His messengers: Go to them and declare unto them what I have said, whether they will hear, or whether they will forbear.

The time is right upon us when persecution will come to those who proclaim the truth. The outlook is not flattering; but, notwithstanding this, let us not give up our efforts to save those ready to perish, for whose ransom the Prince of heaven offered up His precious life. When one means fails, try another. Our efforts must not be dead and lifeless. As long as life is spared, let us work for God. In all ages of the church God's appointed messengers have exposed themselves to reproach and persecution for the truth's sake. But wherever God's people may be forced to go, even though, like the beloved dis-

---

* In this section portions of only a few manuscripts (hitherto unpublished) are given. For other important matter having a direct, vital bearing on religious liberty work, see *Testimonies for the Church,* vol. 5, pp. 449-454, 467-476, 711-720; vol. 6, pp. 394-410; also *The Great Controversy,* chapters 2, 16, 25, 36, 38-40.

ciple, they are banished to desert islands, Christ will know where they are and will strengthen and bless them, filling them with peace and joy.

Soon there is to be trouble all over the world. It becomes everyone to seek to know God. We have no time to delay. With earnestness and fervor the message must be given: "Ho, everyone that thirsteth, come ye to the waters, and he that hath no money; come ye, buy, and eat; yea, come, buy wine and milk without money and without price." Isaiah 55:1. "Thus saith the Lord, Keep ye judgment, and do justice: for My salvation is near to come, and My righteousness to be revealed. Blessed is the man that doeth this, and the Son of man that layeth hold on it; that keepeth the Sabbath from polluting it, and keepeth his hand from doing any evil." Isaiah 56:1, 2.

God's love for His church is infinite. His care over His heritage is unceasing. He suffers no affliction to come upon the church but such as is essential for her purification, her present and eternal good. He will purify His church even as He purified the temple at the beginning and close of His ministry on earth. All that He brings upon the church in test and trial comes that His people may gain deeper piety and more strength to carry the triumphs of the cross to all parts of the world. He has a work for all to do. There must be constant enlargement and progress. The work must extend from city to city, from country to country, and from nation to nation, moving continually onward and upward, established, strengthened, and settled.

"The Word was made flesh, and dwelt among us, . . . full of grace and truth." But those whom Christ came to save, would have none of Him. "He came unto

His own, and His own received Him not." John 1:14, 11. Yielding themselves to Satan's control, they rejected the Messiah and sought opportunity to put Him to death.

Satan and his angels determined to make Christ's death as humiliating as possible. They filled the hearts of the Jewish leaders with feelings of bitter hatred against the Saviour. Controlled by the enemy, priests and rulers stirred the multitude to take part against the Son of God. Aside from Pilate's declaration of His innocence, no one spoke a word in His favor. And even Pilate, knowing His innocence, gave Him over to the abuse of men under the control of Satan.

Similar events will take place in the near future. Men will exalt and rigidly enforce laws that are in direct opposition to the law of God. Though zealous in enforcing their own commandments, they will turn away from a plain "Thus saith the Lord." Exalting a spurious rest day, they will seek to force men to dishonor the law of Jehovah, the transcript of His character. Though innocent of wrongdoing, the servants of God will be given over to suffer humiliation and abuse at the hands of those who, inspired by Satan, are filled with envy and religious bigotry.

Religious powers, allied to heaven by profession, and claiming to have the characteristics of a lamb, will show by their acts that they have the heart of a dragon and that they are instigated and controlled by Satan. The time is coming when God's people will feel the hand of persecution because they keep holy the seventh day. Satan has caused the change of the Sabbath in the hope of carrying out his purpose for the defeat of God's plans. He seeks to make the commands of God of less force in the world than human laws. The man of sin, who thought to change times and laws, and who has always oppressed the people of God, will cause laws to be made enforcing the observance of the first day of the week. But God's people are to stand firm for Him. And the Lord will work in their behalf, showing plainly that He is the God of gods.

The Lord has said: "Verily My Sabbaths ye shall keep: for it is a sign between Me and you throughout your generations." Exodus 31:13. None should disobey His command in order to escape persecution. But let all consider the words of Christ: "When they persecute you in this city, flee ye into another." Matthew 10:23. If it can be avoided, do not put yourselves into the power of men who are worked by the spirit of antichrist. Everything that we can do should be done that those who are willing to suffer for the truth's sake may be saved from oppression and cruelty.

Christ is our example. The determination of antichrist to carry out the rebellion he began in heaven will continue to work in the children of disobedience. Their envy and hatred against those who obey the fourth commandment will wax more and more bitter. But the people of God are not to hide their banner. They are not to ignore the commandments of God and, in order to have an easy time, go with the multitude to do evil.

The Lord encourages all who seek Him with the whole heart. He gives them His Holy Spirit, the manifestation of His presence and favor. But those who forsake God in order to save their lives will be forsaken by Him. In seeking to save their lives by yielding the truth, they will lose eternal life.

The night of trial is nearly spent. Satan is bringing

in his masterly power because he knoweth that his time is short. The chastisement of God is upon the world to call all who know the truth to hide in the cleft of the Rock and view the glory of God. The truth must not be muffled now. Plain statements must be made. Unvarnished truth must be spoken, in leaflets and pamphlets, and these must be scattered like the leaves of autumn.

The remnant church will be brought into great trial and distress. Those who keep the commandments of God and the faith of Jesus will feel the ire of the dragon and his hosts. Satan numbers the world as his subjects, he has gained control of the apostate churches; but here is a little company that are resisting his supremacy. If he could blot them from the earth, his triumph would be complete. As he influenced the heathen nations to destroy Israel, so in the near future he will stir up the wicked powers of earth to destroy the people of God. All will be required to render obedience to human edicts in violation of the divine law. Those who will be true to God and to duty will be menaced, denounced, and proscribed. They will be betrayed "both by parents, and brethren, and kinsfolks, and friends." Luke 21:16.*

"Hearken unto Me, ye that know righteousness, the people in whose heart is My law; fear ye not the reproach of men, neither be ye afraid of their revilings. For the moth shall eat them up like a garment, and the worm shall eat them like wool;" "but My salvation shall be forever, and My righteousness shall not be abolished." Isaiah 51:7, 8, 6.

---

* *Testimonies for the Church,* vol. 5, pp. 472, 473.

SUNDAY LABOR

Sanitarium, California, August 17, 1902.

Dear Brother: I will try to answer your question as to what you should do in the case of Sunday laws being enforced.

The light given me by the Lord at a time when we were expecting just such a crisis as you seem to be approaching, was that when the people were moved by a power from beneath to enforce Sunday observance, Seventh-day Adventists were to show their wisdom by refraining from their ordinary work on that day, devoting it to missionary effort.

To defy the Sunday laws will but strengthen in their persecution the religious zealots who are seeking to enforce them. Give them no occasion to call you lawbreakers. If they are left to rein up men who fear neither God nor man, the reining up will soon lose its novelty for them, and they will see that it is not consistent nor convenient for them to be strict in regard to the observance of Sunday. Keep right on with your missionary work, with your Bibles in your hands, and the enemy will see that he has worsted his own cause. One does not receive the mark of the beast because he shows that he realizes the wisdom of keeping the peace by refraining from work that gives offense, doing at the same time a work of the highest importance.

When we devote Sunday to missionary work, the whip will be taken out of the hands of the arbitrary zealots who would be well pleased to humiliate Seventh-day Adventists. When they see that we employ ourselves on Sunday in visiting the people and opening the Scriptures

(232)

to them, they will know that it is useless for them to try to hinder our work by making Sunday laws.

Sunday can be used for carrying forward various lines of work that will accomplish much for the Lord. On this day open-air meetings and cottage meetings can be held. House-to-house work can be done. Those who write can devote this day to writing their articles. Whenever it is possible, let religious services be held on Sunday. Make these meetings intensely interesting. Sing genuine revival hymns, and speak with power and assurance of the Saviour's love. Speak on temperance and on true religious experience. You will thus learn much about how to work, and will reach many souls.

Let the teachers in our schools devote Sunday to missionary effort. I was instructed that they would thus be able to defeat the purposes of the enemy. Let the teachers take the students with them to hold meetings for those who know not the truth. Thus they will accomplish much more than they could in any other way.

God has given us plain directions regarding our work. We are to proclaim the truth in regard to the Sabbath of the Lord, to make up the breach that has been made in His law. We are to do all that we can to enlighten those in ignorance; but we are never to confederate with men of the world in order to receive financial assistance.

Of the children of Israel we read: "Wherefore I caused them to go forth out of the land of Egypt, and brought them into the wilderness. And I gave them My statutes, and showed them My judgments, which if a man do, he shall even live in them. Moreover also I gave them My Sabbaths, to be a sign between Me and them, that they might know that I am the Lord that sanctify them. But the house of Israel rebelled against Me in the wilderness: they walked not in My statutes, and they despised My judgments, which if a man do, he shall even live in them; and My Sabbaths they greatly polluted: then I said, I would pour out My fury upon them in the wilderness, to consume them.

"But I wrought for My name's sake, that it should not be polluted before the heathen, in whose sight I brought them out. Yet also I lifted up My hand unto them in the wilderness, that I would not bring them into the land which I had given them, flowing with milk and honey, which is the glory of all lands; because they despised My judgments, and walked not in My statutes, but polluted My Sabbaths: for their heart went after their idols. Nevertheless Mine eye spared them from destroying them, neither did I make an end of them in the wilderness. But I said unto their children in the wilderness, Walk ye not in the statutes of your fathers, neither observe their judgments, nor defile yourselves with their idols: I am the Lord your God; walk in My statutes, and keep My judgments, and do them; and hallow My Sabbaths; and they shall be a sign between Me and you, that ye may know that I am the Lord your God." Ezekiel 20:10-20.

The Sabbath is the Lord's test, and no man, be he king, priest, or ruler, is authorized to come between God and man. Those who seek to be conscience for their fellow men, place themselves above God. Those who are under the influence of a false religion, who observe a spurious rest day, will set aside the most positive evidence in regard to the true Sabbath. They will try to compel men to obey the laws of their own creation, laws that are directly opposed to the law of God. Upon those who continue in this course, the wrath of God will fall. Unless they change, they cannot escape the penalty.

The law for the observance of the first day of the week is the production of an apostate Christendom. Sunday is a child of the papacy, exalted by the Christian world above the sacred day of God's rest. In no case are God's people to pay it homage. But I wish them to understand that they are not doing God's will by braving opposition when He wishes them to avoid it. Thus they create prejudice so bitter that it is impossible for the truth to be proclaimed. Make no demonstration on Sunday in defiance of law. If this is done in one place, and you are humiliated, the same thing will be done in another place. We can use Sunday as a day on which to carry forward work that will tell on the side of Christ. We are to do our best, working with all meekness and lowliness.

Christ warned His disciples in regard to what they would meet in their work as evangelists. He knew what their sufferings would be, what trials and hardships they would be called upon to bear. He would not hide from them the knowledge of what they would have to encounter, lest trouble, coming unexpectedly, should shake their faith. "I have told you before it come to pass," He said, "that, when it is come to pass, ye might believe." John 14:29. Their faith was to be strengthened, rather than weakened, by the coming of trial. They would say to one another: "He told us that this would come, and what we must do to meet it."

"Behold," Christ said, "I send you forth as sheep in the midst of wolves: be ye therefore wise as serpents, and harmless as doves." "Ye shall be hated of all men for My name's sake: but he that endureth to the end shall be saved." Matthew 10:16, 22. They hated Christ without a cause. Is it any marvel that they hate those who bear His sign, who do His service? They are counted as the offscouring of the earth.

"When they persecute you in this city, flee ye into another." It is not the will of God that your lives shall be carelessly sacrificed. "Verily I say unto you, Ye shall not have gone over the cities of Israel, till the Son of man be come." Verse 23.

The people must be given the truth, straightforward, positive truth. But this truth is to be presented in the spirit of Christ. We are to be as sheep in the midst of wolves. Those who will not, for Christ's sake, observe the cautions He has given, who will not exercise patience and self-control, will lose precious opportunities of working for the Master. The Lord has not given His people the work of making a tirade against those who are transgressing His law. In no case are we to make a raid on the other churches. Let us remember that, as a people entrusted with sacred truth, we have been neglectful and positively unfaithful. The work has been confined to a few centers until the people in them have become gospel-hardened. It is difficult to make an impression on those who have heard so much truth, and yet have rejected it. . . .

All this is against us now. Had we put forth earnest efforts to reach those who, if converted, would give a true representation of what present truth would do for human beings, how much further advanced our work would now be. It is not right that a few places should have all the advantages while other places are neglected.

At our Avondale school, near Cooranbong, Australia, the Sunday labor question came up for decision. It seemed as if the lines were soon to be drawn so tightly about us that we should not be able to work during Sunday. Our school was situated in the heart of the woods, far from any village or railway station. No one was living near enough to us to be disturbed in any way by anything we might do. Nevertheless, we were watched. The officers were urged to come around to inspect our premises, and they did come. They could have seen many things if they had desired to prosecute us, but they did not appear to notice those who were at work. They had so much confidence in us as a people, and so great respect for us on account of the work we had done in that community, that they believed they could trust us anywhere.

Many recognized the fact that the whole community had been transformed since we went there. A woman who was not a Sabbathkeeper said to me "You would not believe me if I should inform you fully in regard to the transformation that has taken place in this community as the result of your moving here, establishing a school, and holding these little meetings."

So when our brethren were threatened with persecution and thrown into perplexity in regard to what they should do, the same advice was given as was given in answer to the question concerning games. I said "Employ Sunday in doing missionary work for God. Teachers, go with your students. Take them into the bush [this is what we called the sparsely settled districts in the woods, where houses are often a mile or two apart], and visit the people in their homes. Let them know that you are interested in their soul's salvation." They did so and, as the result, were greatly benefited themselves and were able to help others as well. The blessing of God rested upon them as they diligently searched the Scriptures in order to learn how to present the truths of the word in such a way that these truths would be received with favor.

August 20, 1903.

At one time those in charge of our school at Avondale inquired of me, saying: "What shall we do? The officers of the law have been commissioned to arrest those working on Sunday." I replied: "It will be very easy to avoid that difficulty. Give Sunday to the Lord as a day for doing missionary work. Take the students out to hold meetings in different places, and to do medical missionary work. They will find the people at home and will have a splendid opportunity to present the truth. This way of spending Sunday is always acceptable to the Lord."

We are to do all we can to remove the prejudice that exists in the minds of many against our work and against the Bible Sabbath.

Teach the people to conform in all things to the laws of their state when they can do so without conflicting with the law of God.

Sometimes the hearts of persecutors are susceptible of divine impressions as was the heart of the apostle Paul before his conversion.

WORDS OF CAUTION

Christ said to His disciples: "Behold, I send you forth as sheep in the midst of wolves: be ye therefore wise as serpents, and harmless as doves." Matthew 10:16.

Satan's attacks against the advocates of the truth will wax more bitter and determined to the very close of time. As in Christ's day the chief priests and rulers stirred up the people against Him, so today the religious leaders will excite bitterness and prejudice against the truth for this time. The people will be led to acts of violence and opposition which they would never have thought of had they not been imbued with the animosity of professed Christians against the truth.

What course shall the advocates of truth pursue? They have the unchangeable, eternal word of God, and they should reveal the fact that they have the truth as it is in Jesus. Their words must not be rugged and sharp. In their presentation of truth they must manifest the love and meekness and gentleness of Christ. Let the truth do the cutting; the word of God is as a sharp, two-edged sword and will cut its way to the heart. Those who know that they have the truth should not, by the use of harsh and severe expressions, give Satan one chance to misinterpret their spirit.

As a people we must stand as did the world's Redeemer. When in controversy with Satan in regard to the body of Moses, Christ durst not bring against him a railing accusation. He had every provocation to do this, and Satan was disappointed because he could not arouse in Christ a spirit of retaliation. Satan was ready to misinterpret everything that was done by Jesus; and the Saviour would give him no occasion, not the semblance of an excuse. He would not turn from His straightforward course of truth in order to follow the wanderings and twistings and turnings and prevarications of Satan.

We read in the prophecy of Zechariah that when Satan with all his synagogue stood up to resist the prayers of Joshua the high priest, and to resist Christ, who was about to show decided favor to Joshua: "The Lord said unto Satan, The Lord rebuke thee, O Satan; even the Lord that hath chosen Jerusalem rebuke thee: is not this a brand plucked out of the fire?" Zechariah 3:2.

The course of Christ in dealing even with the adversary of souls should be an example to us in all our intercourse with others never to bring a railing accusation against any; much less should we employ harshness or severity toward those who may be as anxious to know the right way as we are ourselves.

Those who have been educated in the truth by precept and example should make great allowance for others who have had no knowledge of the Scriptures except through the interpretations given by ministers and church members, and who have received traditions and fables as Bible truth. They are surprised by the presentation of truth, it is as a new revelation to them, and they cannot bear to have all the truth, in its most striking character, presented to them at the outset. All is new and strange, and wholly unlike that which they have heard from their ministers; and they are inclined to believe what the ministers have told them—that Seventh-day Adventists are infidels and do not believe the Bible. Let the truth be presented as it is in Jesus, line upon line, precept upon precept, here a little and there a little.

Let not those who write for our papers make unkind thrusts and illusions that will certainly do harm and that will hedge up the way and hinder us from doing the work that we should do in order to reach all classes, the Catholics included. It is our work to speak the truth in love and not to mix in with the truth the unsanctified elements of the natural heart and speak things that savor of the same spirit possessed by our enemies. All sharp thrusts will come back upon us in double measure when the power is in the hands of those who can exercise it for injury. Over and over the message has been given to me that we are not to say one word, not to publish one sentence, especially by way of personalities, unless positively essential in vindicating the truth, that will stir up our enemies against us and arouse their passions to a white heat. Our work will soon be closed up, and soon the time of trouble, such as never was, will come upon us, of which we have but little idea.

The Lord wants His workers to represent Him, the great Missionary Worker. The manifestation of rashness always does harm. The proprieties essential for Christian life must be learned daily in the school of Christ. He who is careless and heedless in uttering words or in writing words for publication to be sent broadcast into the world, sending forth expressions that can never be taken back, is disqualifying himself to be entrusted with the sacred work that devolves upon Christ's followers at this time. Those who practice giving harsh thrusts are forming habits that will strengthen by repetition and will have to be repented of.

We should carefully examine our ways and our spirit, and see in what manner we are doing the work given us of God, which involves the destiny of souls. The very highest obligation is resting upon us. Satan is standing ready, burning with zeal to inspire the whole confederacy of satanic agencies, that he may cause them to unite with evil men and bring upon the believers of truth speedy and severe suffering. Every unwise word that is uttered through our brethren will be treasured up by the prince of darkness.

I should like to ask: How dare finite human intelligences speak careless and venturesome words that will stir up the powers of hell against the saints of God, when Michael the Archangel durst not bring against Satan a railing accusation, but said: "The Lord rebuke thee"? Jude 9.

It will be impossible for us to avoid difficulties and suffering. Jesus said: "Woe unto the world because of offenses! for it must needs be that offenses come; but woe to that man by whom the offense cometh!" Matthew 18:7. But because offense will come, we should be careful not to stir up the natural temperament of those who love not the truth, by unwise words and by the manifestation of an unkind spirit.

Precious truth must be presented in its native force. The deceptive errors that are widespread, and that are leading the world captive, are to be unveiled. Every effort possible is being made to ensnare souls with subtle reasonings, to turn them from the truth to fables, and to prepare them to be deceived by strong delusions. But while these deceived souls turn from the truth to error, do not speak to them one word of censure. Seek to show these poor, deluded souls their danger and to reveal to them how grievous is their course of action toward Jesus Christ; but let it all be done in pitying tenderness. By a proper manner of labor some of the souls who are ensnared by Satan may be recovered from his power. But do not blame and condemn them. To ridicule the position held by those who are in error will not open their blind eyes nor attract them to the truth.

When men lose sight of Christ's example and do not pattern after His manner of teaching, they become self-sufficient and go forth to meet Satan with his own manner of weapons. The enemy knows well how to turn his weapons upon those who use them. Jesus spoke only words of pure truth and righteousness.

If ever a people needed to walk in humility before God, it is His church, His chosen ones in this generation. We all need to bewail the dullness of our intellectual faculties, the lack of appreciation of our privileges and opportunities. We have nothing whereof to boast. We grieve the Lord Jesus Christ by our harshness, by our un-Christlike thrusts. We need to become complete in Him.

It is true that we are commanded to "cry aloud, spare not, lift up thy voice like a trumpet, and show My people their transgression, and the house of Jacob their sins." Isaiah 58:1. This message must be given; but while it must be given, we should be careful not to thrust and crowd and condemn those who have not the light that we have. We should not go out of our way to make hard thrusts at the Catholics. Among the Catholics there are many who are most conscientious Christians and who walk in all the light that shines upon them, and God will work in their behalf. Those who have had great privileges and opportunities, and who have failed to improve their physical, mental, and moral powers, but who have lived to please themselves and have refused to bear their responsibility, are in greater danger and in greater condemnation before God than those who are in error upon doctrinal points, yet who seek to live to do good to others. Do not censure others; do not condemn them.

If we allow selfish considerations, false reasoning, and false excuses to bring us into a perverse state of mind and heart, so that we shall not know the ways and will of

God, we shall be far more guilty than the open sinner. We need to be very cautious in order that we may not condemn those who, before God, are less guilty than ourselves.

Let everyone bear in mind that we are in no case to invite persecution. We are not to use harsh and cutting words. Keep them out of every article written, drop them out of every address given. Let the word of God do the cutting, the rebuking; let finite men hide and abide in Jesus Christ. Let the spirit of Christ appear. Let all be guarded in their words, lest they place those not of our faith in deadly opposition against us and give Satan an opportunity to use the unadvised words to hedge up our way.

There is to be a time of trouble such as never was since there was a nation. Our work is to study to weed out of all our discourses everything that savors of retaliation and defiance and making a drive against churches and individuals, because this is not Christ's way and method.

The fact that God's people, who know the truth, have failed to do their duty according to the light given in the word of God makes it a necessity for us to be the more guarded, lest we offend unbelievers before they have heard the reasons for our faith in regard to the Sabbath and Sunday.

TIMELY COUNSELS

"Behold I come quickly: hold that
fast which thou hast, that no man
take thy crown." Revelation 3:11.

FAITHFUL STEWARDSHIP*

Christ has purchased us by the price of His own blood.
He has paid the purchase money for our redemption, and
if we will lay hold upon the treasure, it is ours by the free
gift of God.

"How much owest thou unto my Lord?" Luke 16:5. It
is impossible to tell. All that we have is from God. He
lays His hand upon our possessions, saying: "I am the
rightful owner of the whole universe; these are My
goods. Consecrate to Me the tithes and offerings. As you
bring these specified goods as a token of your loyalty and
your submission to My sovereignty, My blessing shall
increase your substance, and you will have abundance."

God is testing every soul that claims to believe in Him.
All are entrusted with talents. The Lord has given men
His goods upon which to trade. He has made them His
stewards, and has placed in their possession money,
houses, and lands. All these are to be regarded as the
Lord's goods and used to advance His work, to build up
His kingdom in the world. In trading with the Lord's
goods, we are to seek Him for wisdom, that we may not
use His sacred trust to glorify ourselves or to indulge
selfish impulses. The amount entrusted varies, but those
who have the smallest gifts must not feel that because

---

* Manuscript read before the delegates at the San Jose (California) State Conference, January, 1907.

their talent or means is small, they can do nothing with it.

Every Christian is a steward of God, entrusted with His goods. Remember the words: "Moreover it is required in stewards, that a man be found faithful." 1 Corinthians 4:2. Let us be sure that we are not robbing God in any jots or tittles, for much is involved in this question.

All things belong to God. Men may ignore His claims. While He bountifully bestows His blessings upon them, they may use His gifts for their own selfish gratification; but they will be called to give an account for their stewardship.

A steward identifies himself with his master. He accepts the responsibilities of a steward, and he must act in his master's stead, doing as his master would do were he presiding. His master's interests become his. The position of a steward is one of dignity because his master trusts him. If in any wise he acts selfishly and turns the advantages gained by trading with his lord's goods to his own advantage, he has perverted the trust reposed in him.

THE SUPPORT OF THE GOSPEL

The Lord has made the proclamation of the gospel dependent upon the labors and the voluntary gifts of all His people. The one who proclaims the message of mercy to fallen men has another work also—to set before the people the duty of sustaining the work of God with their means. He must teach them that a portion of their income belongs to God and is to be sacredly bestowed to His work. This lesson he should present by both precept and example; he should beware that he does not by his own course lessen the force of his teaching.

That which has been set apart according to the Scriptures as belonging to the Lord constitutes the revenue of the gospel and is no longer ours. It is no better than sacrilege for a man to take from God's treasury in order to serve himself or to serve others in their secular business. Some have been at fault in diverting from the altar of God that which has been especially dedicated to Him. All should regard this matter in the right light. Let no one, when brought into a strait place, take money consecrated to religious purposes and use it for his advantage, soothing his conscience by saying that he will repay it at some future time. Far better cut down the expenses to correspond with the income, to restrict the wants, and live within the means than to use the Lord's money for secular purposes.

THE USE OF THE TITHE

God has given special direction as to the use of the tithe. He does not design that His work shall be crippled for want of means. That there may be no haphazard work and no error, He has made our duty on these points very plain. The portion that God has reserved for Himself is not to be diverted to any other purpose than that which He has specified. Let none feel at liberty to retain their tithe, to use according to their own judgment. They are not to use it for themselves in an emergency, nor to apply it as they see fit, even in what they may regard as the Lord's work.

The minister should, by precept and example, teach the people to regard the tithe as sacred. He should not feel that he can retain and apply it according to his own judgment because he is a minister. It is not his. He is not at liberty to devote to himself whatever he thinks is his due. He should not give his influence to any plans for diverting from their legitimate use the tithes and offerings dedicated to God. They are to be placed in His treasury and held sacred for His service as He has appointed.

God desires all His stewards to be exact in following divine arrangements. They are not to offset the Lord's plans by performing some deed of charity or giving some gift or some offering when or how they, the human agents, shall see fit. It is a very poor policy for men to seek to improve on God's plan, and invent a makeshift, averaging up their good impulses on this and that occasion, and offsetting them against God's requirements. God calls upon all to give their influence to His own arrangement. He has made His plan known, and all who would co-operate with Him must carry out this plan instead of daring to attempt an improvement on it.

The Lord instructed Moses, for Israel: "Thou shalt command the children of Israel, that they bring thee pure oil olive beaten for the light, to cause the lamp to burn always." Exodus 27:20. This was to be a continual offering, that the house of God might be properly supplied with that which was necessary for His service. His people today are to remember that the house of worship is the Lord's property and that it is to be scrupulously cared for. But the funds for this work are not to come from the tithe.

A very plain, definite message has been given to me for our people. I am bidden to tell them that they are making a mistake in applying the tithe to various objects which, though good in themselves, are not the object to which the Lord has said that the tithe should be applied. Those who make this use of the tithe are departing from the Lord's arrangement. God will judge for these things.

One reasons that the tithe may be applied to school purposes. Still others reason that canvassers and colporteurs should be supported from the tithe. But a great misake is made when the tithe is drawn from the object for which it is to be used—the support of the ministers. There should be today in the field one hundred well qualified laborers where now there is but one.

A SOLEMN OBLIGATION

The tithe is sacred, reserved by God for Himself. It is to be brought into His treasury to be used to sustain the gospel laborers in their work. For a long time the Lord has been robbed because there are those who do not realize that the tithe is God's reserved portion.

Some have been dissatisfied and have said: "I will not longer pay my tithe; for I have no confidence in the way things are managed at the heart of the work." But will you rob God because you think the management of the work is not right? Make your complaint, plainly and openly, in the right spirit, to the proper ones. Send in your petitions for things to be adjusted and set in order; but do not withdraw from the work of God, and prove unfaithful, because others are not doing right.

Read carefully the third chapter of Malachi and see what God says about the tithe. If our churches will take their stand upon the Lord's word and be faithful in paying their tithe into His treasury, more laborers will be encouraged to take up ministerial work. More men would give themselves to the ministry were they not told of the depleted treasury. There should be an abundant supply in the Lord's treasury, and there would be if selfish hearts and hands had not withheld the tithes or made use of them to support other lines of work.

God's reserved resources are to be used in no such haphazard way. The tithe is the Lord's, and those who meddle with it will be punished with the loss of their heavenly treasure unless they repent. Let the work no longer be hedged up because the tithe has been diverted into various channels other than the one to which the Lord has said it should go. Provision is to be made for these other lines of work. They are to be sustained, but not from the tithe. God has not changed; the tithe is still to be used for the support of the ministry. The opening of new fields requires more ministerial efficiency than we now have, and there must be means in the treasury.

Those who go forth as ministers have a solemn responsibility devolving upon them which is strangely neglected. Some enjoy preaching, but they do not give personal labor to the churches. There is great need of instruction concerning the obligations and duties to God, especially in regard to paying an honest tithe. Our ministers would feel sadly aggrieved if they were not promptly paid for their labor; but will they consider that there must be meat in the treasure house of God wherewith to sustain the laborers? If they fail to do their whole duty in educating the people to be faithful in paying to God His own, there will be a shortage of means in the treasury to carry forward the Lord's work.

The overseer of the flock of God should faithfully discharge his duty. If he takes the position that because this is not pleasant to him, he will leave it for someone else to do, he is not a faithful worker. Let him read in Malachi the words of the Lord charging the people with robbery toward God in withholding the tithes. The mighty God declares: "Ye are cursed with a curse." Malachi 3:9. When the one who ministers in word and doctrine sees the people pursuing a course that will bring this curse upon them, how can he neglect his duty to give them instruction and warning? Every church member should be taught to be faithful in paying an honest tithe.

"Bring ye all the tithes into the storehouse, that there may be meat in Mine house, and prove Me now herewith, saith the Lord of hosts, if I will not open you the windows of heaven, and pour you out a blessing, that there shall not be room enough to receive it." Verse 10.

———————

I pray that my brethren may realize that the third angel's message means much to us and that the observance of the true Sabbath is to be the sign that distinguishes those who serve God from those who serve Him not. Let those who have become sleepy and indifferent, awake. We are called to be holy, and we should carefully avoid giving the impression that it is of little consequence whether or not we retain the peculiar features of our faith. Upon us rests the golden obligation of taking a more decided stand for truth and righteousness than we have taken in the past. The line of demarcation between those who keep the commandments of God and those who do not is to be revealed with unmistakable clearness. We are conscientiously to honor God, diligently using every means of keeping in covenant relation with Him, that we may receive His blessings—the blessings so essential for a people who are to be so severely tried. To give the impression that our faith, our religion, is not a dominating power in our lives is greatly to dishonor God. Thus we turn from His commandments, which are our life, denying that He is our God and we His people.

"The Lord thy God, He is God, the faithful God, which keepeth covenant and mercy with them that love

Him and keep His commandments to a thousand generations; and repayeth them that hate Him to their face, to
destroy them: He will not be slack to him that hateth Him,
He will repay him to his face." Deuteronomy 7:9, 10.

Where shall we be before the thousand generations
mentioned in this scripture are ended? Our fate will have
been decided for eternity. Either we shall have been pro-
nounced worthy of a home in the everlasting kingdom of
God or we shall have received sentence of eternal death.
Those who have been true and faithful to their covenant
with God; those who, remembering Calvary, have stood
firmly on the side of truth, ever striving to honor God,
will hear the commendation: "Well done, good and faithful servant." But those who have given God only
halfhearted service, allowing their lives to be conformed
to the ways and practices of the world, will hear the sad
words: "Depart from Me; I know you not."

BENEFICENCE

"Honor the Lord with thy substance, and with the first fruits of all thine increase: so shall thy barns be filled with plenty, and thy presses shall burst out with new wine." Proverbs 3:9, 10.

"There is that scattereth, and yet increaseth; and there is that withholdeth more than is meet, but it tendeth to poverty. The liberal soul shall be made fat: and he that watereth shall be watered also himself." Proverbs 11:24, 25.

"The liberal deviseth liberal things; and by liberal things shall he stand." Isaiah 32:8.

Divine wisdom has appointed, in the plan of salvation, the law of action and reaction, making the work of beneficence, in all its branches, twice blessed. He who gives to the needy blesses others and is blessed himself in a still greater degree.

THE GLORY OF THE GOSPEL

That man might not lose the blessed results of benevolence, our Redeemer formed the plan of enlisting him as His co-worker. God could have reached His object in saving sinners without the aid of man, but He knew that man could not be happy without acting a part in the great work. By a chain of circumstances which would call forth his charities, He bestows upon man the best means of cultivating benevolence, and keeps him habitually giving to help the poor and to advance His cause. By its necessities a ruined world is drawing forth from us talents of means and of influence, to present to men and women the truth, of which they are in perishing need. And as we heed these calls, by labor and by acts of benevolence, we are assimilated to the image of Him who for our sakes became poor. In bestowing we bless others and thus accumulate true riches.

It is the glory of the gospel that it is founded upon the principle of restoring in the fallen race the divine image by a constant manifestation of benevolence. This work began in the heavenly courts. There God gave to human beings an unmistakable evidence of the love with which He regarded them. He "so loved the world, that He gave His only-begotten Son, that whosoever believeth in Him should not perish, but have everlasting life." John 3:16. The gift of Christ reveals the Father's heart. It testifies that, having undertaken our redemption, He will spare nothing, however dear, which is necessary to the completion of His work.

The spirit of liberality is the spirit of heaven. Christ's self-sacrificing love is revealed upon the cross. That man might be saved, He gave all that He had and then gave Himself. The cross of Christ appeals to the benevolence of every follower of the blessed Saviour. The principle there illustrated is to give, give. This, carried out in actual benevolence and good works, is the true fruit of the Christian life. The principle of worldlings is to get, get, and thus they expect to secure happiness; but carried out in all its bearings, the fruit is misery and death.

The light of the gospel shining from the cross of Christ rebukes selfishness and encourages liberality and benevolence. It should not be a lamented fact that there are increasing calls to give. God in His providence is calling His people out from their limited sphere of action, to enter upon greater enterprises. Unlimited effort is demanded at this time when moral darkness is covering the world. Many of God's people are in danger of being ensnared by worldliness and covetousness. They should understand that it is His mercy that multiplies the demands for their means. Objects that call benevolence into action must be placed before them, or they cannot pattern after the character of the great Exemplar.

THE BLESSINGS OF STEWARDSHIP

In commissioning His disciples to go "into all the world, and preach the gospel to every creature," Christ assigned to men the work of extending the knowledge of His grace. But while some go forth to preach, He calls upon others to answer His claims upon them for offerings with which to support His cause in the earth. He has placed means in the hands of men, that His divine gifts may flow through human channels in doing the work appointed us in saving our fellow men. This is one of God's ways of exalting man. It is just the work that man needs, for it will stir the deepest sympathies of his heart, and call into exercise the highest capabilities of the mind.

Every good thing of earth was placed here by the bountiful hand of God as an expression of His love to man. The poor are His, and the cause of religion is His. The gold and the silver are the Lord's, and He could rain them from heaven if He chose. But instead of this He has made man His steward, entrusting him with means, not to be hoarded, but to be used in benefiting others. He thus makes man the medium through which to distribute His blessings on earth. God planned the system of beneficence in order that man might become like his Creator, benevolent and unselfish in character, and finally be a partaker with Christ of the eternal, glorious reward.

MEETING AROUND THE CROSS

The love expressed on Calvary should be revived, strengthened, and diffused among our churches. Shall we not do all we can to give power to the principles which Christ brought to this world? Shall we not strive to establish and give efficiency to the benevolent enterprises which are now called for without delay? As you stand before the cross and see the Prince of heaven dying for you, can you seal your heart, saying: "No; I have nothing to give"?

Christ's believing people are to perpetuate His love. This love is to draw them together around the cross. It is to divest them of all selfishness and bind them to God and to one another.

Meet around the cross of Calvary in self-sacrifice and self-denial. God will bless you as you do your best. As you approach the throne of grace, as you find yourself bound to this throne by the golden chain let down from heaven to earth to draw men from the pit of sin, your heart will go out in love for your brethren and sisters who are without God and without hope in the world.

THE SPIRIT OF INDEPENDENCE*

Before leaving Australia, and since coming to this country, I have been instructed that there is a great work to be done in America. Those who were in the work at the beginning are passing away. Only a few of the pioneers of the cause now remain among us. Many of the heavy burdens formerly borne by men of long experience are now falling upon younger men.

This transfer of responsibilities to laborers whose experience is more or less limited is attended with some dangers against which we need to guard. The world is filled with strife for the supremacy. The spirit of pulling away from fellow laborers, the spirit of disorganization, is in the very air we breathe. By some, all efforts to establish order are regarded as dangerous—as a restriction of personal liberty, and hence to be feared as popery. These deceived souls regard it a virtue to boast of their freedom to think and act independently. They declare that they will not take any man's say-so, that they are amenable to no man. I have been instructed that it is Satan's special effort to lead men to feel that God is pleased to have them choose their own course independent of the counsel of their brethren.

Herein lies a grave danger to the prosperity of our work. We must move discreetly, sensibly, in harmony with the judgment of God-fearing counselors; for in this course alone lies our safety and strength. Otherwise God cannot work with us and by us and for us.

Oh, how Satan would rejoice if he could succeed in his efforts to get in among this people and disorganize

---

*Manuscript read before the delegates at the General Conference, Washington, D. C., May 30, 1909.

the work at a time when thorough organization is essential and will be the greatest power to keep out spurious uprisings and to refute claims not endorsed by the word of God! We want to hold the lines evenly, that there shall be no breaking down of the system of organization and order that has been built up by wise, careful labor. License must not be given to disorderly elements that desire to control the work at this time.

Some have advanced the thought that, as we near the close of time, every child of God will act independently of any religious organization. But I have been instructed by the Lord that in this work there is no such thing as every man's being independent. The stars of heaven are all under law, each influencing the other to do the will of God, yielding their common obedience to the law that controls their action. And, in order that the Lord's work may advance healthfully and solidly, His people must draw together.

The spasmodic, fitful movements of some who claim to be Christians are well represented by the work of strong but untrained horses. When one pulls forward, another pulls back, and at the voice of their master one plunges ahead and the other stands immovable. If men will not move in concert in the great and grand work for this time, there will be confusion. It is not a good sign when men refuse to unite with their brethren and prefer to act alone. Let laborers take into their confidence the brethren who are free to point out every departure from right principles. If men wear the yoke of Christ, they can not pull apart; they will draw with Christ.

Some workers pull with all the power that God has given them, but they have not yet learned that they should not pull alone. Instead of isolating themselves, let them draw in harmony with their fellow laborers. Unless they do this, their activity will work at the wrong time and in the wrong way. They will often work counter to that which God would have done, and thus their work is worse than wasted.

UNITY IN DIVERSITY

On the other hand, the leaders among God's people are to guard against the danger of condemning the methods of individual workers who are led by the Lord to do a special work that but few are fitted to do. Let brethren in responsibility be slow to criticize movements that are not in perfect harmony with their methods of labor. Let them never suppose that every plan should reflect their own personality. Let them not fear to trust another's methods; for by withholding their confidence from a brother laborer who, with humility and consecrated zeal, is doing a special work in God's appointed way, they are retarding the advancement of the Lord's cause.

God can and will use those who have not had a thorough education in the schools of men. A doubt of His power to do this is manifest unbelief; it is limiting the omnipotent power of the One with whom nothing is impossible. Oh, for less of this uncalled-for, distrustful caution! It leaves so many forces of the church unused; it closes up the way so that the Holy Spirit cannot use men; it keeps in idleness those who are willing and anxious to labor in Christ's lines; it discourages from entering the work many who would become efficient laborers together with God if they were given a fair chance.

To the prophet the wheel within a wheel, the appearance of living creatures connected with them, all seemed

intricate and unexplainable. But the hand of Infinite
Wisdom is seen among the wheels, and perfect order is
the result of its work. Every wheel, directed by the
hand of God, works in perfect harmony with every
other wheel. I have been shown that human instrumentalities are liable to seek after too much power and try
to control the work themselves. They leave the Lord
God, the Mighty Worker, too much out of their methods and plans, and do not trust to Him everything in
regard to the advancement of the work. No one should
for a moment fancy that he is able to manage those
things that belong to the great I AM. God in His providence is preparing a way so that the work may be done
by human agents. Then let every man stand at his post
of duty, to act his part for this time and know that God
is his instructor.

THE GENERAL CONFERENCE

I have often been instructed by the Lord that no man's
judgment should be surrendered to the judgment of any
other one man. Never should the mind of one man or the
minds of a few men be regarded as sufficient in wisdom
and power to control the work and to say what plans shall
be followed. But when, in a General Conference, the
judgment of the brethren assembled from all parts of the
field is exercised, private independence and private judgment must not be stubbornly maintained, but surrendered. Never should a laborer regard as a virtue the persistent maintenance of his position of independence,
contrary to the decision of the general body.

At times, when a small group of men entrusted with
the general management of the work have, in the name
of the General Conference, sought to carry out unwise

plans and to restrict God's work, I have said that I could no longer regard the voice of the General Conference, represented by these few men, as the voice of God. But this is not saying that the decisions of a General Conference composed of an assembly of duly appointed, representative men from all parts of the field should not be respected. God has ordained that the representatives of His church from all parts of the earth, when assembled in a General Conference, shall have authority. The error that some are in danger of committing is in giving to the mind and judgment of one man, or of a small group of men, the full measure of authority and influence that God has vested in His church in the judgment and voice of the General Conference assembled to plan for the prosperity and advancement of His work.

When this power, which God has placed in the church, is accredited wholly to one man, and he is invested with the authority to be judgment for other minds, then the true Bible order is changed. Satan's efforts upon such a man's mind would be most subtle and sometimes well-nigh overpowering, for the enemy would hope that through his mind he could affect many others. Let us give to the highest organized authority in the church that which we are prone to give to one man or to a small group of men.

A DISTRIBUTION OF RESPONSIBILITY*

God would have His people an understanding people. He has so arranged matters that chosen men shall go as delegates to our conferences. These men are to be tried and proved. They are to be trustworthy men. The choosing of delegates to attend our conferences is an important matter. These men are to lay the plans that shall be followed in the advancement of the work; and therefore they are to be men of understanding, able to reason from cause to effect.

"And it came to pass on the morrow, that Moses sat to judge the people: and the people stood by Moses from the morning unto the evening. And when Moses' father-in-law saw all that he did to the people, he said, What is this thing that thou doest to the people? why sittest thou thyself alone, and all the people stand by thee from morning unto even? And Moses said unto his father-in-law, Because the people come unto me to inquire of God: when they have a matter, they come unto me; and I judge between one and another, and I do make them know the statutes of God, and His laws. And Moses' father-in-law said unto him, The thing that thou doest is not good. Thou wilt surely wear away, both thou, and this people that is with thee: for this thing is too heavy for thee; thou art not able to perform it thyself alone. Hearken now unto my voice, I will give thee counsel, and God shall be with thee: Be thou for the people to Godward, that thou mayest bring the causes unto God: and thou shalt teach them ordinances and laws, and shalt show them the way wherein they must walk, and the

---

*Manuscript read before the delegates at the General Conference, Washington, D. C., May 30, 1909.

work that they must do. Moreover thou shalt provide out of all the people able men, such as fear God, men of truth, hating covetousness; and place such over them, to be rulers of thousands, and rulers of hundreds, rulers of fifties, and rulers of tens: and let them judge the people at all seasons: and it shall be, that every great matter they shall bring unto thee, but every small matter they shall judge: so shall it be easier for thyself, and they shall bear the burden with thee.

"If thou shalt do this thing, and God command thee so, then thou shalt be able to endure, and all this people shall also go to their place in peace.

"So Moses hearkened to the voice of his father-in-law, and did all that he had said. And Moses chose able men out of all Israel, and made them heads over the people, rulers of thousands, rulers of hundreds, rulers of fifties, and rulers of tens. And they judged the people at all seasons: the hard causes they brought unto Moses, but every small matter they judged themselves." Exodus 18:13-26.

In the first chapter of Acts, also, instruction is given regarding the choosing of men to bear responsibilities in the church. The apostasy of Judas had left one place vacant in the ranks of the apostles, and it was necessary that another be chosen to take this place. Speaking of this, Peter said:

"Wherefore of these men which have companied with us all the time that the Lord Jesus went in and out among us, beginning from the baptism of John, unto that same day that He was taken up from us, must one be ordained to be a witness with us of His resurrection. And they appointed two, Joseph called Barsabas, who was surnamed Justus, and Matthias. And they prayed, and said, Thou, Lord, which knowest the hearts of all men, show whether of these two Thou hast chosen, that he may take part of this ministry and apostleship, from which Judas by transgression fell, that he might go to his own place. And they gave forth their lots; and the lot fell upon Matthias; and he was numbered with the eleven apostles." Acts 1:21-26.

From these scriptures we learn that the Lord has certain men to fill certain positions. God will teach His people to move carefully and to make wise choice of men who will not betray sacred trusts. If in Christ's day the believers needed to be guarded in their choice of men for positions of responsibility, we who are living in this time certainly need to move with great discretion. We are to present every case before God and in earnest prayer ask Him to choose for us.

The Lord God of heaven has chosen experienced men to bear responsibilities in His cause. These men are to have special influence. If all are accorded the power given to these chosen men, a halt will have to be called. Those who are chosen to bear burdens in the work of God are not to be rash or self-confident or selfish. Never is their example or influence to strengthen evil. The Lord has not given men or women liberty to advance ideas that will bring commonness into His work, removing the sacredness that should ever surround it. God's work is to become increasingly sacred to His people. In every way we are to magnify the exalted character of the truth. Those who have been set as guardians of the work of God in our institutions are ever to make the will and way of God prominent. The health of the general work depends upon the faithfulness of the men appointed to carry out the will of God in the churches.

Men must be placed in charge who will obtain an enlarged experience, not in the things of self, but in the things of God, an enlarged knowledge of the character of Christ. The more they know of Christ, the more faithfully they represent Him to the world. They are to listen to His voice and give heed to His words.

A WARNING

"Then began He to upbraid the cities wherein most of His mighty works were done, because they repented not: Woe unto thee, Chorazin! woe unto thee, Bethsaida! for if the mighty works, which were done in you, had been done in Tyre and Sidon, they would have repented long ago in sackcloth and ashes. But I say unto you, It shall be more tolerable for Tyre and Sidon at the day of judgment, than for you.

"And thou, Capernaum, which art exalted unto heaven, shalt be brought down to hell: for if the mighty works, which have been done in thee, had been done in Sodom, it would have remained until this day. But I say unto you, That it shall be more tolerable for the land of Sodom in the day of judgment, than for thee.

"At that time Jesus answered and said, I thank Thee, O Father, Lord of heaven and earth, because Thou hast hid these things from the wise and prudent, and hast revealed them unto babes. Even so, Father: for so it seemed good in Thy sight. All things are delivered unto Me of My Father: and no man knoweth the Son, but the Father; neither knoweth any man the Father, save the Son, and he to whomsoever the Son will reveal Him.

"Come unto Me, all ye that labor and are heavy-laden, and I will give you rest. Take My yoke upon you, and learn of Me; for I am meek and lowly in heart: and ye shall find rest unto your souls. For My yoke is easy, and My burden is light." Matthew 11:20-30.

It is always safe to be meek and lowly and tenderhearted, but at the same time we are to be as firm as a rock to the teachings of Christ. His words of instruction are to be strictly heeded. Not one word is to be lost sight of. The truth will abide forever. We are not to place our trust in any lie or pretense. Those who do this will find that it has been done at the loss of eternal life. We are now to make straight paths for our feet, lest the lame be turned out of the way. When the lame are turned from safe paths, who is accountable but those who have misled them? They have set at nought the counsel of the One whose words are life eternal, for the works of deception originating with the father of lies.

I have words for all who may suppose that they are safe in obtaining their education in Battle Creek. The Lord has blotted out two of our largest institutions that were established in Battle Creek, and has given warning after warning, even as Christ gave warning to Bethsaida and Capernaum. There is a necessity of giving earnest attention to every word that proceedeth out of the mouth of God. There can be no sinless departure from the words of Christ. The Saviour urges the erring ones to repent. Those who humble their hearts and confess their sins will be pardoned. Their transgressions will be forgiven. But the man who thinks that should he confess his sins he would show weakness, will not find pardon, will not see Christ as his Redeemer, but will go on and on in transgression, making blunder after blunder and adding sin to sin. What will such a one do in the day that the books are opened and every man is judged according to the things written in the books?

The fifth chapter of Revelation needs to be closely studied. It is of great importance to those who shall act a part in the work of God for these last days. There are some who are deceived. They do not realize what is coming on the earth. Those who have permitted their minds to become beclouded in regard to what constitutes sin are fearfully deceived. Unless they make a decided change they will be found wanting when God pronounces judgment upon the children of men. They have transgressed the law and broken the everlasting covenant, and they will receive according to their works.

"And I beheld when he had opened the sixth seal, and, lo, there was a great earthquake; and the sun became black as sackcloth of hair, and the moon became as blood; and the stars of heaven fell unto the earth, even as a fig tree casteth her untimely figs, when she is shaken of a mighty wind. And the heaven departed as a scroll when it is rolled together; and every mountain and island were moved out of their places. And the kings of the earth, and the great men, and the rich men, and the chief captains, and the mighty men, and every bondman, and every free-man, hid themselves in the dens and in the rocks of the mountains; and said to the mountains and rocks, Fall on us, and hide us from the face of Him that sitteth on the throne, and from the wrath of the Lamb: for the great day of His wrath is come; and who shall be able to stand?" Revelation 6:12-17.

"After this I beheld, and, lo, a great multitude, which no man could number, of all nations, and kindreds, and people, and tongues, stood before the throne, and before the Lamb, clothed with white robes, and palms in their hands; and cried with a loud voice, saying, Salvation to our God which sitteth upon the throne, and unto the

Lamb. . . . These are they which came out of great tribulation, and have washed their robes, and made them white in the blood of the Lamb. Therefore are they before the throne of God, and serve Him day and night in His temple: and He that sitteth on the throne shall dwell among them. They shall hunger no more, neither thirst any more; neither shall the sun light on them, nor any heat. For the Lamb which is in the midst of the throne shall feed them, and shall lead them unto living fountains of waters: and God shall wipe away all tears from their eyes." Revelation 7:9-17.

In these scriptures two parties are brought to view. One party permitted themselves to be deceived and took sides with those with whom the Lord has a controversy. They misinterpreted the messages sent them and clothed themselves in robes of self-righteousness. Sin was not sinful in their eyes. They taught falsehood as truth, and by them many souls were led astray.

We need now to take heed to ourselves. Warnings have been given. Can we not see the fulfillment of the predictions made by Christ and recorded in the twenty-first chapter of Luke? How many are studying the words of Christ? How many are deceiving their own souls and cheating themselves out of the blessings that others might secure if they would believe and obey? Probation still lingers, and it is our privilege to lay hold of the hope set before us in the gospel. Let us repent and be converted and forsake our sins, that they may be blotted out. "Heaven and earth shall pass away: but My words shall not pass away. And take heed to yourselves, lest at any time your hearts be overcharged with surfeiting, and drunkenness, and cares of this life, and so that day come upon you unawares. For as a snare shall it come on all them that dwell on the face of the whole earth. Watch ye therefore, and pray always, that ye may be accounted worthy to escape all these things that shall come to pass, and to stand before the Son of man." Luke 21:33-36.

Shall the warnings given by Christ be passed by unheeded? Shall we not make diligent work for repentance now, while Mercy's gracious voice is still heard?

"Watch therefore: for ye know not what hour your Lord doth come. But know this, that if the good man of the house had known in what watch the thief would come, he would have watched, and would not have suffered his house to be broken up. Therefore be ye also ready: for in such an hour as ye think not the Son of man cometh. Who then is a faithful and wise servant, whom his lord hath made ruler over his household, to give them meat in due season? Blessed is that servant, whom his lord when he cometh shall find so doing. Verily I say unto you, That he shall make him ruler over all his goods. But and if that evil servant shall say in his heart, My lord delayeth his coming; and shall begin to smite his fellow servants, and to eat and drink with the drunken; the lord of that servant shall come in a day when he looketh not for him, and in an hour that he is not aware of, and shall cut him asunder, and appoint him his portion with the hypocrites there shall be weeping and gnashing of teeth." Matthew 24:42-51.

IN HUMILITY AND FAITH*

Special instruction has been given me for God's people, for perilous times are upon us. In the world, destruction and violence are increasing. In the church, man power is gaining the ascendancy; those who have been chosen to occupy positions of trust think it their prerogative to rule.

Men whom the Lord calls to important positions in His work are to cultivate a humble dependence upon Him. They are not to seek to embrace too much authority; for God has not called them to a work of ruling, but to plan and counsel with their fellow laborers. Every worker alike is to hold himself amenable to the requirements and instructions of God.

WISE COUNSELORS

Because of the importance of the work in Southern California and the perplexities which now surround it, there should be selected no less than five men of wisdom and experience to consult with the presidents of the local and union conferences regarding general plans and policies. The Lord is not pleased with the disposition some have manifested to rule those of more experience than themselves. By this course of action some have revealed that they are not qualified to fill the important positions which they occupy. Any human being who spreads himself out to large proportions and who seeks to have the control of his fellows, proves himself to be a dangerous man to be entrusted with religious responsibilities.

Let no one cling to the idea that unless money is in

---

*Read at the Los Angeles, California, camp meeting, August 15-31, 1907, and afterward published in the tract, *Jehovah Is Our King*.

hand, no move should be made that calls for the investment of means. If in our past experience we had always followed this method, we would often have lost special advantages, such as we gained in the purchase of the Fernando school property and in the purchase of the sanitarium properties at Paradise Valley, Glendale, and Loma Linda.

GO FORWARD

To make no move that calls for the investment of means unless we have the money in hand to complete the contemplated work should not always be considered the wisest plan. In the upbuilding of His work the Lord does not always make everything plain before His servants. He sometimes tries the confidence of His people by having them move forward in faith. Often He brings them into strait and trying places, bidding them go forward when their feet seem to be touching the waters of the Red Sea. It is at such times, when the prayers of His servants ascend to Him in earnest faith, that He opens the way before them and brings them out into a large place.

The Lord wants His people in these days to believe that He will do as great things for them as He did for the children of Israel in their journey from Egypt to Canaan. We are to have an educated faith that will not hesitate to follow His instructions in the most difficult experiences. "Go forward" is the command of God to His people.

Faith and cheerful obedience are needed to bring the Lord's designs to pass. When He points out the necessity of establishing the work in places where it will have influence, the people are to walk and work by faith. By their godly conversation, their humility, their prayers and earnest efforts, they should strive to bring the people to appreciate the good work that the Lord has established among them. It was the Lord's purpose that the Loma Linda Sanitarium should become the property of our people, and He brought it about at a time when the rivers of difficulty were full and overflowing their banks.

The working of private interests for the gaining of personal ends is one thing. In this, men may follow their own judgment. But the carrying forward of the Lord's work in the earth is entirely another matter. When He designates that a certain property should be secured for the advancement of His cause and the building up of His work, whether it be for sanitarium or school work, or for any other branch, He will make the doing of that work possible if those who have experience will show their faith and trust in His purposes, and will move forward promptly to secure the advantages He points out. While we are not to seek to wrest property from any man, yet when advantages are offered, we should be wide awake to see the advantage, that we may make plans for the upbuilding of the work. And when we have done this we should exert every energy to secure the freewill offerings of God's people for the support of these new plants.

Often the Lord sees that His workers are in doubt as to what they should do. At such times, if they will put their confidence in Him, He will reveal to them His will. God's work is now to advance rapidly, and if His people will respond to His call, He will make the possessors of property willing to donate of their means and thus make it possible for His work to be accomplished in the earth.

"Faith is the substance of things hoped for, the evidence of things not seen." Hebrews 11:1. Faith in the word of God will place His people in the possession of property which will enable them to work the large cities that are waiting for the message of truth.

The cold, formal, unbelieving way in which some of the laborers do their work is a deep offense to the Spirit of God. The apostle Paul says: "Do all things without murmurings and disputings: that ye may be blameless and harmless, the sons of God, without rebuke, in the midst of a crooked and perverse nation, among whom ye shine as lights in the world; holding forth the word of life; that I may rejoice in the day of Christ, that I have not run in vain, neither labored in vain. Yea, and if I be offered upon the sacrifice and service of your faith, I joy, and rejoice with you all." Philippians 2:14-17.

We are to encourage in one another that living faith which Christ has made it possible for every believer to have. The work is to be carried forward as the Lord prepares the way. When He brings His people into strait places, then it is their privilege to assemble together for prayer, remembering that all things come of God. Those who have not yet shared in the trying experiences that attend the work in these last days will soon have to pass through scenes that will severely test their confidence in God. It is at the time His people see no way to advance, when the Red Sea is before them and the pursuing army behind, that God bids them: "Go forward." Thus He is working to test their faith. When such experiences come to you, go forward, trusting in Christ. Walk step by step in the path He marks out. Trials will come, but go forward. This will give you an experience that will strengthen your faith in God and fit you for truest service.

THE EXAMPLE OF CHRIST

A deeper and wider experience in religious things is to come to God's people. Christ is our example. If through living faith and sanctified obedience to God's word we reveal the love and grace of Christ, if we show that we have a true conception of God's guiding providences in the work, we shall carry to the world a convincing power. A high position does not give us value in the sight of God. Man is measured by his consecration and faithfulness in working out the will of God. If the remnant people of God will walk before Him in humility and faith, He will carry out through them His eternal purpose, enabling them to work harmoniously in giving to the world the truth as it is in Jesus. He will use all—men, women, and children—in making the light shine forth to the world and calling out a people that will be true to His commandments. Through the faith that His people exercise in Him, God will make known to the world that He is the true God, the God of Israel.

"Let your conversation be as it becometh the gospel of Christ," the apostle Paul exhorts, "that whether I come and see you, or else be absent, I may hear of your affairs, that ye stand fast in one spirit, with one mind striving together for the faith of the gospel; and in nothing terrified by your adversaries: which is to them an evident token of perdition, but to you of salvation, and that of God. For unto you it is given in the behalf of Christ, not only to believe on Him, but also to suffer for His sake."

"If there be therefore any consolation in Christ, if any comfort of love, if any fellowship of the Spirit, if any bowels and mercies, fulfill ye my joy, that ye be likeminded, having the same love, being of one accord, of one mind. Let nothing be done through strife or vain glory; but in lowliness of mind let each esteem other better than themselves.

"Look not every man on his own things, but every man also on the things of others. Let this mind be in you, which was also in Christ Jesus: who, being in the form of God, thought it not robbery to be equal with God: but made Himself of no reputation, and took upon Him the form of a servant, and was made in the likeness of men: and being found in fashion as a man, He humbled Himself, and became obedient unto death, even the death of the cross. Wherefore God also hath highly exalted Him, and given Him a name which is above every name: that at the name of Jesus every knee should bow, of things in heaven, and things in earth, and things under the earth; and that every tongue should confess that Jesus Christ is Lord, to the glory of God the Father. Wherefore, my beloved, as ye have always obeyed, not as in my presence only, but now much more in my absence, work out your own salvation with fear and trembling. For it is God which worketh in you both to will and to do of His good pleasure." Philippians 1:27-29; 2:1-13.

I have been instructed to present these words to our people in Southern California. They are needed in every place where a church is established, for a strange experience has been coming into our ranks.

It is time now for men to humble their hearts before God and to learn to work in His ways. Let those who have sought to rule their fellow workers study to know what manner of spirit they are of. They should seek the Lord by fasting and prayer, and in humility of soul.

Christ in His earthly life gave an example that all can

safely follow. He appreciates His flock, and He wants no power set over them that will restrict their freedom in His service. He has never placed man as a ruler over His heritage. True Bible religion will lead to self-control, not to control of one another. As a people we need a larger measure of the Holy Spirit, that we may bear the solemn message that God has given us, without exaltation.

Brethren, keep your words of censure for your individual selves. Teach the flock of God to look to Christ, not to erring man. Every soul who becomes a teacher of the truth must bear in his own life the fruit of holiness. Looking to Christ and following Him, he will present to the souls under his charge an example of what a living, learning Christian will be. Let God teach you His way. Inquire of Him daily to know His will. He will give unerring counsel to all who seek Him with a sincere heart. Walk worthy of the vocation wherewith you are called, praising God in your daily conversation as well as in your prayers. Thus, holding forth the word of life, you will constrain other souls to become followers of Christ.

TO THE WORKERS IN SOUTHERN CALIFORNIA*

This morning I cannot rest. My mind is troubled over the situation in Southern California. God has given to every man his work, but there are some who are not prayerfully considering their individual responsibility.

When a worker is selected for an office, that office of itself does not bring to him power of capability that he did not have before. A high position does not give to the character Christian virtues. The man who supposes that his individual mind is capable of planning and devising for all branches of the work reveals a great lack of wisdom. No one human mind is capable of carrying the many and varied responsibilities of a conference embracing thousands of people and many branches of work.

But a greater danger than this has been revealed to me in the feeling that has been growing among our workers that ministers and other laborers in the cause should depend upon the mind of certain leading workers to define their duties. One man's mind and judgment are not to be considered capable of controlling and molding a conference. The individual and the church have responsibilities of their own. God has given to every man some talent or talents to use and improve. In using these talents he increases his capability to serve. God has given to each individual judgment, and this gift He wants His workers to use and improve. The president of a conference must not consider that his individual judgment is to control the judgment of all.

---

*Published first in *Special Testimonies,* Series B, No. 10, *Jehovah Is Our King.*

In no conference should propositions be rushed through without time being taken by the brethren to weigh carefully all sides of the question. Because the president of a conference suggested certain plans, it has sometimes been considered unnecessary to consult the Lord about them. Thus propositions have been accepted that were not for the spiritual benefit of the believers and that involved far more than was apparent at the first casual consideration. Such movements are not in the order of God. Many, very many matters have been taken up and carried by vote, that have involved far more than was anticipated and far more than those who voted would have been willing to assent to had they taken time to consider the question from all sides.

We cannot at this time afford to be careless or negligent in the work of God. We must seek the Lord earnestly every day if we would be prepared for the experiences that come to us. Our hearts are to be cleansed from every feeling of superiority, and the living principles of the truth are to be planted in the soul. Young and aged and middle-aged should now be practicing the virtues of Christ's character. They should daily be making spiritual development, that they may become vessels unto honor in the Master's service.

"And it came to pass, that, as He was praying in a certain place, when He ceased, one of His disciples said unto Him, Lord, teach us to pray, as John also taught his disciples." Luke 11:1. The prayer that Christ gave to His disciples in answer to this request is not made in high-flown language, but expresses in simple words the necessities of the soul. It is short and deals directly with the daily needs.

Every soul has the privilege of stating to the Lord his

own special necessities and to offer his individual thanksgiving for the blessings that he daily receives. But the many long and spiritless, faithless prayers that are offered to God, instead of being a joy to Him, are a burden. We need, oh, so much! clean, converted hearts. We need to have our faith strengthened. "Ask, and it shall be given you," the Saviour promised; "seek, and ye shall find; knock, and it shall be opened unto you." Matthew 7:7. We need to educate ourselves to trust in this word and to bring the light and grace of Christ into all our works. We need to take hold of Christ and to retain our hold of Him until we know that the power of His transforming grace is manifested in us. We must have faith in Christ if we would reflect the divine character.

Christ clothed His divinity with humanity and lived a life of prayer and self-denial, and of daily battle with temptation, that He might help those who today are assailed by temptation. He is our efficiency and power. He desires that, through the appropriation of His grace, humanity shall become partakers of the divine nature and thus escape the corruption that is in the world through lust. The word of God in the Old and New Testaments, if faithfully studied and received into the life, will give spiritual wisdom and life. This word is to be sacredly cherished. Faith in the word of God and in the power of Christ to transform the life will enable the believer to work His works and to live a life of rejoicing in the Lord.

Again and again I have been instructed to say to our people: Let your faith and trust be in God. Do not depend on any erring man to define your duty. It is your privilege to say: "I will declare Thy name unto my brethren: in the midst of the congregation will I praise Thee.

Ye that fear the Lord, praise Him; all ye the seed of Jacob, glorify Him; and fear Him, all ye the seed of Israel. For He hath not despised nor abhorred the affliction of the afflicted; neither hath He hid His face from him; but when he cried unto Him, He heard. My praise shall be of Thee: . . . I will pay my vows before them that fear Him. The meek shall eat and be satisfied: they shall praise the Lord that seek Him: your heart shall live forever." Psalm 22:22-26.

These scriptures are right to the point. Every church member should understand that God is the one to whom to look for an understanding of individual duty. It is right that brethren counsel together; but when men arrange just what their brethren shall do, let them answer that they have chosen the Lord as their counselor. Those who will humbly seek Him will find His grace sufficient. But when one man allows another to step in between him and the duty that God has pointed out to him, giving to man his confidence and accepting him as guide, then he steps from the true platform to a false and dangerous one. Such a man, instead of growing and developing, will lose his spirituality.

There is no power in any man to remedy the defective character. Individually our hope and trust must be in One who is more than human. We need ever to remember that help has been laid on One who is mighty. The Lord has provided the needed help for every soul who will accept it.

Sanitarium, California, October 3, 1907.

"I AM BUT A LITTLE CHILD"*

At the beginning of his reign Solomon prayed: "O Lord my God, Thou hast made Thy servant king instead of David my father: and I am but a little child: I know not how to go out or come in." 1 Kings 3:7.

Solomon had succeeded his father David to the throne of Israel. God greatly honored him, and, as we know, he became in later years the greatest, richest, and wisest king that had ever sat upon an earthly throne. Early in his reign Solomon was impressed by the Holy Spirit with the solemnity of his responsibilities, and, though rich in talents and ability, he realized that without divine aid he was helpless as a little child to perform them. Solomon was never so rich or so wise or so truly great as when he confessed to the Lord: "I am but a little child: I know not how to go out or come in."

It was in a dream, in which the Lord appeared to him, saying, "Ask what I shall give thee" (verse 5), that Solomon thus gave expression to his feeling of helplessness and need of divine aid. He continued: "Thy servant is in the midst of Thy people which Thou hast chosen, a great people, that cannot be numbered nor counted for multitude. Give therefore Thy servant an understanding heart to judge Thy people, that I may discern between good and bad: for who is able to judge this Thy so great a people?

"And the speech pleased the Lord, that Solomon had asked this thing. And God said unto him, Because thou hast asked this thing, and hast not asked for thyself long life; neither hast asked riches for thyself, nor hast asked

---

*Published first in *Special Testimonies*, Series B, No. 10, *Jehovah Is Our King*.

the life of thine enemies; but hast asked for thyself understanding to discern judgment; behold, I have done according to thy words: lo, I have given thee a wise and an
understanding heart; so that there was none like thee before thee, neither after thee shall any arise like unto thee.
And I have also given thee that which thou hast not
asked, both riches, and honor: so that there shall not be
any among the kings like unto thee all thy days." Now
the conditions: "And if thou wilt walk in My ways, to
keep My statutes and My commandments, as thy father
David did walk, then I will lengthen thy days.

"And Solomon awoke; and, behold, it was a dream.
And he came to Jerusalem, and stood before the ark of the
covenant of the Lord, and offered up burnt offerings, and
offered peace offerings, and made a feast to all his
servants." Verses 8-15.

All who occupy responsible positions need to learn the
lesson that is taught in Solomon's humble prayer. They
are ever to remember that position will never change the
character or render man infallible. The higher the position a man occupies, the greater the responsibility he has
to bear, the wider will be the influence he exerts and the
greater his need to feel his dependence on the wisdom
and strength of God and to cultivate the best and most
holy character. Those who accept a position of responsibility in the cause of God should always remember that
with the call to this work God has also called them to
walk circumspectly before Him and before their fellow
men. Instead of considering it their duty to order and
dictate and command, they should realize that they are to
be learners themselves. When a responsible worker fails
to learn this lesson, the sooner he is released from his
responsibilities the better it will be for him and for the

work of God. Position never will give holiness and excellence of character. He who honors God and keeps His commandments is himself honored.

The question which each should ask himself in all humility is: "Am I qualified for this position? Have I learned to keep the way of the Lord to do justice and judgment?" The Saviour's earthly example has been given us that we should not walk in our own strength, but that each should consider himself, as Solomon expressed it, "a little child."

FOLLOWERS OF GOD, AS DEAR CHILDREN

Every truly converted soul can say: "I am but a little child; but I am God's child." It was at infinite cost that provision was made whereby the human family might be restored to sonship with God. In the beginning, God made man in His own likeness. Our first parents listened to the voice of the tempter and yielded to the power of Satan. But man was not abandoned to the results of the evil he had chosen. The promise of a Deliverer was given. "I will put enmity between thee and the woman," God said to the serpent, "and between thy seed and her seed; it shall bruise thy head, and thou shalt bruise his heel." Genesis 3:15. Before they heard of the thorn and the thistle, of the sorrow and toil that must be their portion, or of the dust to which they must return, they listened to words that could not fail of giving them hope. All that had been lost by yielding to Satan could be regained through Christ.

The Son of God was given to redeem the race. At infinite suffering, the sinless for the sinful, the price was paid that was to redeem the human family from the power of the destroyer and restore them again to the image of God. Those who accept the salvation brought to them in Christ will humble themselves before God as His little children.

God wants His children to ask for those things that will enable Him to reveal His grace through them to the world. He wants them to seek His counsel, to acknowledge His power. Christ lays loving claims on all for whom He has given His life; they are to obey His will if they would share the joys that He has prepared for all who reflect His character here. It is well for us to feel our weakness, for then we shall seek the strength and wisdom that the Father delights to give to His children for their daily strife against the powers of evil.

While education, training, and the counsel of those of experience are all essential, the workers are to be taught that they are not to rely wholly upon any man's judgment. As God's free agents, all should ask wisdom of Him. When the learner depends wholly upon another's thoughts, accepting his plans and going no further, he sees only through that man's eyes and is, so far, only an echo of another.

THE REWARD OF EARNEST EFFORT

"If any man's work abide, . . . he shall receive a reward." 1 Corinthians 3:14. Glorious will be the reward bestowed when the faithful workers gather about the throne of God and of the Lamb. When John in his mortal state beheld the glory of God, he fell as one dead; he was not able to endure the sight. But when the children of God shall have put on immortality, they will "see Him as He is." 1 John 3:2. They will stand before the throne, accepted in the Beloved. All their sins have been blotted out, all their transgressions borne away. Now they can look upon the undimmed glory of the throne of God. They have been partakers with Christ in His sufferings, they have been workers together with Him in the plan of redemption, and they are partakers with Him in the joy of seeing souls saved in the kingdom of God, there to praise God through all eternity.

My brother, my sister, I urge you to prepare for the coming of Christ in the clouds of heaven. Day by day cast the love of the world out of your hearts. Understand by experience what it means to have fellowship with Christ. Prepare for the judgment, that when Christ shall come, to be admired in all them that believe, you may be among those who will meet Him in peace. In that day the redeemed will shine forth in the glory of the Father and the Son. The angels, touching their golden harps, will welcome the King and His trophies of victory—those who have been washed and made white in the blood of the Lamb. A song of triumph will peal forth, filling all heaven. Christ has conquered. He enters the heavenly courts, accompanied by His redeemed ones, the witnesses that His mission of suffering and sacrifice has not been in vain.

The resurrection and ascension of our Lord is a sure evidence of the triumph of the Saints of God over death and the grave, and a pledge that heaven is open to those who wash their robes of character and make them white in the blood of the Lamb. Jesus ascended to the Father as a representative of the human race, and God will bring those who reflect His image to behold and share with Him His glory.

There are homes for the pilgrims of earth. There are robes for the righteous, with crowns of glory and palms of victory. All that has perplexed us in the providences of God will in the world to come be made plain. The things hard to be understood will then find explanation. The mysteries of grace will unfold before us. Where our finite minds discovered only confusion and broken promises, we shall see the most perfect and beautiful harmony. We shall know that infinite love ordered the experiences that seemed most trying. As we realize the tender care of Him who makes all things work together for our good, we shall rejoice with joy unspeakable and full of glory.

Pain cannot exist in the atmosphere of heaven. In the home of the redeemed there will be no tears, no funeral trains, no badges of mourning. "The inhabitant shall not say, I am sick: the people that dwell therein shall be forgiven their iniquity." Isaiah 33:24. One rich tide of happiness will flow and deepen as eternity rolls on.

We are still amidst the shadows and turmoil of earthly activities. Let us consider most earnestly the blessed hereafter. Let our faith pierce through every cloud of darkness and behold Him who died for the sins of the world.

He has opened the gates of paradise to all who receive and believe on Him. To them He gives power to become the sons and daughters of God. Let the afflictions which pain us so grievously become instructive lessons, teaching us to press forward toward the mark of the prize of our high calling in Christ. Let us be encouraged by the thought that the Lord is soon to come. Let this hope gladden our hearts. "Yet a little while, and He that shall come will come, and will not tarry." Hebrews 10:37. Blessed are those servants who, when their Lord comes, shall be found watching.

We are homeward bound. He who loved us so much as to die for us hath builded for us a city. The New Jerusalem is our place of rest. There will be no sadness in the city of God. No wail of sorrow, no dirge of crushed hopes and buried affections, will evermore be heard. Soon the garments of heaviness will be changed for the wedding garment. Soon we shall witness the coronation of our King. Those whose lives have been hidden with Christ, those who on this earth have fought the good fight of faith, will shine forth with the Redeemer's glory in the kingdom of God.

It will not be long till we shall see Him in whom our hopes of eternal life are centered. And in His presence, all the trials and sufferings of this life will be as nothingness. "Cast not away therefore your confidence, which hath great recompense of reward. For ye have need of patience, that, after ye have done the will of God, ye might receive the promise. For yet a little while, and He that shall come will come, and will not tarry." Verses 35-37. Look up, look up, and let your faith continually increase. Let this faith guide you along the narrow path that leads through the gates of the city of God into the great beyond, the wide, unbounded future of glory that is for the redeemed. "Be patient therefore, brethren, unto the coming of the Lord. Behold, the husbandman waiteth for the precious fruit of the earth, and hath long patience for it, until he receive the early and latter rain. Be ye also patient; stablish your hearts: for the coming of the Lord draweth nigh." James 5:7, 8.

SCRIPTURAL INDEX

GENERAL INDEX

Drugs, poisonous, healing without, to be brought into prominence 169

  instruction in our school regarding non use of 175, 176

  not to be used in ministry to people 168, 169, 172

Drunkenness at time of end 44

See also Intemperance.

Duty, allowing another to interfere with 280

  performance of, increases our usefulness 220

Dwarfs in work of Christ 184

Dyspepsia, causes of 160

EARNESTNESS, greater, in soulsaving 44

  intense, to take possession of us 44-48

  reward of 285-288

Earthquake, San Francisco 94-96

East, cities of 98-100, 134

Eating and drinking, as one pleases results in carelessness about truth 156

  erroneous, leads to erroneous thinking 160

Economy, in, behalf of missions 53-59, 76-80

  daily living to help cause 131

  personal expenditure 54, 55

  to be practiced by students 76, 77

Editors, cautions to, in view of times of trial 239-244

  danger of imbibing false theories 68

Education, for gospel service 171, 172

  formal, God can use learners without 259

  medical missionary training is in harmony with 174

  of medical missionary evangelists 173-178

  our purpose now to prepare to receive, in school above 172

  true higher, Christ is foundation and source of 174, 175

  workers receive, from the Great Teacher 32

  worldly, for medical students 175

  See also Schools; Training schools.

Educators, physicians should be wise 161

Efficiency through faith and submission 141

Effort, intensity of 141

Efforts, determined, not without fruit 100

  for following up interest developed at camp meetings 120, 121

Eggs, use of 162, 163

End, "be ye also ready" 48

  diligent work needed in view of 101, 167

  is near, 24, 25

  nearness of, predictions of fulfilling 268, 269

  talk about, to neighbors 38

  unmistakable evidences of 55

  walk carefully in view of 203

  warning after warning of 27

  stealing upon us 11-17, 135

  See also Second advent.

Endowments, God has in store health and spiritual 165

  See also Talents.

Enemies, of truth, discretion referring to 241, 242

  kindness toward 239-244

  thrusts at, come back in double measure 241

  See also Opposers.

Enterprise, private, men may follow their judgment in 272

Enterprises, missionary, to be carried forward 100, 101

Enthusiasm, holier, from a new heart 152

lessons, on organization from 262-264

to be learned from experiences of 165, 262-265

Movements, final, will be rapid ones 11

spasmodic, like untrained horses 258

Murder a sign of the times 89

Music, instrumental, to praise of God 144

that is only form 143, 144

Mysteries, divine, to be made clear 194

of grace will unfold 194

of incarnate love communicated through human agency 30

Mystery, scientific, leads men from truth 68

NATIONALITY, difference in, not to separate brethren 195-198

Nationalities, Christ's relation to 190

conferences for various, in America 195-198

different, can work in harmony 184-198

Nature, divine, partakers of 187, 188

human, Christ took our 190

Negro race, ideas of morality among 223

men of talent and ability among 202

representatives of, at assemblies 209

workers of, consideration for 223, 224

Negroes, meetinghouses for 210

of South, missionary work for 225, 226

schools and work for 200, 201

work to be done for 199-226

See also Colored people.

Neighborhood work, youth to be active in 118-120

Neighbors, duty to labor for 30-42, 45, 125-136

New birth essential preparation for God's service 156

See also Conversion.

New Jerusalem, place of rest 287

New York City, centers of influence in 115

fireproof buildings in 12, 13

work of mission 137-140

Nurses, lady, more needed who treat without drugs 176

Loma Linda to be strong in training of 174

Nutrition, diet lacking 161

See also Diet; Food.

OCCUPATIONS, men of diverse, called to work 170

Offerings, annual, for colored work 225, 226

for mission fields 80

See also Benevolence; Gifts and offerings; Giving; Liberality.

Office does not give capabilities 277

Old Testament gives spiritual wisdom 279

Opponents, avoid trouble with 241

Christ's way is best way to meet our 148

how to meet 147-149

repeating false statements of 148

Opportunities, for service, along the great thoroughfares of travel, were improved by Christ 121

among all classes and nationalities in our day 121, 122

are opening on every side 130

Christians in centers of commerce and travel have special 122

churches are blessed and encouraged by improving 127

Teachers—*continued*

danger of, in imbibing false theories through reading 68

for colored people in South 201, 214, 226

for Loma Linda who depend wholly upon God 177

qualification of, is consecration to God 176

should stand firmly on Bible ground regarding health reform 158

work of, to lead out in sale of relief books 86

Teaching, hold to affirmative in 147, 148

Tear down, not to 227

Temper, health essential for acquirement of an even 160

Temperance and health, instruction in 153-166, 177

can be given on Sunday 233

Temple, Jewish, a type of God's spiritual 180

Temptation, Christ, met, with word of God 68

pities those who fall under 222

resistance of, repulse enemy with word 68, 69

Tenderness, of Christ manifested by undershepherds 54

toward one another 193

Test, last, to all on earth 149

of fellowship, meat eating not to be 159

Tests, fearful, await people of God 17

Testimonies, acceptance of portions and rejection of portions 154

recipients of, of reproof tempted to seek human sympathy 182

Thank offerings in return for great love 50

Theories, false, danger of, to ministers, teachers, editors 68

Satan exercises deceptive powers through 67-69

fascinating influence of new, erroneous 67, 68

pantheistic 68

satanic, make nonentity of God 68

Third angel's message, belief in theory of, not sufficient 155

call to proclaim truths of 25

carried to foreign fields under difficult circumstances 78

colored people to be given light of 209, 210

multitudes to hear, through books 78, 86

presented, plainly and decidedly 109

so decidedly as to startle hearers 137

proclaimed through sanitariums 173

teachers to be true to 113

white people of South need 210

See also Message.

Thoroughfares of travel, evangelistic and colporteur work in 121, 122

medical work in 84, 85

Thrusts, refrain from making sharp 241, 243

Time, a gift from God 38

is precious 48, 117

of trouble, on very verge of 43-48, 227-231

unmoved in 17

protection for saints in 17

shortness of 200

wasted, remorse over 106, 107

Times, instruction in view of perilous 270-276

Timidity in advancing work 141

Tithe, constitutes revenue of gospel 246, 247

not all workers to be paid from 248, 249

not to be applied promiscuously 247-251

Witnesses, called to be 19-29, 53, 54

called to save sinners 43

Women, work of, as Bible workers 120, 121

    in families 128, 129

    in homes of neighbors 36, 37

    in medical lines 176

Words, frivolous, deprive of spiritual strength 133

    not to be rugged and sharp 239

Work, of God, building up, not tearing down 227

    finished if all had done part 29

    formality in, danger of 273

    hasten, in view of nearness of end 101

    importance of, at impending crisis 19

    many do not realize importance of 57

    not to retrench 55, 56

    sense of sacredness of, is to increase with God's people 264

    urgency of 60

    See also Cause of God.

    spiritual, all lines of, to be united 169, 170

    appointed by God for all to do 26-29, 37

    appointed persons to do 138

    eternity to be kept in view while engaged in 47

    looking for great, while neglecting small duties 129

    measuring of, not to be by eight-hour system 45

    reveals what Christ has placed in heart 135

    reward of, souls saved 285-288

    untiring effort called for in 40

    wholehearted, result of 32, 33

Works, good, Christianity revealed in 56

Workers, blend together in perfect whole 26

co-operation among ministerial, medical, educational 169, 170

duties and responsibilities of, distributing literature 61-88

    laboring for wealthy 115

    representing Christ, the great Missionary Worker 241

failures and mistakes of, coldness, selfishness, self-exaltation 218, 219

    condemning individual methods 259

hour service not to be rendered by 45

in Southern California, instruction to 270-276

lack of faith brings lack of means and 105

lay members may become 117-120

    See also Laymen.

older, experienced, association of youth with 119

promises to, to see eye to eye when unselfish 33

qualifications of, deep Christian experience 26

    education by Great Teacher 32

    efficiency and consecration 27

    prayerfulness 110

    realization of nearness of end 27

    sympathy with others 26, 45

    union with one another in Christ 184-188

    unselfishness 26

    willingness to spend and be spent for others 56

    wisdom 26

    zeal 118

support of, by tithes and offerings 49-60